# All My Friends Will Buy It

*A Bottlefield Tour*

# ALL MY FRIENDS WILL BUY IT

## A BOTTLEFIELD TOUR

by

Leo Cooper

SPELLMOUNT
Staplehurst

ISBN 1-86227-284-0

First published in the UK in 2005 by
Spellmount Limited
The Village Centre
Staplehurst
Kent TN12 0BJ

Tel: 01580 893730
Fax: 01580 893731
E-mail: enquiries@spellmount.com
Website: www.spellmount.com

1 3 5 7 9 8 6 4 2

Typeset in Palatino by MATS, Southend-on-Sea, Essex
Printed in Great Britain by
Oaklands Book Services
Stonehouse, Gloucestershire GL10 3RQ

# Contents

To Jilly
who made it all possible

Writing your memoirs will not only make some useful additional cash, it will enable you to do two things that can be immensely satisfying.

1.  Polish your own image to an even greater brilliance as you describe your masterstrokes of business strategy.

2.  Rubbish the careers and reputations of many people who have stood in your way in the past.

From *How to Get Seriously Rich While Failing in Business* by Philip Sadler, published by kind permission of Souvenir Press.

# *Foreword*

Leo Cooper cannot explain what sparked his interest in military history. Nor can I. In neither case has it been a passing interest but has persisted throughout life. As a result, Leo and I know many of the same people. Whereas, however, I came to meet them generally in formal circumstances, in the Officers' Mess at The Royal Military Academy Sandhurst where I taught for over twenty years, or on the touchline at the Sovereign's Parade, Leo's immensely varied life, as publisher, clubman and touring cricketer ensured that his wide acquaintance was made in much more haphazard – and interesting ways. The result is that the people he brings to life in these pages appear in guises quite different from those I recognise. It is the same cast of characters, but transformed by Leo's genius for conviviality and friendship, and his extraordinary ability to change direction in his passage through life.

Leo is a publisher but like almost no other publisher in the London book world. I lost count of the number of publishers for whom, at the beginning of his career, he worked, Longmans, Hamish Hamilton, André Deutsch, or for the variety of jobs he did, in editorial, publicity, production departments, and eventually as head of his own firm.

It was only when he was able to strike out for himself that he came into his own. As a trainee he did as he was told, often peremptorily, by publishing tyrants for whom the production of books provided an opportunity to indulge their temperaments. The names are familiar. The picture of their working methods is not. Jamie Hamilton, a 'drawing room' publisher, liked big names and fawned on them, as he did on his juniors, which sometimes led to unintended consequences. Leo's efforts to convey to Jamie the news, transmitted in person on the telephone, that Sir Malcolm Sargent was dying led to his being ordered downstairs, several times, until what should have been Jamie's last chance to speak to the great conductor became a death announcement. André Deutsch, the professional immigrant, bullied all his staff every day and frequently sacked them. Leo does not bear a grudge. Indeed, unsurprisingly in view of his sunny temperament, he appears to bear no grudges against anyone. He writes in the kindest fashion about men I would have paid money to avoid, such as Brigadier 'Mad' Mike Calvert, war hero, professional killer and predatory homosexual.

As Leo's little business grew, its output of battle narratives, regimental history and autobiographical tales of derring-do attracted the characters on whose company Leo thrived. Some were pukka gentleman officers, such as the delightful Valentine ffrench-Blake and the almost certifiable Loopy Kennard. Others were military rough trade, old sweats with blood on their hands but a gift for words. Leo had the gift of turning their stories into publishable manuscripts. By the 1980s Leo had become almost as well known in military circles as some of the famous generals whose biographies he published, and the sort of books in which he specialised, particularly his 'Famous Regiment' series, could be found in every military library.

Leo was not only known for what he produced but because of his personality, which made him welcome wherever he chose to spend his leisure time, particularly the pubs on the fringes of Bloomsbury behind his office and in the Garrick Club. I happen to share his membership of that club and came to recognise the signs that Leo was 'in'. There would be a benevolent atmosphere in the upstairs bar and a distinctive cluster around the bar itself behind which the Garrick's famous barman, Tony Wild, would be filling Leo's orders at lightning speed. The drinkers congregated, however, not for the chance of a treat but for the pleasure of Leo's company and conversation, an inimitable mixture of anecdote, reminiscence and character sketch. There was also his unfailing good humour. I can truthfully say that Leo is that unusual human being, someone who is never downcast or put out, someone the mere sight of whom automatically lightens the atmosphere and generates good cheer.

Given Leo's appetite for company and a glass it is astonishing that he has achieved anything serious in life. Yet he has. Huge areas of military history have been illuminated by his instinct for a story that needs to be told and bookshelves have been filled with the results. Some is light-hearted, some is lightweight. Some, however, is very serious indeed and will stand the test of time. Leo will be honoured as a publisher if only for staying with the Marquess of Anglesey while he completed his magnificent eight-volume history of British cavalry. Not all his friends will buy that book which requires a serious outlay to acquire. All his friends, however, will want this book, will search eagerly in its pages to see if they get a mention and, if lucky, will grin at his portrait of them. This is a marvellous picture of two worlds, that of publishers and soldiers and, unintentionally, a memorable self-portrait of someone who, in his time, has been one of the most popular men in London.

John Keegan
2005

# Introduction and Acknowledgements

This book is really an acknowledgement in itself. I wish to thank especially all those who have helped me, worked with me or for me during the past years. Naturally I have been unable to thank everyone who enjoyed this pleasure: a furtive look at the index will suffice to tell the reader whether he or she has been included or not. I would though like to single out a few people in particular.

Firstly I mention Mandy Williams who typed this manuscript God knows how many times. Without her there would be no book. Nor indeed would there be a book had Tom Hartman not been riding shotgun over this enterprise. Originally I intended to give much more space to Tom, my business partner, and his views but it turned out that the sort of book I have written did not fit in entirely with what he expected so we compromised. In the Appendices you will find a very funny account of what went on behind the scenes from his point of view. Tom, being the modest man that he is, hid under his bushel a light which was always flickering and sometimes roaring. He was equally good with the printers and binders, in fact he was probably better than I was. I feel though that he deserves to have his say and his delightful essay, I suggest, adds tone to the book. I also owe an enormous amount of gratitude to Simon McMurtrie, my protégé, for all his good advice and encouragement over the years and even more recently. There are, alas, undoubtedly those who get no mention. This is because they were far too many. If you feel left out please complain and I will buy you lunch, or at least a drink.

I want to pay a special tribute to Henry Anglesey, Jack Smithers, Charles Whiting, Ewen Southby-Tailyour, the late John Terraine, Ronald Lewin and the late Michael Glover, all authors who gave the Leo Cooper imprint so much momentum, help and advice and also remained loyal to the imprint throughout its trials and tribulations.

Some there be who have no memorial but I could not let these acknowledgements stand were I not to thank, among many others, Tom Rosenthal, Kate (Gavron) Gardiner, Peter Gross, Victor Briggs,

Beth Macdougall, Helen Watson, John Mitchell, my production amanuensis, and Terry Mansell my bookkeeper for their advice and helpful information and friendship over the years. I want to thank, too, the Karamani family, my London landlords, for all the hospitality and helpful support they have given me and many of the players in the drama over the years.

Next I come to the category of the many people who have helped me, although they probably did not realise it at the time. I don't forget good deeds and I often think of those people and would hate them to think that I had forgotten them. For instance, I always had a soft spot for those poor chaps who had to go around the publishing houses selling advertising space. They are a dead breed now I suspect, but I remember with affection, among others, Frank Derry of *The Times*, the late Michael Roberts of the *New Statesman*, Christopher Lorne from *The Times*, Bob Dwyer-Joyce from *The Telegraph* and Andrew Wauchope. Many is the jolly drink we've had in the local pubs and many times has an order for a half double been placed out of sheer sympathy for the poor chap having to sell his soul to obtain it. The king of these was Michael Roberts whose sessions on bottles of Guinness or Bass knew no end. I miss him very much. One day he and I had been having some drinks in a pub in Tottenham Court Road over a period of one and a half to two hours. As we came out of the pub we were accosted by a survey lady with a clipboard who said: 'May I ask you a few questions?' To which we replied: 'Yes'. 'Have you had any Guinness today?' she asked. Michael said 'Yes'. She said: 'May I ask what quantity?' and he replied 'sixteen bottles between us'. She said: 'Come off it I am trying to do a decent survey here.' And he said: 'Well if you don't believe me come into the pub and we'll show you.' So we marched back into the pub and there in the corner was the table, still empty, at which we'd been sitting and on it were sixteen empty Guinness bottles. Game, set and match to Roberts and Cooper. An indication of the high regard in which Michael Roberts was held is borne out by the attendance at his funeral which included Derek Cross; Jeremy Lewis; Euan Cameron; John Gammons; Gwyn Hedley; Marian Fleizcher; Miles Huddleston; Fred Nolan and Richard Johnson. Many of these rallied later at the Cheshire Cheese in his memory, but they are all friends of mine as well whom I came across in various circumstances during the course of my publishing career and I am happy to include them here quite simply because I acknowledge that they were good friends.

I have listed people in alphabetical order and I want to start off by thanking Joan Astley OBE, who was at one stage Maurice

Buckmaster's assistant in SOE. She was always very kind to me and to Tom. Also, although she probably doesn't realise it, Diana Athill, whom I met at Deutsch, albeit briefly, was a great inspiration to me, particularly through her two books *Instead of a Letter* and *Stet*. Also helpful to me was the terrifying Vera Atkins of SOE. Then there was John Banks who taught me more about mercenaries than I cared to know. Michael Barber who briefly worked in the warehouse and later became a very useful outlet for authors' interviews which he was able to get exposed on the radio, not least for Forces' Broadcasting and the BBC. He is now the proud author of a life of Simon Raven called *The Captain* and his new book on Anthony Powell has just been released. I count him as a friend and I admire him very much. Other people beginning with 'B' include Mary and Andy Baylis who are in charge of the pub in my village and who provide the necessary fuel to allow me to tick over. Although I don't know him, I am obviously grateful to Eric de Bellaigue for the permission to quote from his wonderful book, *The British Book Publishing Business since the 1960s*. Nigel Brooke was a constant fan of mine as far as military books were concerned, i.e. he bought them!

In category 'C' Clive Carr deserves a mention for being one of my many Radleian friends who were kind to me when I was not well. I am glad that I am still in touch with most of them. There was, too, James Colquhoun who could claim to be my oldest friend. He is certainly one of the six and I believe I am godfather to one of his children, although I can't remember which one! James is probably the most constant friend of all. I first met him on National Service out in Kenya and we have been close ever since. I must mention Bruce Coward, the king of all space sellers in the good old days and the sustainer of the Publishers -v- *The Times* cricket match. I should also mention his delightful wife who, sailing under the name of Nicolette Milnes-Walker, was the first woman to cross the Atlantic single handed.

Category 'D' includes Ted Dexter who has also been a constant inspiration, although he probably doesn't know it, to me, at least on the cricket field. Then there is Christopher Duffy, the historian from Sandhurst. Good advice was constantly available from Professor M R D Foot. Susie and Bill Franklyn, my cousins, who are to be remembered for all the social support they have given, as is Professor Paul Fussel, the American historian who enjoyed (I think he did anyway) a hilarious trip to the battlefields in France with Tom Hartman in his mother's about to be sold, magnificent Daimler.

'G' is for Gray, Edwyn the submarine expert, constantly reprinting on the Pen & Sword list. Pat Grubb I want to thank for lending us the

Lebegue wine cellar to launch *The Queen's Malabars*. Then there was Shahid Hamid, alas no longer with us, a formidable Pakistani General, and Sir Stephen Hastings MC who was so helpful to us when we were looking after his excellent memoir. I thank Ernie Hecht for his encouragement and also for letting me use a paragraph from one of his books. Of all the independent publishers and solo acts surely Ernie must be the longest surviving member and the best. Overseas Jay Howland, née Williams, who used to work for Longmans in the old days on the exchange scholarship between Longmans and American publishers, has remained a friend ever since. Michael Hoyle was an early editor and useful because he had a brother who was a film star whose one success was a cameo performance in the film *Battle of Britain*. I remember too Miles Huddleston, the youngest looking of all old publishers who, for years, was a friend on the drinking circuit and indeed the publishing circuit. I thank Bobby Hunt for being a constant source of inspiration where picture research was concerned. I have written about Tim Jaques, but under 'J' must come Phillip Jones, originally working for Longmans in Australia and then coming over for a brief period and working in London, who became a close friend and who has just published his own autobiography in Australia.

Henry Keown-Boyd is a class act and should have started writing earlier. He was great fun to deal with. Fortunately for me I am still in touch with Lady Elizabeth Longman and owe her a deep debt of gratitude for sorting out the Longman family for me so I could get it right on how many there were when I first joined the firm. She has been a constant encouragement. Then there is Terry Lucas, who is mentioned later in the book and who was my pal at Longmans and has remained in touch ever since. I owe a lot to Martin Marix-Evans who first worked with me at Longmans and then shared those dreadful dark days at Frederick Warne. Subsequently he has been a constant friend and adviser and I am very grateful to him for all his help.

More locally there is Rosemary Nunneley, a regular source of comfort to me because I live in what used to be her house and we have our own little British Legion meetings in the pub every Monday. She never fails to turn up. Living overseas now, once a stalwart of the HAC (Honourable Artillery Company) rugby club is Simon Parker who has always kept a watchful eye on my publishing, mainly as a customer. I also thank Michael Pollock for advising me on aspects of the German hierarchy as far as the Nazis were concerned. He was an invaluable translator of documents.

John Scott has been a constant friend and an encourager. He is one of my heroes, being a Radleian, who was capped at rugby football for

England. We have remained in close touch. Also John Service of Seeley Service who was very much involved with us in the early days on the social side and was at one stage an apprentice of dazzling initiative in the old firm, an initiative which sometimes got us in into danger.

I thank Dave Todd who has been such a help in putting together the prints, pictures and photographs and for being the general factotum in and around the house while this book was being prepared. Also in category 'T' I must mention Lady Travers (Copper) whose husband was one of the officers in charge of the cadet cadre at Buller Barracks, Aldershot when I was a cadet and later became the Quartermaster General during the Falklands Campaign. Unfortunately he died prematurely otherwise he would have risen to the top of the army. His widow has always been kind to me. Then there is Michael Virtue, a fellow member of the HAC. He actually played in an HAC rugby fifteen, three of whom in the back row were called Virtue, Justice and Christian. That is really true. In Australia are John Waddilove and Christopher Walton, ironically the opening pair for the great Radley cricket eleven of 1951/52. Christo went on to captain Oxford and play for Middlesex and emigrated, as did John, to Australia; all those miles don't separate us because we see each other as often as we can. I do not forget Bob Wormald, a fellow Yorkshireman, a good customer and my ex fly-half. Lastly, but not least, there is Ilsa Yardley who was a colleague at André Deutsch and was one of the first people to read this book and be encouraging about it. She is godmother to my daughter Emily, but far more than that she was an ally against the forces of darkness in the Deutsch days.

No doubt by the time this book has gone to the printer I will discover a list of people I have left out, but all those mentioned I thank in enthusiastic terms, not least because the book couldn't have existed without their help and advice.

The work is dedicated to Jilly, my wife, who does not appear until half way through. The reason for this is quite simply that I was not married to her at the time the narrative began. As the Dedication says, I could not have survived without her love, affection, common sense and strong business experience. All this whilst pursuing her own path with distinction, wit and wisdom.

# Fall of Innocence

*Go, little booke; God send thee good passage,*
*And specially let this be thy prayere*
*Unto them all that thee will read or hear,*
*Where thou art wrong after their help to call,*
*Thee to correct in any part or all.*

Geoffrey Chaucer
*Troilus and Criseyde*

My first real memory is of a military nature. I was lying in my pram in the back garden of our house in the Yorkshire Dales. I must have been about 2½ to 3 years old. I remember this whole episode distinctly. I even remember the inside of the pram hood under which I tried to take shelter. I became aware of an extraordinary noise which was unfamiliar to me. It sounded like a drilling engine or something similar, not that I would have known, but it was relentless and it was coming nearer. I seem to remember nothing about what I did, but what I saw was enough to put the fear of God into anyone, let alone a young child. Suddenly, framed between the chimneys of our house, there appeared an absolutely astonishing sight. It was the *Graf Zeppelin* no less, and it was 1937. On a tour of Great Britain under the excuse of goodwill, this infernal machine was crossing England to visit Manchester and other industrial cities of the north. Goodwill is, up to a point, a not unreasonable way of looking at it, but it was later discovered that the airship had been on an intelligence mission, namely to photograph all industrial cities in the North of England from the air. Actually, you can forget the goodwill. I can hear the noise of those engines to this day. It looked deeply menacing, silver-grey and very long. It must have been only about 600 feet up. I was absolutely terrified and I cannot say any more than that. If one is absolutely terrified, one is.

I was, of course, far too young to explain to anybody what I had seen and for all I know I was gathered up and comforted, but I don't recall that part of it. I was in shock!

Quite by chance, some time ago I came across a cutting from one of the Northern papers reproducing an account of that visit by the *Graf Zeppelin* and its route passing over our house. Sure enough there was the very date on which this happened. She or he, whatever sex Zeppelins are, was blazoned over the front page of the *Yorkshire Post* and the dates and times coincided with my subsequent researches. No doubt tucked away in the bowels of some photographic collection, or indeed in the *Bundesarchiv* itself, there exists an aerial picture of an English infant bawling his head off in his pram as the *Graf Zeppelin* sailed between the two chimneys of his heavily defended (as you will see later) house.

My next experience of a military nature was the arrival of my maternal grandparents to stay in Yorkshire for the duration of the Second World War and with a self-appointed mission to start the third. The pace was too hot for them living in 'leafy' Chislehurst, and they descended on our household, much to the annoyance of my father, not only with all their goods and chattels, but, very fortunately for me, with a large collection of Britain's model soldiers, which had belonged to my mother's two brothers. They were a fine set, including Zulus, cavalry, coronation coaches, Royal Horse Artillery, you name it. All their arms moved. The sad thing is that, whilst I came to know all the uniforms of the regiments and details of their weapons, all I did was shoot them to pieces with my artillery and then replace their heads with matchsticks. What a stupid thing to do. A large set of Britain's soldiers such as I had (not to mention my Dinky Toys) are worth a fortune today to collectors. I have not one solitary soldier left, only a milkmaid and a turkey from the 'Britain's farm characters'*. Nevertheless I learnt a great deal, not least about military history.

My next experience was far more interesting. The war, as I've said, was upon us, as indeed were my grandparents, and my father, having been invalided out of the army, very carefully managed to become a local bigwig in the Home Guard, or LDV** as it was first called. Anybody who thinks Captain Mainwaring in the television series *Dad's Army* is an exaggeration should have seen my father. He was in charge of the local unit and, with his shiny boots, his sword (yes, he carried a sword on ceremonial days in the TA) and all his khaki finery he cut quite a dash. That image remains firmly planted in my memory,

* SOE Agents I suspect!
** Local Defence Volunteers.

as do the weapons belonging to the Home Guard which were stored temporarily in my nursery under the bed. There was a Blacker Bombard, a Northover Projector, a box of Mills grenades, a Patchett submachine gun and several Lee Enfield 303s, but not any ammunition. Little did the Germans know that I was harbouring a cache of such modest weapons of mass destruction and it's just as well that the *Graf Zeppelin* never looked under my bed.

My father's chief duty was to guard the Ribblehead Viaduct, which was the mainstay of the Settle/Carlisle line. This was all very well, but at the time there were rumours of parachutists dressed as nuns and therefore a twenty-four hour watch was kept on the Viaduct. However, my mother, who would have made a good nun, finally found out that, whilst he should have been guarding the arches, my father was quietly ensconced underneath them in the Ashfield Hotel in Settle with his cronies drinking himself to death, which he signally failed to do. I used to go out on manoeuvres with the Home Guard and learnt all about map reading and fieldcraft and, indeed, a little bit of tactical training, and this stayed with me all my life. I was aged 8. Part of me still is.

Later, when I went to prep school, I would become more aware of the war itself and the course it was following, because every Sunday evening after we had blubbed our way through 'The day thou gavest', the headmaster would call us to attention and read the latest dispatches from the front, or wherever, and read out too a list of those old boys who had so far perished in the conflict.

A small clinker-built rowing boat floats on the placid, mirror-smooth surface of a dark and deep man-made lake. Here the waters flowing down from Ingleborough and Gaping Ghyll are collected before plunging into the valley below, which leads on to the Ribble. The still water reflects the racing clouds on the lake's surface. Otherwise there is not a sound except the slow drip of the water off the two light oars which lie just above the surface, fixed in the rowlocks, and each of the two oars in the hands of a small boy aged 8 or 9. In the stern of *Amazon*, or it might have been *Swallow*, is hunched the figure of a man wearing a crumpled battledress and carrying the insignia on his shoulder flash, RAMC (the Royal Army Medical Corps). He wears the rank of Captain, three pips on his shoulder epaulette. He gazes intensely at the two boys who are sitting facing him, awaiting instructions. Suddenly the man bursts into tears with a huge gulp of emotion and turns his head away from the boys to hide his embarrassment. Who is he? Captain Booth RAMC has just been repatriated from a German Prisoner of War Camp, having been captured in the fighting around

Dunkirk. Of the two small boys, one is his son whom he has not seen since 1939 – it was now 1942. I was the other child.

What on earth were we doing that day, sitting in a small boat on a lake in the middle of the Yorkshire Dales? The answer is that, as a special privilege, Captain Booth was allowed to take out his son for the day, together with one friend. This was called a 'leave out'. But there is really not much to do in such circumstances – no shops, no pubs, no cafés, nothing. The Captain shook from side to side with emotion, hiding his head in his hands, and the boat began to wobble. What on earth the management of the prep school who had sanctioned the trip thought they were doing allowing such an unsupervised boating trip for two young boys and a disturbed doctor was beyond belief. They could ill afford to lose any more pupils. Neither of us could swim and we could hardly row. 'I think we had better turn round,' said Captain Booth now recovered. I had never seen a man cry before but in this case there was no escape, short of jumping overboard. We were trapped. Eventually we managed to paddle to the shore and disembarked. I never saw Captain Booth again and his son (Booth, Anthony) was never a bosom pal. He was an untidy child with a shock of snow-white hair and a pair of metal-rimmed glasses. His socks were always round his ankles and he dressed like a scarecrow. His nickname at the school was 'Professor'. The first time I'd set eyes on him was the day I was first delivered to the school. Some weeks later, after the boat trip, Booth approached me in the corridor and said, 'Have you been to the library yet? There are some jolly good books there.' I was far more interested in what was going on up the corridor, where a boy called Gretton Doidge was attempting to drown a mouse in a wash basin. 'When the bubbles stop,' he said, 'it will be dead.' I turned away, imagining the rowing boat – Captain Booth, his son and myself sinking to the bottom of the lake in a trail of bubbles.

I have no idea what happened to Captain Booth, but I do know that Anthony, that most unprepossessing of schoolboys, became a successful medical professor at one of the great teaching hospitals in London. I wonder if his bubbles have stopped now.

Why am I telling you all this? I have had plenty of time to think about it. That vision of the man bursting into tears in the middle of a lake has never left my mind. Whether he was crying out of relief at finding his son who was clearly not what he expected. (I felt *de trop*), or whether it was in the sheer horror of what he'd found, I didn't bother to find out. I think it was the first time I realised that grown-ups had emotions, other than those that one experienced from the daily interaction of one's parents.

It was a strange time of my life. Almost symbolic was the rowing boat in the middle of the lake going nowhere, and even more so was the fact that the episode was never mentioned again by anybody to anybody until now. You may think this is a trivial incident, but it made me realise that beyond us all were things that we couldn't control, least of all war and warfare, loneliness, despair and longing. Part of this book is about those emotions.

The episode made a great impression on me, as did all the fieldcraft games that we played as boy cubs and scouts in the daft and happy hunting grounds of Ingleborough Hall, which was a wild, wild place, set in the bosom of the limestone Pennines and belonging to the Farrer family. The garden had been designed and laid out by that old queen, the eccentric horticulturist Reginald Farrer. The headmaster was called Oliver Farrer.* He only lasted one term for me. He had served on the Somme and occasionally ran off into the woods where he would howl and scream, the horrors of 1 July 1916 never having left him. During my first school holidays he died suddenly and there is a memorial plaque to him in the Clapham (Yorks) village church, which the expansion of the stonework has managed to split in half. The school had been evacuated from Broadstairs at the start of the war to Clapham, near Settle, where I was born. I remember all too much about this prep school, but I don't feel like writing about it except to tell you why I am the only person I know who can play the piano with one hand alone. This is because my music master, who shall remain nameless, usually had one hand up my trousers so I was constantly fending him off. I was oven-ready. I am not going to write much more about my childhood here either because that is another book. Suffice it to say that after leaving my prep school, which had returned to Broadstairs, I then went on to be educated at Radley where I achieved some military notoriety, not least being in charge of the Military Band. I also achieved the utmost glory on the cricket and rugby pitches and was capped later on for Yorkshire as a schoolboy. Little attention was given to academic prowess.

My early training in the CCF (Combined Cadet Force) was very useful because it meant, when I later went to do my National Service, I had a background which enabled me to play the trumpet and use a 303 rifle, understand the normal elements of drill and map reading, and hence, when eventually I did roll up in Aldershot for my statutory two years, I was, like many other public school boys, seized on by the

---

* Coincidentally the Chief Editor at Secker & Warburg, where I went to work in the future, was Oliver Farrer's brother, David, a delightful and brilliant editor, particularly of fiction.

instructing staff to help them knock the edges off those poor young fellow National Servicemen, many of whom had never been away from home in their lives. Some had never seen pyjamas or owned a toothbrush. Most cried themselves to sleep at night, asking for their mothers. Within six weeks the system had turned them into a cohesive unit, such is the power and experience of the British Army's training skills, and even at that stage in my military career I was enormously impressed by how quickly attitudes changed and the intense competition between huts over keeping the hut floors clean; how quickly men respond to discipline when there is so much at stake over reliance on your mate to help you out. You were lost without a mate. I remember, even now, the names of many of my fellow trainees. There was Betteridge, King, the Austin twins, Finn (just out of Wormwood Scrubs), Cunningham, Chritchlow, Jefferies, Price, Whale, Smith, Wandless, Kelland, Wax, Pevan, Olden, to name just a few. Smith eventually achieved fame as the young Mr Grace in the television series *Are You Being Served?* Olden was Ted Ray's son Robin who was later to achieve fame on television.

After call-up I went through the normal basic training as a soldier and passed out with fairly good marks. The rest, as they say, is history and here it is. My story really begins here.

I took passage aboard HMT *Empire Windrush* on New Year's Eve in 1953. This ill-fated vessel (destination Kenya and Singapore) was, in a roundabout way, on her last voyage, although we were not to know it at the time. I myself was heading for a totally fresh experience. A newly commissioned subaltern, I had chosen to serve out most of my National Service in one of the more beautiful countries in the world. Kenya at that time, though, was suffering from a blight which is now known as the Mau Mau rebellion, although that is almost exaggerating its importance. Here is not the place to discuss the whys and wherefores of that campaign but I was not heading for a cushy number. Far from it. The day after I arrived Lord Wavell's son was killed in action serving with the Black Watch. The Mau Mau were represented by the British press as a bunch of hooligans, but the army was having a hard time trying to knock the hell out of them. For instance, the regiments sent from Germany had only been trained in nuclear warfare – not much use in the forest. Nor were a flight of Lincoln Bombers, a flight of Harvards normally used as trainers but adapted for dropping bombs by hand over the side, or a flight of Vampire Jets which flew in from Aden and set the forest on fire with their rockets. The other thing that these raids did was injure forest animals; there is a terrible story of an elephant that had had its trunk blown off and came down marauding in the villages because it couldn't eat as it had lost its KFS*, so to speak.

To clarify the emergency situation, 2,000 loyal Africans were killed and only thirty-two British or European civilians. Thirty-two British combatants were killed, nineteen of whom were shot by their own side – friendly fire. The real casualties were the Africans themselves. Over 10,000 lost their lives during the conflict, black on black. It is worth pointing out here that, based on figures from 1945, white National Serviceman took part in six major campaigns and during that time 345 were killed in action. I don't have the figures for wounded. Back to the ship.

I was totally wet behind the ears when I boarded HMT *Empire Windrush*. I had never been overseas before, an innocent going abroad. I had never drunk spirits. I had virtually no experience with the opposite sex, although that was not for want of trying. Having been educated at boarding schools I was perfectly prepared for the uncomfortable conditions in which one had to serve during basic training. I was lucky, however, because I was going to serve in a transport unit which, to my joy, would give me, I hoped, the ability to swan all round East Africa at the War Office's expense. I was lucky also to be offered such a posting, acquired by passing out second in my cadet course which gave me a wider choice. Passing out first was Robin Olden who had opted to serve in Grantham, because he thought it would be 'less noisy'.

As I said I had never been abroad before and indeed my knowledge of East Africa, or any other part of the world for that matter, was limited. I'd been launched into a world of routine post-boarding school indecision, not really knowing what I was going to do with my life. In many ways the army, which I had almost decided to join as a regular, seemed as good an option as any, although of course being a National Serviceman the choice of units was, up to a point, small.

This original desire to join the regular army had been somewhat hindered by the fact that I was totally deaf in one ear and have been since I was 6. This meant that I was kept back after my initial training and told that I would never get a commission. By some judicious wire-pulling I soon managed to get this decision reversed. The Old Boy Net had swung into action. In fact I arrived at Mons Officer Cadet School before some of my contemporaries. 22867795 later became 432316. You never forget your number.

* Army slang for knife, fork and spoon.

During the time I served in Kenya I was fortunate as far as travelling was concerned. With access to plenty of expected War Office fuel I could go where I wanted, within reason, not least because I was the person who signed the work tickets. I had been posted to an up-country town called Nyeri* which was at the centre of the Kikuyu Reserve and indeed very much the centre of the Mau Mau's terror campaign. Whilst flitting from place to place as part of my duties running an independent transport platoon of the 70th East African Brigade, I had a great deal more opportunity to see the countryside than many of my contemporaries. This also meant that by visiting all the various military units which I was required to do during the course of my duties, I was able to see a great deal of the British Army, not always successfully in action so to speak.

Many of the regiments that came to take part in the campaign had been gently simmering on the hob in Germany or the UK – dull postings with not much activity. Some of those, it is true, had taken part in the Korean War which was ending just as I started. We passed a troopship homeward bound as we entered the harbour at Aden. 'Get your knees brown,' they shouted at us and it was also in Aden that I set foot on foreign shores for the first time. Never to be forgotten. Earlier we had been stuck for a day in the Suez Canal. Other regiments sent for had served in Malaya and various trouble spots such as Cyprus. Kenya was very much a second XI campaign, but many distinguished British regiments (eleven in fact) were to have the opportunity of serving there before it was all over.

I was fortunate enough, by virtue of my occupation, constantly to be able to compare one regiment with another. There was always something distinctively different about their image, attitude, efficiency and not least hospitality. As time went on, I became more and more intrigued by the way the army worked and indeed with the regiments themselves and their histories. At any one time I might find myself visiting the Black Watch, The Royal Northumberland Fusiliers, The King's Own Shropshire Light Infantry (Simon Raven's mob), The King's Own Yorkshire Light Infantry (my father's old regiment and one which I had hoped to join as a regular), The Buffs, The Royal Inniskilling Fusiliers, The Gloucestershire Regiment and The Devonshire Regiment, not to mention several battalions of the King's African Rifles. There were two full brigades in the field at this time. 92 Company EAASC, commonly known as 'white officers with black privates', was based in Nairobi. It was a ramshackle outfit. I was given

* Baden Powell is buried there and the Outspan Hotel and Treetops are adjacent.

responsibility for 'A' Platoon and promptly sent north after I had attended a quick language course in Swahili and had myself measured for the statutory desert boots and khaki drill uniform. I should point out here that most people, settlers and the army, adopted a pretty unusual style of dress, more like cowboys and indeed sometimes like Indians. They were only carrying on the tradition of the original Desert Rats. Many of them were from the Kenya Regiment whose knowledge of the countryside and the ground was absolutely invaluable to the British Infantry. Each British battalion had two or three Kenya Regiment men attached and they were usually in the thick of events, although they did not necessarily respond to British military discipline in the way that might have been expected. Nearly everyone (army or civvy) toted a loaded gun. Life could be very dangerous at times.

Just before I left for the north, I was given a somewhat unpleasant job as acting escort to a man under trial by court martial for cruelty to prisoners. Captain Griffiths had captured some terrorists in the forest and linked them together through the lobes of their ears with piano wire as he led them to captivity. It is the right of an officer who is awaiting court martial to have two escorts, one of similar rank and a subaltern. I was this subaltern. There is no point in going into the details of the case, but it made an impact on me to have to sit on a veranda drinking neat gin (which I had never had before I arrived in Kenya) listening to the reminiscences and ramblings of a chap who was plainly a misfit. He was duly sent to prison, followed not long after by a string of officers from various base units who never quite got over the last war and were often caught with their hands in the PRI* till. Very much buckshee Majors, if you know what I mean.

One morning I came down to breakfast to find one of these characters fast asleep with his face in a bowl of cornflakes. Someone had written 'Good Morning' in lipstick on his bald head. There were other eccentrics one had to tolerate. One man never stopped describing how during the Desert War he'd captured a mobile brothel from the Italians with soldiers actually on the job at the time. Another officer, who had served in the Navy and was now in the King's African Rifles, used to drink Pink Gin and onions at lunch time. He only ever went into lunch when the glass was full to the top with onions. As a result he wasn't much use to anybody in the afternoon. There were plenty of these characters and one was safest to be away from them because most had got into bad habits as a result of their experiences in

---

* The Army Welfare Fund, PRI standing for President of the Regimental Institute. It is a unit's or regiment's private bank service.

the war. They were a sad group of people who wore the General List badge. Gradually as time went on they became fewer and fewer. I was lucky to have the posting north because there was far less interference from the directing staff and I was very much able to be my own master.

Although my brigade headquarters was in Nyeri, my camp, at the supply point, was about three miles outside, so I had my own perimeter, my own security problems and indeed responsibility at the tender age of 19 for more than thirty-three lorries, three 15cwt trucks, two Land Rovers, three staff cars, four ambulances, a recovery vehicle, three motorcycles and the occasional water tanker. Aligned with this motley collection of vehicles were sixty odd African Askaris and three white NCOs. Most of them were drivers and some of them were cast in the role of storemen which was from their point of view a very useful job to have, because it was virtually impossible in the camp to keep track of anything that was portable.

I mentioned earlier the fact that all the British regiments had such different characteristics. This is where I acquired my continuing curiosity and interest in the whole structure of the British Army and its history by working alongside them or in parallel with them. Let me give you an example of an eccentricity which was not untypical. The Devonshire Regiment had one National Service subaltern who was a brilliant pianist. Somewhere or other the Battalion had managed to obtain a grand piano, and on the several occasions that I was called in to move the Regiment from one location to another, I was amused to see that the grand piano usually went with the advance party. This was confirmed when I once went up into the forest to a location that the Devons had just occupied. There was a clearing in the forest at a place that I think was called Karatina. Trees had been chopped down and the essential corrugated iron buildings such as latrines, cook houses, etc. had been erected by the PWD* and the bush cleared. The only tent erected, however, was that of the officer's mess and as I drove up I could hear the mellifluous sound of a Chopin Nocturne as it floated through the forest out of the GS Marquee in which the piano was placed. I never forgot that moment any more than I forgot that Regiment's nickname, 'the Bloody Eleventh'. Nothing could be further from the truth to judge by how they behaved towards me. I was welcomed with open arms, fed and watered and asked to dine and stay the night with them. This was in stark contrast to a visit to The Buffs sometime later where I was treated like a servant. I know that the

* Known as the Piss and Wind Department. Actually the Public Works Department.

Royal Army Service Corps, or indeed the East African Army Service Corps, were not exactly fashionable units, but the Royal Logistic Corps* (as they are today) are seated well above the salt. The measure of a decent regiment as far as I was concerned was how they treated me and the men, the emphasis being very much on the men. Incidentally, I dare say the Devons were not quite so pleased with me the following morning when I discovered that my two dogs (one of which used to belong to the gin and onion man) had devoured a large proportion of the meat ration of the Devons during the course of a rampaging night when everyone was having a singsong. I crept away muttering about marauding forest creatures and often wonder whether they realised who the real culprit was.

It was not a cushy posting and I witnessed certain unpleasantnesses. One of these was turning up at breakfast one morning where I was messing with the 23rd KAR to find twenty-six bodies, all of them needless to say black, laid out in rows outside the breakfast tent. Nearly all of them appeared to have been shot through the head. There was a sheen on their skin like a damson plum. They represented the night's catch. This created a certain amount of trouble at the time because some English politicians got hold of the fact that regiments were having competitions to see how many terrorists they could kill. A scoreboard was being kept. It was also the first time I had seen any dead bodies and it is quite a shock to see twenty-six first go. It left a nasty taste in my mouth.

On another occasion I was called up in the middle of the night to provide transport urgently to take most of the brigade to surround a house which belonged to Professor L S B Leakey of anthropology fame. There had been a Mau Mau raid on his house. His daughter managed to hide in the attic but his wife was left dead on the lawn. She had been strangled and was lying staring awfully with wide open eyes, wearing a grey chiffon dress on which the dew had already begun to settle. There was no sign of Professor Leakey and indeed he was not found until several weeks later. His captors had buried him alive. He was an honorary member of the Kikuyu tribe and spoke their language and was much loved by them all, in keeping with their policy towards those who were sympathetic to them. I watched the medical people move in and followed them into the house which had been ransacked. One thing caught my eye. On the mantelpiece was a Victoria Cross in a frame which had been won by Professor Leakey's son in the Abyssinian Campaign at the beginning of the last war. Of all

---

* Now jokingly known as The Really Large Corps.

the items that the terrorists could have taken one would have thought that a Victoria Cross would have been the first among them, but it was rescued and is now in safe hands.

Not long after this episode, I had to appear twice in the Nyeri Civil Court as a prosecution witness. My first appearance was to identify a scruffy looking gang whom we captured on the outskirts of our camp. The second was as an observer only at the trial of 'General' China who, being the local milkman, had promoted himself rapidly. He was nevertheless sentenced to death, as were the gang because they were carrying arms. 'General' China, who was later reprieved, appears in the illustration section.

In this prologue I have tried to set out some sort of background which explains why I became so closely linked with the Army and indeed with military history. I suppose, on reflection, because my deep desire to become a regular soldier was not to be fulfilled, the nearest I could get was to take an interest in the history of the regiments. You will see later how my experiences with and alongside the armed forces helped to prepare me for my eventual career as a specialist publisher of military and particularly regimental history, of which I have published under my own name over 120 individual volumes.

# CHAPTER I

# *In at the Shallow End*

*The sole pardon one can extend to rebels
Is to kill them promptly.*

Jean-Baptiste Carrier

Looking back, Kenya was one glorious dream. I have been able to return there twice in recent years, and part of my heart is still buried there. As the RAF Hermes crossed the English Channel flying directly over Worthing on whose beaches Hitler had planned to land in his invasion of the United Kingdom (I wonder what Granny now back in 'leafy' Worthing would have thought of it all), I suddenly became aware that everything had now changed, even trooping by sea was no longer the form – hence my seat on the aircraft. It was now 1955. As the fate of the HMT *Empire Windrush** was probably partly responsible for ending trooping by ship, it might be worth recording that she blew up and sank on her return voyage having dumped me in Mombasa some time earlier. HMT *Empire Windrush* lies, for the second time, at the bottom of the sea, off the coast of Algiers. Four crew were killed in the explosion and all the rest of the passengers (many still wearing dinner jackets at six o'clock in the morning) were rescued in an amazing performance by the crew and lots of little boats. Apparently there had been some competition about the amount of mileage the ship could make in one day and the chief engineer had drawn a bow at a venture and thrown a particular switch in the engine room which nobody had used before. The mileage of the ship increased to over 400 miles in a day and then she blew up. So that was the end of that.

* She had previously sailed under the name *Monte Rosa* and another of her claims to fame was that she was one of the ships we used to bring the large numbers of West Indians to these shores after the war in which she had been scuttled by the German owners. All Africa got in exchange was me!

1

The aircraft plumped itself down on the tarmac at Blackbushe and taxied to a halt outside the terminal building. A new life was about to begin. Here were my family to meet me, and after the initial embarrassed greetings a stony silence descended on the car as we headed back to London. My only request was to see a 'Teddy Boy' who had come into fashion since I'd left the country and sure enough there was one walking up Camberley High Street so I felt that I was back in civilization again.

There was a 21st birthday dinner to come at the Savoy and various telephone calls to be made, and then finally I arrived back home in Yorkshire to contemplate my future. As I always do when I go home, I made a point of walking up the hill to the moorlands behind our house to an area known as the Tops. From here on a clear day you can see in a complete circle. Over to the left there is Hellifield, farther to the right Clitheroe, then the Ribble valley itself with the oxbow bends of the river which glisten in the sunlight, and then Settle where I was born. Behind me the great limestone crags of the Pennines forcing their way to the skyline. Curlews were as usual in full and mournful cry and the sky-larks twittered their way up into the air leading me away from their nesting grounds. There was a lot of thinking to be done. It was plainly obvious that I wasn't going to be able to get much further with my life if I stayed in Yorkshire. At the back of my mind there lurked a memory. A great friend of my parents asked me before I went off to Africa what I intended to do with my life and I murmured something about becoming a writer. 'You'd be wasting your time,' she said. 'Your father's a writer and he has never made a penny. If you ask me the people who make the money are the publishers.' This seemed an intriguing idea but I didn't really know very much about what publishers did, although I had received some slight introduction to the literary world thanks to my two maiden aunts who lived in London. They were my father's sisters and in their own way a very talented duo. From the age of 15, journeying between Yorkshire and Broadstairs, and later Radley, I always stopped off in London and spent a night or so with them. For me these visits were quite wonderful and the aunts themselves founts of wisdom, enthusiasm for the arts and good living. They always entertained me royally. They took me to theatres, concerts and restaurants. They introduced me to Fitzrovia, to writers and artists, and I met a whole gallery of people who later became, or already were, household names during my publishing career*.

* Aunt Barbara once took me to lunch at the Café Royal with L A G Strong. I had been given a book called *The Man Who Asked Questions* which was a life of Socrates. I dropped a terrible brick by saying that I found the book very difficult to read and I never saw him again. I didn't like him anyway. I was a pompous little squirt.

Aunt Lettice* was the chief aunt. She had published eighteen novels in her lifetime and a fair number of other books. She was also one of the three writers** responsible for lobbying the government in support of the public lending right for which she quite deservedly earned an OBE. She died aged 97, having been a very early influence in my life. I shall always be grateful to her. Her sister, Barbara, was a different cup of tea. Unlike Lettice she was high Tory, whereas Aunt Lettice was deeply left and had a diploma from Lady Margaret Hall, Oxford. Barbara had studied singing in Leeds and then gone south and tried to write. Sadly, twice she had books within an ace of being published and twice publishers went broke on her which was ominous to my way of thinking. Nevertheless she did have a very important job. She was secretary to an extraordinary man called John Lehmann. John, who had been at Eton, was the brother of two well known figures in the arts world, Rosamand, a novelist and Beatrix, an actress. He, in 1936, started Penguin New Writing and during the war there were very few officers in the army who were without the odd copy of New Writing in their knapsacks.

Later John founded the *London Magazine* which he ran with inimitable style from a delightful house in Pimlico. The ballet dancers Alexis Racine and Nadia Nerina lived upstairs. I had done the odd day's work for John Lehmann during some of my visits to London in previous years and was well aware that he was what you might call today gay, but in a fairly predatory fashion. I am afraid Aunt Barbara used to pimp for him and he wasn't averse to a bit of rough trade. Curiously enough this is where Tom Hartman, my business partner, first comes in because not long after we had met, Tom was approached by a builder who was doing some work on the roof of his house who said to him: 'Tom, I've got a cheque here but I haven't got a bank account. Could you cash it for me?' Tom said, 'Show me the cheque.' He was more than surprised to see it was made out to '*The Bearer*' (a strange misnomer under the circumstances) and was signed by John Lehmann. On another occasion John summoned me up to his office. 'Come here dear boy,' he said 'I want a word with you.' Wondering what I'd done wrong I went up to his study and walked across the room and stood by his desk and to my horror I heard the door being locked behind me. Some minutes later it was made plain by myself that I was not rough trade or indeed any sort of trade and I was released, but that didn't help our relationship very much. As time drew on, I often saw John and he always boomed a hopeful greeting

* During the war Lettice was private secretary to Lord Woolton, Minister of Food.
** Brigid Brophy and Maureen Duffy were the other two.

across the bar at the Garrick, but in his later years he became rather a sad figure and eventually had to resign from the Club because he couldn't afford the membership. Nevertheless, he helped lots of writers and publishers in their early days and many young men such as myself cracked their teeth by working in the office for virtually no money, among them Martin Seymour-Smith, David Hughes, Charles Osborne, et al, who later made their own literary reputations. John died not many years ago and I shall remember him, but not necessarily for the right reasons. But I digress.

So I went south leaving behind for ever my beloved Yorkshire. First stop was the aunts. They were magnificent. To start with they showed me how to try and find somewhere to live and secondly they gave me a list of people to contact, friends in publishing in most cases. I was sent to see Victor Gollancz who dismissed me with a puff of cigar smoke. I met the famous bookseller J G Wilson of Bumpus's Bookshop and a whole gaggle of publishers too numerous to mention here. They were all very kind. Finally my Aunt Lettice suggested I write to some-body called Noel Brack at Longmans and this I did.

I had never heard of Longmans but they were one of the most firmly established publishing houses (founded in 1724*) in London and before I knew where I was Noel Brack had offered me a job with a view to being sent out to Africa to sell educational books. This never came to fruition and I didn't get back to Africa that way, but what I was offered was a job in the invoicing department on the trade side. Here began my life in publishing. Nobody could have been more ill-suited to the job than I, whose sole educational qualification was one 'A' level in Art and whose knowledge of mathematics and calculation was worse than pathetic. I could speak Swahili moderately well but that was little help. I had in fact achieved a first by failing to answer any questions in the Common Entrance paper on maths at all and here was I, eleven years later, at the centre of a busy office checking invoices to see whether they had been cast off correctly.

I was to remain at Longmans for ten years and I ask forgiveness for offering a brief account of the time I spent there. I was learning all the time, but it took me rather longer than most to realise that the way to the top was not to sit and just wait for things to come to you. Looking back I bitterly regret that I stuck with my job at Longmans for as long as I did. On the other hand there were compensations, some of them being the people with whom I came into contact through work, and of course, above all, there were the authors themselves.

* They were once called Longmans, Rees, Orme, Brown & Green.

Telegrams
Longmans, Piccy, London
Cables
Freegrove, London

Directors
W. Longman
K. B. Potter, C. S. S. Higham,
T. M. Longman, M. F. K. Longman,
J. C. Longman

# Longmans, Green & Co Limited
## 6 & 7 Clifford Street, London, W.1

Ref. M/HG        June 20th,        1955

*Telephone: Regent 7431 (10 lines)*

New York
Toronto
Bombay
Calcutta
Madras
Melbourne
Cape Town

Leonard Cooper, Esq1,
229, Goldhurst Terrace,
N.W.6.

Dear Cooper,

    I now write formally to confirm that we are pleased to engage you as a clerk in our Home Sales department, as arranged earlier last week.

    As you know, our standard office hours are 9 a.m. to 5.30 p.m. with an hour for lunch, and we are closed on Saturdays. We have a canteen on the premises. Everyone receives a fortnight's holiday a year with pay, and later on depending upon age plus length of service, or the particular post held, there are provisions for the granting of three weeks' holiday with pay. The Company give, and require to receive, one month's notice of termination of employment.

    Initially, your salary will be £6. 10. 0. per week. In addition, however, it has been the Company's practice, in recent years, when business has been good, to pay a bonus to all members of the staff. The payment, and the actual size of this bonus, which is calculated as a percentage of salary is dependent upon trading conditions generally. Three months after you join us, you will be required to join the Pension Scheme, and your weekly contribution to this will amount to 5/-.

    I am enclosing a duplicate copy of this letter, and if you agree that I have correctly set out the arrangements made between yourself and the Company, perhaps you would write "Agreed" on the duplicate, sigh it, and return it to me.

                  Yours very truly,

                  N.D.J. Brack,
                  Manager.

Longmans at this time was emerging from the effects of the war, having been virtually wiped out during the blitz in the famous publishers' fire at Paternoster Row. The firm had been run by one K B Potter (who earlier had rescued the business by investing £25,000) and C S S Higham. During the war they had managed to corner large parts of the educational markets, not least in Africa, west and east, and in the Far East. The emphasis on educational books was beginning to be like the tail that wagged the dog. With the freedom from colonialism giving the opportunity for the emergent nations to educate themselves, educational publishing was a boom trade, particularly as very little had been done during the course of the war. Longmans had their sights on this market and they grabbed the initiative with both hands, while their main rivals' behaviour in trying to steal the Longman market by subterfuge and bribery was dubious to say the least.

Whilst I sat in the ex-billiard room of No 6/7 Clifford Street, surrounded by smelly young typists (there was no air conditioning), making the wrong calculations, I began to wake up to my surroundings and to find my feet in London. One aspect of Longmans' location in Mayfair, where I first went to work, was that the office was opposite Cork Street which was home to all the art galleries. Even more interestingly, it was the frequent beat of some fairly dramatic ladies of the night, many of whom I used to know and who became bosom friends, if you will forgive the expression. Likewise I used to go into all the art galleries so I had a fairly good knowledge of painting, with my one 'A' level tucked under my belt. There was a constant flow of exhibitions available and I was only a few hundred yards from the Royal Academy so this was a bonus.

What wasn't a bonus, though, was the tedious work I was having to do. My colleagues, Terry Lucas and Michael Wymer, both ex-National Servicemen, deduced from our researches that there was a person above us who checked the work that we had been doing. So we worked out that if we 'checked' an average of say 300 invoices a day we would be bound to make mistakes, but the knowledge that a Mrs Jackson sat checking our work meant that we just didn't bother to add the things up properly, and we lived a life of quiet serenity. There were some good pubs around the corner and we used to go out into Green Park and play catch with a tennis ball. There were also secretaries to pounce on, the attraction of which became more of a challenge once 'modesty' panels were fitted to their desks.

Such frivolity was not going to last and fortunately the person who occupied the job I had my eye on left. There was a void in the publicity department and I was moved sideways, which was a great blessing because I came under the influence of a tremendous man in all senses of the word, Laurence Cotterell who, among other things, had served as a trooper in the war in Palestine. He had at one stage been the transport manager of a laundry. He had lost the job by being rude to his superior, but the said superior had made a misjudgement and didn't realise that Laurence was a light heavyweight champion boxer; not only that, he was to prove it by knocking his transport manager out in the car park. So Laurence was a man of substance, a great bear of a man. He was also a minor poet and a legend in publishers' publicity circles. I worked under him for nearly five years and this was really my beginning in publishing.

One of the perks of working for Laurence Cotterell was that I was given a secretary, my first. I treated her like I would a delicate ornament and was very impressed by her because she was obviously a well-bred filly. My admiration for her grew enormously on the day that I overheard her on the telephone. It was a Friday and the conversation went, 'Daddy, hello Daddy, Can you hear me?' Obviously she was ringing up her father. Next came the immortal line. 'Daddy, will you arrange to have the train stopped. I'm coming on the five thirty'. This was in the days when feudalism still reigned. When the railways crossed people's private land they were entitled to have a train stopped at their local station should they so wish. I believe this is now discontinued because they'll stop anywhere but at the station. Her name was Caroline. I often wonder what happened to her.

Later on, Cotterell taught me, among other things, to eat and drink well at decent restaurants as long as Longmans picked up the bill. They were in fact very generous and had a reputation for good parties and good hospitality, partly due to one Mark Longman who was in overall charge of the firm but not what one might call an active publisher or an entrepreneur. He was dashingly handsome, and was married to one of the Queen's bridesmaids, Lady Elizabeth Lambart, with whom I fell madly in love. Mark, when he did any publishing work at all, was used as a flying ambassador by Longmans to go all round the world, very often with Lady Liz, chasing the educational business. But his real feeling was for general publishing and it was in that area that I had been firmly placed.

Mark Longman is best summed up by the following anecdote. On Fridays I used to wear my only suit and hang around on the stairs hoping to be noticed. One day I met Mr Mark, as he was called. I had him cornered and I ventured to say to him, 'Oh Mr Mark, I have just finished reading *The Trap* by Dan Billany. What a marvellous book it is and how much I enjoyed *Broken Images* by John Guest.' Mark looked somewhat astounded and beckoned me into his newly decorated office. Signs of affluence were beginning to show themselves as a result of Longmans' success in the educational market. Nowhere did it show more than in the extravagant decoration of Mark's office. The office walls were dragged in dark green and the woodwork picked out in gold.

'Come in and sit down,' he said. Then he gave me a piece of advice that I have never forgotten. 'I am very glad that you take an interest in the books, but whatever you do don't talk to me about them when there are other people around. You see I don't actually read them.' How true that was.

The Longmans general list at this time was a fascinating one. It contained many categories of books with a strong leaning towards the humanities and religion. Tucked away in various rooms in the office buildings were private little empires run by experts in their field. For instance the late James Kennaway (a brilliant novelist) used to run the humanities department and was succeeded by Jocelyn Baines, a delightful man who sadly committed suicide. Kennaway was killed in a car crash. Then there was one called Cyprian Blagden who was in charge of history and had undertaken to write Longmans' official history. This book is not yet published! I could go on listing them. The real shop window though was the general books department to which I was posted. Apart from Gavin Maxwell, whom I will say more about later, there existed a stable of absolutely excellent writers.

There was the novelist Francis King, carefully nurtured by John Guest, our chief editor. John was very squeamish. He often gave me manuscripts to read and he once singled out one by Colin Spencer. I can't remember the title of the book but it had a particularly unpleasant scene in which somebody disposes of a miscarriage down a lavatory. John gave me the manuscript but he stapled together a five-page section. He didn't want to upset me, having found the whole passage deeply distasteful. Of course the first thing one did was to break the staple and see what all the fuss was about. Then there was Christopher Hibbert on the way up and Walter Lord, famous for writing the book about the sinking of the Titanic, *A Night to Remember*.

Another eccentric author, but a delightful one, was Fred Majdalany who was the *Daily Mail* film critic. He had fought at the Battle of Cassino and he produced an absolutely superb history of that battle. The jacket was designed by Lynton Lamb who also fought at Cassino. Fred was also a *bon viveur* and once gave me a marvellous description of how he and his wife managed to struggle home to Suffolk from Liverpool Street station. They were both so drunk that all they could do was travel the whole journey with their heads stuck out of the train window and they emerged at the other end covered in smuts and looking like chimney sweeps.

Another star was a brilliant but grumpy old lesbian novelist who wrote the most superb historical novels. She was called Mary Renault and was best known for her two books *The King Must Die* and *The Last of the Wine*. She was probably the best writer on the list, but difficult, and, thank God, she lived in South Africa. We also published books by David Garnett, Robin Maugham and Christopher Hassall, Ivor Novello's lyricist. Hassall died in a railway train on his way to Ramsgate. Someone heard of his death and remarked what a joy it must have been setting out for Ramsgate and waking up in heaven. Other authors on the list were M M Kaye (*Shadow of the Moon*) and the magnificent industrial revolution historian L T C Rolt whose books on Isambard Kingdom Brunel and Telford were masterpieces of the biographer's art. There is a lovely story told about John Guest who was Rolt's editor. There appeared on the office notice board one day a limerick which went as follows:

> *Oh doctor please help me it's* hell
> *Digging tunnels 'neath the Westbury Hotel,*\*
> *But you see my name's Guest*
> *And I'm wholly obsessed*
> *With Isambard Kingdom Brunel.*

Not long after the phantom lyricist struck again with a limerick about one of our typists.

> *A love story addict is Janet.*
> *She's read every one in the planet.*
> *When a new one appears*
> *She goes rushing downstairs*
> *To get it before they can ban it.*

The general lethargy of the office at this time was beautifully summed up by the lyricist (now identified as a clever young girl called Mary Rayner). This one, describing various people in an editorial office, read:

---

\* The Westbury Hotel was being built on a site behind the office in Clifford Street.

*Two editors, Steven and Hugh,*
*Lacked things constructive to do*
*So they flicked rubber bands*
*With their rulers and hands*
*At each other, and Herbert Rees too*

I cannot give a description of Longmans without mentioning one Herbert Rees who had been a minor canon of St Paul's and was defrocked for some misdemeanour with a member of his confirmation class. He also had a brain tumour removed. We frequently found him fast asleep at his desk and had to wake him up when the boss came round. He was very, very funny and had an encyclopaedic knowledge of the English language. He was the author of a book called *The Rules of Printed English* or *Rope* as it was commonly known. He was a guinea a minute.

One of the books I was very fond of on the Longmans list was called *Onward Christian Soldier*, a life of the Reverend Sabine Baring-Gould, who was a parson, a squire, a novelist and an antiquary. Born in 1834 he died in 1924. He had many children and lived in a rectory in the West Country. One day he, or his wife, gave a children's party. Descending that afternoon from his study he met a little girl on the half landing and patting her on the head said, 'And whose little girl are you?' 'I'm yours, Daddy,' she replied.

Then there was G M Trevelyan's *History of England (Illustrated)* and a series of *The Social History of England* in several volumes. That reminds me of an episode which took place one day in the early evening in the office. We were giving one of our publicity parties and Mark Longman, who had an eye for this sort of thing, spotted a well-known reviewer and drunk called John Raymond walking out of the front door with a copy of Trevelyan tucked under his arm. Mark said, 'Where do you think you are going with that?' Raymond replied, 'Oh, Mr Longman, I'm just taking it out into the sunlight to see if I can read it in better light\*.' Mark let him go and sent him an invoice the next day. He never again reviewed a book of ours in the *Sunday Times*.

Other distinguished writers included the Jesuit Philip Caraman, Edward Hyams, Rayne Kruger and Gerald Green. We published quite a lot of American fiction which was not always successful, but I remember one book called *By Love Possessed* by James Gould Cozzens. We were still living in a fairly prudish age in those days, the f-word was certainly never used and references to sex were sanitised to say

---

\* It was early evening.

the least. There appeared in the middle of the novel a description of 'a semen stained mattress'. This was regarded as obscene by some members of the staff and not least by W H Smith & Son who refused to stock the book. Mark Longman did a very brave thing. He crashed a W H Smith board meeting and lectured them on the whole business of changing attitudes and said that they would be making public fools of themselves if they banned such a book. His brave ruse worked and the book, which was incredibly boring and had nothing else particularly titillating in it, went on to sell something like 27,000 copies, all because it was hinted that it was dirty. That was a lot of books in those days.

During my time the staff of Longmans were poorly treated. Mr Brack had an assistant called Joyce Nairn who was knee-high to a grasshopper. What she lacked in stature she made up for in busyness. She was I suppose what they now call human resources. She called all the girls by their surname and was very much involved in setting up traps for people who came in late. That sort of management. Fortunately I had an ally in the office postal department. Bill Andrews had been Mark Longman's batman in the war and he ran the central post like a private kingdom. Once you were in with him no harm could come to you. Almost invariably he would tip me off that there was a time check coming up on a certain day of the week and I would then get in about an hour and a half early before they put anybody on the door. On one occasion I was hauled up and asked how it was that I never appeared to arrive in the office and I was able simply to reply that I was working very hard on a project for the education department. It was thanks to Bill Andrews that I always managed to avoid any trouble at work. He was also a mastermind with the drink at office parties and managed to siphon off large quantities of spirits into lemonade bottles when nobody was looking. On one occasion Lady Liz asked me to get her a glass of water. This I did but unfortunately Bill poured it from the wrong bottle and what she got was a mouthful of neat gin which left her spluttering all over the showroom. I kept well away for the rest of the evening.

Nairn was aided and abetted by a really unpleasant man called Adrian Beckett who was very tall and looked like a vulture. He became enamoured of the time and motion people to the extent that we found our waste paper baskets being searched at the end of every day and all sorts of *systems* imposed on us which did not work. Mr Brack was even discovered on his hands and knees in the boardroom reeling out a roll of Bronco and a roll of a somewhat softer lavatory paper to see how many sheets were on each roll in an attempt to cut down the consumption. The staff were treated in some cases with contempt.

Every Christmas there was excitement as bonus day approached. One day a poor little man called Mr Hose was summoned to the office to be told of his annual increase. He came back into the department and the poor man was crying. He had been offered another 2s 6d a week. A couple of members of staff, including myself, went and complained to Phillip Wallis, the delightful production manager, and he rectified the situation by having Hose's salary put up by 5 shillings a week. Big deal. Poor Mr Hose was typical of a down-trodden Dickensian clerk. He came to work every day with a briefcase and we often wondered what he kept in it. One day a colleague of mine less squeamish than I opened his briefcase and found it full of crumbs. Nothing else.

It is worth saying a little bit more about the Longman family because they were such a diverse bunch. There were, apart from Mr Mark, Mr Michael, a religious fanatic who eventually defected and founded a firm called Darton, Longman and Todd (religious publishers). Then there was Mr Willy, who was a very old man, not entirely up to date with events. It was rumoured that all he ever did was organise the All England Croquet Tournament at Hurlingham. Sure enough when Terry and I crept into his office in a lunch hour we discovered an oak chest where he kept a set of croquet balls and croquet mallets. It is said of Mr Willy that one day a member of the staff said 'Good morning' to him on the stairs. He was so shocked he didn't come into the office for a fortnight. Mr John was a fellow director and Mr Peregrine didn't last long. But Longmans, as I have said, was one of the oldest English publishing firms, founded in 1724 at the sign of the ship, and publishers of Johnson's English Dictionary. I was lucky to be trained by them for as long as I was, although perhaps I stayed rather too long. They were an extraordinary organisation, almost feudal one might say. For instance we used to have to come into the office on Saturday mornings but we were allowed to wear a 'change coat'. There was very little to do because none of the senior executives were in and the more louche male members of staff came in because they got extra work moonlighting on the newspapers in Fleet Street, packing the Sunday papers for distribution throughout the countryside.

Noel Brack was a nice old thing really and he offered me £6.10 a week to begin with. Technically, he was the managing director but time was catching up on him. He wore a brown suit every day of the week and I never saw him wear anything different. He had been at school at Hailebury, a fact that he never ceased to point out to us when we were driving down to Harlow where Longmans were relocating and building a vast new warehouse on the profits of the educational publishing. We always had to divert to pass the gates of Hailebury and be treated to a lecture on the qualities of that great school. He had a wife who had lost a hand in an accident. Quite by chance she won a Mini car in a Heinz baked bean competition. The prize, or rather 57 prizes, were presented to the winners at a party at the Dorchester, but the vehicles were themselves lined up along Park Lane to be driven away by the winners. I had volunteered to help Mrs Brack and was sent to escort her to the party. I eventually discovered her in the melee and she was looking rather distressed so I said to her, without thinking: 'Can I give you a hand?' Talk about bricks I have dropped. Fortunately I don't think she heard me, but we decided that I would drive the mini away and park it behind Clifford Street where presumably somebody took it back to wherever they lived, possibly to Hailebury.

I should add at this stage that, while starting my publishing career, I was also in the process of getting married to my housemaster's daughter from Radley. The less said about this the better. It was not a success but I am happy to say that we are still on speaking terms.

Another encounter with a vehicle, not a Mini, told a somewhat different story. No pun intended. I got to know the novelist David Storey very well. He wrote a book called *This Sporting Life* which was turned into an excellent film. I had been given the manuscript to read by John Guest as he had wrongly assumed that I was a Rugby League player. I was Union. I read the book with a degree of enthusiasm since it was set in my part of the world, but I can't say that I recommended it, much as I'd like to take credit for its subsequent success. As I said, David and I became very friendly and one day there was a telephone call from the receptionist downstairs at Clifford Street 'Mr Storey is here to see you. He'd like you to come down if you can spare a moment.' I went downstairs eagerly because he was always fun to be with and saw him there smiling all over his face. 'Come 'ere,' he said, 'Come and 'ave a look.' I went out into the street with him and there parked outside the office was an enormous white Jaguar, gleaming in the sun. I said 'David, you can't drive.' He said, 'I know, you're going to teach me.' And I did. He went on to write several more novels and of course eventually became a talented playwright. David's hero in *This Sporting Life* achieves moderate success as a Rugby League professional and the first thing he does, when he is in the big money, is to go out and buy a large white Jaguar. This was art repeating history. David in his past had played Rugby League for Wakefield Trinity.

I have mentioned John Guest several times. He was the chief editor of the general list at Longmans. One day I was sitting in my office adding up things wrong when a silver head poked itself round the door and said, 'I'm looking for Leo Cooper. My name is John Guest.' That encounter enabled me to get my foot in the door of the general list and removed from mashing up the figures. John became a bosom friend; he had been tipped off to look me up by the aunts, needless to say.

At that time John lived with Raleigh Trevelyan. This was an unusual relationship, largely because both of them had had what one might call 'interesting wars'. John had written a brilliant book called *Broken Images*, a winner of the Heinemann Award for Literature. I had read *Broken Images* before I got to Longmans, thanks to the aunts again. At the same time Raleigh Trevelyan had written a splendid piece of military history about the Battle of Anzio called *The Fortress*. It was incongruous to my mind to see these two living together when both of them had played such a large part in the war itself and had gone on to produce classic books about it. I firmly believe that John Guest's was one of the funniest memoirs of WW2 that I have ever read, and Raleigh's book is in my top ten.

I was to work alongside John Guest for five or six years before I left Longmans and I always kept up my friendship with him. He was easier to get on with than Raleigh, but Raleigh was just shy. John and I often had lunch together and sometimes at weekends I'd go round and see him. It was to Raleigh and John that I crept one day to announce the break-up of my first marriage and to ask them what to do. It may seem a strange choice but they were kind to me and gave me good advice. John said to me, 'What you've got to do next time is marry a rich woman.' How right he was! Apart from his book on the Anzio battle Raleigh went on to write other successful titles, not least *A Hermit Disclosed* about a real life hermit who lived in a village in Essex, and then a rather strange novel which was based on the Collins family of publishers called *The Big Tomato*. It was a thinly disguised portrait, written from a deep hatred, because Raleigh was so unhappy working for them. It was also very funny.

In one scene, at the Collins Christmas party, thinly disguised in the book, was the fact that Raleigh got himself into trouble by winning the musical chairs event, a victory which was specifically reserved for members of the Collins family. This was an appalling piece of bad form on Raleigh's part. Later he went on to write a whole succession of well-reviewed non-fiction titles, but I don't think he ever tried a novel again and John's book, *Broken Images*, was his only published work. I had the pleasure in my later career of republishing both those books and both went into two editions, having originally appeared under other imprints. It was books like these that gradually began to reawaken in me my interest in military history and indeed the possibility that I might be able to work more closely with authors on that type of subject. It was the beginning of my decision to go it alone, although there was plenty of rough water between my ambition and reality.

As I have shown, the Longmans general list at this time was very strong. I was fortunate to work with Laurence Cotterell in promoting a number of titles which went on to be famous, not least Gavin Maxwell's *Ring of Bright Water, Raven Seek Thy Brother, The House at Elrig, Harpoon at a Venture,* and *A Reed Shaken by the Wind,* to name but a few. I got to know Gavin Maxwell very well. He was an impossible man to deal with, permanently in debt and neurotic to say the least. He was heavily under the influence of a monstrous poet called Kathleen Raine. He did however have a heart of gold when it came to looking after his otters. When I met him he kept them in a large glass tank in the back garden of a house in Paulton's Square just off the King's Road. Every morning a van from Harrods would turn up and deliver live trout which visitors were invited to feed to the otters. I never penetrated the lowlands of Scotland to visit Gavin up there, but, having worked with him for a long time, I am glad that I played a part in the promotional success of his remarkable books.

A less professional success, or one which gave rise to a series of rather odd incidents, was an account of Gavin's journey with the explorer Wilfred Thesiger to the Marsh Arabs of Iraq. Thesiger, an incredible character both physically and intellectually, was more at home journeying alone or with nomads across deserts than he was in Chelsea wearing an old Etonian tie which he always did. He wrote *Arabian Sands,* which John Guest described as a masterpiece when he gave me the original manuscript to read. Thesiger then rather unwisely teamed up with Gavin Maxwell and they mounted a joint expedition to visit the Marsh Arabs again. As a result of this Gavin wrote a beautiful book called *A Reed Shaken by the Wind* but he and Thesiger fell out in a tempestuous way. One of the final episodes in their relationship took place in the showroom at Longmans in Grosvenor Street where we had recently moved. To my horror Wilfred Thesiger turned up at the same time as Gavin Maxwell. Gavin was sitting at a table waiting to see John Guest and Thesiger took a copy of *A Reed Shaken by the Wind* off the display shelf, threw it down on the table in front of Gavin Maxwell and said, 'This is absolute drivel'. I made an excuse and left and quickly warned John that something would have to be done to make sure that the two didn't start fighting. I then went and hid, which was rather cowardly of me.

Gavin died a horrible death of cancer. He was dogged by bad luck. He never had any money. When *Ring of Bright Water* was published he owed Longmans a fairly considerable sum. Although the book earned a tidy amount, all it did was mop up the debts and Gavin was constantly coming round to the back door to see what he could screw out of John who always had to go to Mark Longman for permission. Anyway, I was glad that I had worked with both of them. I was sitting in the Garrick a couple of years ago, and to my astonishment in came the gaunt figure of Wilfred Thesiger* wearing a black tie. He looked exactly as I remembered him forty years earlier, a magnificent craggy face with a boxer's broken nose. He ignored me – quite rightly!

One of my favourite stories about Raleigh Trevelyan dates from when he was working at Collins and Field Marshal Montgomery was having his *History of Warfare* published by them. Monty was invited by Billy Collins to visit the office and was given a guided tour. When they reached Raleigh's desk Collins said to Monty, 'Field Marshal, you may be interested to meet Raleigh Trevelyan. He wrote that marvellous book on Anzio, *The Fortress*.' Monty looked quizzically at Raleigh, said, 'Not my show' and walked on.

Another Collins story concerns Lady Collins who had a Peke called Wellington. Sometimes during the lunch hour (she worked in the religious department at Collins) she would take Wellington out for a walk in Green Park. Wellington often ran away. One day he ran too far and was heading in the direction of Hyde Park Corner when she started shouting at him. 'Wellington,' she cried 'Wellington,' in a stentorian voice. There was no reaction from the dog so Lady Collins started running and shouting, 'Wellington, Wellington, you naughty little boy.' Eventually a tall, distinguished looking man who was walking just in front of her turned round and said, 'Madam, are you addressing me?' It was in fact the Duke of Wellington himself out for a constitutional from No. 1 London which was, and still is, his London family home.

I was gradually getting to know people at Longmans, particularly on the editorial and general side and one of the most delightful people working there as an editor, who was also renowned for writing crime novels, was Lord (George) Hardinge, the most modest of men and one of the most socially awkward I had ever met. He always made a point

---

* Thesiger died in August 2003.

of standing up when you went into his office and you stood there expecting him to sit down which he never did. This made me deeply uneasy and I caught myself at one stage saying to him, 'Please do sit down.' George promptly sat down and then said, 'Why don't you?' This was repeated every time one went to see him so I tended to deal with him on the telephone instead. Then I didn't need to know whether he was standing up or sitting down!

One of the best books we published at Longmans during that period was *In Flanders Fields* by Leon Wolfe, an American. It was based on the First World War and is today a classic. I read it at a sitting and it had an enormous effect on me because it was really the beginning of my love affair with the First World War, although 'love affair' may seem an odd expression to use. It was probably one of the first books published in the very early '60s which started people rethinking the Great War and led of course to the works of Correlli Barnett and John Terraine and the impressive television series. Wolfe's book was a huge success and very much the leader in the attempt to try and reassess the effect of that horrendous conflict.

Military encounters were now coming thick and fast to Longmans thanks to the interest shown in Leon Wolfe's book, and they were not all about the First World War. One such was a splendid book by Christopher Hibbert, probably one of the most readable of all contemporary popular historians. This was *The Destruction of Lord Raglan* and it achieved a tremendous critical success. That and a book called *The Court at Windsor* helped to put Christopher on the map, as did his *Mussolini* and *The Great Mutiny*.

One day, now being in charge of publicity, I was told to go and arrange a window display for the Raglan book at Hatchards. This was in the days of the late Tommy Joy, who sanctioned the display. I had ascertained that several items of clothing and equipment belonging to Lord Raglan were available to use as display material in the shop window. I arranged for the current Lady Raglan to come and meet me at the office and I would then take her down to Hatchards and we would put the window together. Alas she couldn't get a taxi and I caught sight of her, because I was waiting on the steps, as she came sailing like a stately galleon up Grosvenor Street carrying, or should I say trailing, a large sword and its scabbard, a sabre-tache and, above all, Lord Raglan's actual uniform worn at the charge with the missing arm empty and sewn up against the chest. The arrival of Lady Raglan convinced me that, had we used her in the Crimean War, we would have won without any trouble at all. She was absolutely furious about there being no taxi and even more furious when she found she had to go all the way back to Hatchards to arrange the display. This was not one of my more successful moments in publishing and to this day I carry the vision of this formidable lady heading in my direction with evil intent and a sword.

It would be remiss not to say something about the educational side of Longmans because that is really where they made their reputation. I was surprised early on to realise that I was working for the publishers who were responsible for *Kennedy's Revised Latin Primer* (known at all prep schools as Kennedy's Revised Eating Primer because you could change the letters with your pen). And then there were North & Hillard and Hillard & Botting, both Latin textbooks, and Backhouse & Holdsworth on Maths and many titles by Eckersley and Kauffman on teaching English to foreigners. They were an interesting couple because Eckersley had met Kauffman when he was a prisoner of war in England and didn't speak any English. Between them Eckersley and his prisoner devised a way of teaching English which led to the enormous success of these texts.

Every year Longmans gave a Christmas party for the educational authors. They were completely different from other authors. They wore shabby raincoats and often carried brown paper parcels. They looked extremely scruffy and in many cases were wildly inarticulate. This didn't stop the party being a rave of its sort because very few of them could take their drink and the inebriation factor was much to be admired. I will never forget seeing them all foregoing orange squash and diving for the red wine. The irony of it is that all of them earned about ten times as much money as the general list authors and certainly many thousands of pounds more than the publishers who brought them such fame and fortune. The genial host of the educational party, apart from Mark Longman, was one E W Parker who had nurtured the Longmans list until it became one of the most powerful forces in educational publishing. He was a dear old man, chiefly renowned, apart from his publishing, for the fact that he had a hole in his wrist, which you could see right through, acquired on the Somme in 1916. He wrote an excellent memoir called *Into Battle,* one of the better books I re-published when I set up on my own. It is certainly a classic of its genre.

You can see from the books mentioned that it was a fairly wide-ranging general list, but it was very much our shop window and it was a tragedy when Pearsons, who took Longmans over in 1968, finally decided to close down the general list and move it to Viking Penguin because it was too expensive to run, and that was the end of that. John

Guest went with the list, as did Peter Carson, the only surviving member of Longmans' graduate training scheme and still one of the best publishers in London. So the great general list died and, my goodness, how Longmans could have done with it later on.

The responsibility of handling this destruction was given to Tim Rix, an old mate of mine from Radley days, later to become Longmans' Chief Executive.

Enough about Longmans. I learnt an enormous amount there, but I was due for a shock and, sensing that the general list was in trouble and with the general feeling that I wasn't getting anywhere, I decided it was time for me to make a break. For the first and only time in my career I myself made a decision about my job. I offered my resignation and bade farewell to that extraordinary organisation which never really seemed to achieve what it set out to do. I had made many friends. Later I found that I had learnt less than I thought and the experience that I was in for would be hard for me to sustain. I had heard on the old boy net that there was a job going at André Deutsch and that he was looking for a personal assistant, so I applied for that post and much to my surprise was offered the job at £2,000 a year, which I considered to be a princely sum. Little did I know what was waiting for me round the corner. I had sold my soul to the devil, or devils as it turned out!

# CHAPTER II

# The Post War Publishing Scene

*Publishing pays as long as you don't charge for
your time.*

The book trade had taken quite some time to recover from the ravages
of the Second World War, both in human terms and in technological
adaptation. During that conflict a lot of key executives had gone off to
fight for King and country and the domestic battlements were manned
by people who in all probability had done their service in the First
World War or were deemed unfit for the Second. Whilst conducting
perfectly satisfactory stewardships, the executives who remained
tended to be the dead wood among the directors of the publishing
houses. These were in many cases people with old fashioned views
who had acquired a position in the business rather on the presumption
of Buggins' turn or were recent arrivals from war-torn Europe. By the
1970s they stood like rocks in a stream, diverting the currents and not
actually taking on board a great deal of new thinking. Soon they were
somewhat surprised by the arrival of new production techniques,
mainly from overseas and it is arguable that in some cases, particularly
Germany and Italy (and to a lesser extent Hong Kong and Singapore),
despite having been defeated or occupied in the war, had become,
much to their surprise, the beneficiaries of this technological revolution. But new ideas certainly took a long time to take root in the UK.

One forgets all too easily that the country was still in the throes of
rationing up until the end of 1952. Among the commodities that was
very much a battleground was the manufacture and sale of paper. The
UK has never been a large paper-producing nation. It has also always
been vulnerable to the ups and downs of economic recession in other
countries. During the war publishers had been given, or rather
allocated, the quantity of paper they were permitted to use during any
one year, and they could also apply for a special allocation for needy

causes. As a result there was a great deal of trading between individual publishers who became more like paper merchants, themselves jobbing off their surplus or desperately trying to buy a new art paper from some fellow publisher who had some left from his allowance or was seeking some of a different quality. There was a whiff of the black market in the air. Finally, thank goodness, the so called 'utility mark', which had to appear in the front of every book throughout the war and indeed for some time afterwards, was abolished. The gates were open at last.

It is extraordinary now to look back on those days and remember how one was using the word photolithography, or litho for short, with little idea of what it actually meant. It wasn't long before the businesses gradually picked up speed, but even then it was striking how old-fashioned were some of the techniques still being used. For instance, nearly all clerical work was hand-driven. Computers didn't exist. The new edition of *Roget's Thesaurus* was being compiled at Longmans by a retired Indian judge by the name of Dutch and a shifting population of American students on work experience. They used strange printed cards with holes in. I never quite understood how the system worked, but eventually a new edition of *Roget* appeared which was a huge success. At that time colour printing in the UK was in the hands of a small number of firms, and the best who, either by luck or foresight, had acquired the relevant machinery were few and far between. Most quality work was coming from abroad, as was of course the paper. There was also competition with the United States who, needless to say, had different paper sizes and different book shapes. By this time I was fortunate enough to be out of the Longmans' production department where I had been training and found myself on the marketing side rather than the technical side, but I did pick up quite a lot of information as I went along. It seems funny now, but when I used the word 'half-tones' and 'hot metal' in a conversation the other day, the person I was talking to didn't know what I was talking about.

You could sell almost anything in those heady days at the end of the '50s and at last there came the flower burst of the '60s and everything changed irrevocably, not least in the way people behaved towards one another. Certainly there was a degree more freedom and openness and not so much bullying of the staff in offices who had, until recently, been treated like dirt by management. Even then brutality was not far beneath the surface and one saw this, particularly in the larger firms, now under the control of soldiers returning from the wars. They did not fit in easily. They did a lot of damage in staff relationships during those post-war years, because anybody who had been commissioned was used to marching round telling people what to do and expecting absolute obedience and this is not the way offices work*.

Good relationships between printers and publishers, on the other hand, were even more vital because they had to be. Tom has written about this better than I can, but a production manager was operating very much in the twilight world of backhanders to place orders when nobody was looking. The production department at one firm I knew had so much free drink aimed at it from the printer's public relations side over Christmas that they had, at a certain stage, to beseech the printers to go steady as more and more bottles came flowing through the post room. One particular firm, which will remain anonymous because the person who perpetrated this is still living, when he saw the way the wind was blowing auctioned the surplus bottles in the basement of the office when the Board was out at Christmas lunch. The management got to hear about it, and the person in question disappeared alongside the surplus bottles, never to be seen again. One production manager I know was given a set of silver backed hairbrushes and other items for the dressing table. This was discovered and the poor man was hauled up in front of the Directors and told to give them back. Alas he had already sold them.

The Frankfurt Book Fair was just beginning to find its feet again. Only the Germans could have managed to get that phoenix to rise from the ashes so quickly. Now it is probably the most sophisticated trade fair in the world and you simply aren't anyone in publishing unless you have been there several times. Rather like Ascot or Henley. So there we were surrounded by a change of attitude and indeed changes in business ethics and lumbered with new machinery which caused a great many publishers headaches as they struggled for an equal share of the expanding market.

At this stage the paperback industry was in its infancy. Penguin, of course, started before the war and there were one or two other desultory efforts including Four Square Books, Panther and Consul, but very soon along came all the other hardback houses crowding the market place and determined to have their own paperback imprints. At the beginning, when I started, a paperback right sold was considered to be an astonishing achievement.

Nor were there book clubs as we know them. There used to be one called The Book Society before the war and then there were World

* I found this disastrous to my business when I employed two retired Army Officers – they were not very good with people.

Books and The Reprint Society. We were yet to be besieged by Doubleday and persuaded to allow the book clubs into the market place. The booksellers did all they could to prevent progress being made. This was sheer Luddism. About this time also the Net Book Agreement began to come under fire from all sides and a bloody battle ensued – Luddism again. Doubleday's efforts led to a completely different approach to the length of print runs, particularly short ones. It was eventually realised by some lazy unadventurous directors and production executives, and indeed some bigoted managing directors, that the addition of another 750 copies on the end of a print run could make all the difference to the profitability and price of a title even if it did mean that one had to accept a very low offer from the book club. It took a long time to sink in and indeed one of the new book clubs, like a dragonfly, began in a blaze of glory and disappeared in a whiff of sulphur. This outfit was somewhat inappropriately called The Leisure Circle and went as far as trying to sell items other than books by direct mail. They got their sums wrong and that was the end of that. On the other hand Book Club Associates (BCA) were backed by Doubleday and W H Smith and at last things really took off.

In more recent times the operations of such outfits as Amazon and the Internet ordering facilities have redefined methods of selling within the trade. One is now able to assess with more accuracy the marketing information that comes back from direct supplying, making sales figures and forecasts far more comprehensive. The only problem is that we publishers never know when to stop and at the time of writing I think it is fair to say that we are still overproducing. Some 100,000 new titles were published during the last year which is indicative to my mind of gross overproduction. There's simply not enough room in the shops to cope with all the titles. As a result, authors receive lower advances and lower royalties as the price juggling affects the actual royalty situation. Where, once upon a time, 10% of the published price of a book was the author's share, now very often deals are based contractually on a percentage of the amount received and not on the published price. The authors have had to bear the burden. But more of this later.

There were at this time a number of efforts to improve and sex up the marketing side of publishing. One of these was an operation called The World Book Fair. I attended the opening ceremony, but at the same time had to be careful not to be seen because Mark Longman had decreed that no members of the staff were to attend, adding a few pensive remarks about book clubs and warning that direct selling would never catch on. However, I had managed to creep in and I did witness one of the early publicity events which consisted of a man doing a pole vault jump. I don't know what it was meant to be promoting but I doubt if it was pole vaulting. If anything it was promoting a brush with death because the poor fellow with his bendy stick missed the mattress and came splat down on the concrete floor just opposite the publicity person who was declaring the occasion open. I shall remember that thud all my life. This was considered to be, not least by Mark Longman, an ill omen. In the end the World Book Fair was transformed into some other stunt and the name of The Book Bang was next. The London Book Fair now at least works with some momentum behind it and has also become respectable.

I earlier mentioned the Net Book Agreement. This simply dictated that publishers and booksellers agreed to supply only through recognised outlets, i.e. no publisher could supply a book directly to a member of the public nor could booksellers offer cut-price titles. Price fixing was the rule. Everything had to go through bookshops and all deals were made at the same price. This was, I believe, one of the great drag anchors that prevented our trade developing fast enough after the war. The situation caused bitter battles and a lot of enmity. I myself (as Leo Cooper Ltd), made it publicly known that I would supply anybody at any time and within reason at any price as long as it made sense. This led to my being ostracised by a number of my most valued customers, not least Harrods, who refused to stock any of my books for a period of two years. Where are you now, Mr Van Danzig? Mr Van Danzig was the chief book buyer at Harrods at the time.

It was an uphill struggle to convince the old and bold that direct marketing was the name of the game, as was direct mail. Thank goodness, before I decided to give up my business, I saw that the trade had begun to understand that there were no direct threats to their livelihood and soon everybody fell in quietly behind the leaders. Before we knew where we were, the Net Book Agreement had been abolished and a pernicious practice vanished. I firmly believe that it did more damage than anything else on the post-war publishing scene as I knew it.

There was one way of responding to complaints, as I found out when a bookseller in Somerset accused me of taking away his livelihood by selling direct to the members of the Somerset Light Infantry Old Comrades Association copies of the history of that regiment. I had offered him a new deal in which he had exclusive rights to sell the book in the county. He still complained. I squashed him flat by hinting that any profit made from direct selling was going to help the refurbishment of the outside of Wells Cathedral. I got a letter of apology. I am not ashamed to say that I was not entirely honest, but I always made it plain in other such deals that I regarded direct selling as essential and certainly, when dealing with regimental histories, it was virtually the only way to make a profit because booksellers were so idle and uninterested.

There was a firm called Gale & Polden* in Aldershot who had dominated the market for regimental histories and other military books over the years, but in many cases the regiments were being ripped off. No attempt was made by Gale & Polden to persuade regiments to market the books and many piles of regimental histories have I seen sitting damply in some ancient RHQ. I remember once visiting Norton Barracks in Worcestershire and being taken down to see the stock of their published history which had been lying around in their basement for several years. When you picked up one book another nine came up with it because the dampness was such that all the books had fused together. I saw what was happening and decided that the only way to publish regimental histories or indeed any specialist military history was to stick my neck out and not only publish a quantity for the regiment themselves but to market to the general public, who, I was certain, were interested, but always experienced great difficulty in obtaining such books through the bookshops. The booksellers simply were not interested in such ideas. I can safely say that by the time I retired almost any regimental history could sell at least 750 copies at about £25 a copy in the general trade market on top of what we call the domestic market, i.e. the regiment itself, and most shops have a military section now. This enabled the histories to be published with a degree of opulence which was the envy of some publishers who didn't know quite how to go about it. Almost invariably I was able to prove that a regimental history could be profitable. This was very much the case with most of my army business and most of the regiments I dealt with would thoroughly endorse my claim that they, having admittedly put up some money to underpin the venture, got it nearly all back or at least broke even.

You may know that the Famous Regiment** series was originally invented by me when I was still with Hamish Hamilton, with his full backing, at the price of 21 shillings each. Volumes are now fetching at least £40 a copy in the second-hand market and I heard the other day that a copy of *The Light Dragoons* by one Allan Mallinson, whose name

* Later subsumed by the late Captain Maxwell MC.
** More about this series in Chapter IV.

will be familiar to readers of military fiction, was fetching £200 a copy and there was call for a reprint. This was partly due to the fact that it was a beautifully written and produced book, but I see no reason why such marketing ploys should not continue to help specialist publishing in this subject to do more than just survive.

To sum up, it is plain to me that we publishers did not spring off the starting blocks fast enough after the war and it goes without saying that very little notice was initially taken of new techniques. However, there was a glimmer on the horizon and very soon things were to change. They certainly were to change for me. I said at the end of the previous chapter that I had sold my soul to the devils and the next chapter takes us into the Bloomsbury jungle where they lived.

# CHAPTER III

# *André*

*It is essential for a General to be tranquil and obscure, upright and self-disciplined, and able to stupefy the eyes and ears of the officers and the troops, keeping them in ignorance. He alters his management of affairs and changes his strategies to keep other people from recognising him. He shifts his position and traverses in direct routes to keep the other people from being able to anticipate him.*

Sun Tzu (*The Art of War*)

André Deutsch resembled a boiled canary. He was small and birdlike but with a permanent twinkle in his eye – though never in his soul. He had come to England just before the war – from Hungary – along with a great many other men-of-letters-to-be, who, with their Jewish origins, in most cases brought with them a huge impetus of business blood, one might almost say business bloody mindedness, leading to the revitalisation of the mess which was the post-war London literary scene. André came to England to study Economics but was initially interned as an alien on the Isle of Man. He was most certainly an alien, but he didn't waste much time and after his release soon set up a publishing firm called Allan Wingate which turned into André Deutsch – quite a feat. To continue the avian analogy he could very quickly change from being a boiled canary to a fierce robin with puffed-up feathers when crossed, particularly when he had one of his daily losses of temper. He did not suffer fools gladly. He was some-times very funny, occasionally very kind to unfortunate people. He was not well read; he had limitations which suggested an inadequate education. He was a bad employer with a constantly changing staff and absolute hell to work for.

## André Deutsch Limited *Publishers*

*105 Great Russell Street London WC1 Telephone:Langham 2746*

CABLES: ADLIB LONDON WC1    TELEGRAMS: ADLIB WESTCENT LONDON

ad/js

PRIVATE AND CONFIDENTIAL

Leo Cooper Esq
17 Redliffe Square
LONDON SW10                          8th December 1965

Dear Mr. Cooper

This is just to confirm our conversation this morning.  We hope
you will be joining us early in January, preferably on Monday,
3rd, but we will wait if this is not possible.

I don't think I have to go into details of your job here, but
I'd like to confirm some technical points:  Your starting salary
will be £2,000.  You will have three weeks' holiday.  I promise
that we will look into the question of a car and I am sure we can
arrange it so that the car is not entirely your responsibility, and
the office will have some use of it.  This will, of course, have
to wait until you have settled in.

You know how much I am expecting from you and I hope, for both
our sakes that neither of us will be disappointed.  If you stand
up to the demands of the job you will be very happy and prosperous,
if occasionally overworked.

I very much look forward to receiving your confirmation and welcoming
you here.

Yours sincerely

P.S.  Oh yes, just in case, I suggest a month's notice on either
side.


PRIVATE AND CONFIDENTIAL


DIRECTORS: ANDRE DEUTSCH  DIANA ATHILL  NICOLAS BENTLEY  GEORGE DEPOTEX  F. P. KENDALL

I had little idea what I was letting myself in for when I stepped through the portals of Number 105 Great Russell Street. It did not take long to surmise that I was about to face a difficult period in my life. No one can deny the impact that André made on publishing. He was, it has to be said, a very good publisher, with an eye for a book, but his business methods were often enough to raise eyebrows and he treated his employees, especially the males, with total disdain. Like all small men he had tremendous energy and frequently changed moods. His principal support and referee was one Diana Athill, two of whose books, *Instead of a Letter* and *Stet*, are pretty substantial contributions to the history of publishing. Besides being autobiographical, they have had a tremendous impact in trade circles. It was Diana who really kept the show on the road, although André said to me in an introductory letter (some staff were given this when they joined) that he found Diana to be 'a partner, founder, close friend, brilliant editor and copyrighter [sic]. Not the best business woman'. She was also, for a very short time, his mistress. His other pillar of support was the cartoonist Nicolas Bentley, who was a cheerful soul and very much keeper of the peace. He was also that rare thing in publishing – a gentleman. Like Diana he had a marvellous ability to escape if there was any trouble and his influence (at arm's length) in the office was considerable, although very often he wasn't there when he was needed, like McCavity.

The rest of the staff were hard-working and lived with a constant threat of being shouted at. Hence the atmosphere in the office was never very happy. Every Tuesday we had an editorial lunch at which all the proposals to publish were submitted and all the various editors emerged from their offices in the building to give their views on future plans and current projects. It was plain that André very seldom read any of the submissions himself, but he did listen to his editors and he trusted them and I think, to be fair, they were very good. Lunch was usually accompanied by André giving us his views on the quality of the pâté or salami that we had been served. He also preached against bananas. He was very lucky to have such a loyal staff.

One of them, Ilsa Yardley, is my daughter's godmother, a relationship born out of suffering and a mutual tongue-lashing from André on more than one occasion. Among other things, Ilsa reminded me the other day of the occasion when she was sent out to buy lunch for eight people and was given £2.10! Another person who deserves a mention is Mr Tammer, the accountant. Small and round like a deflated Michelin man, he made André look tall. I once found André and Tammer standing in the office hallway; Mr Tammer was perched on a chair and held at the ankles by André. They were changing light bulbs from 60 watt to 40 watt to save electricity. They looked like two escapees from Le Cirque du Soleil. André said in his encyclical of Mr Tammer:

> He has been with me for two years; he is the chief accountant and secretary of the company, a most useful little man – loyal, hard-working and enthusiastic but in certain directions a little daft. Can and will improve and I am sure if you help me to keep an eye, not so much on him, as on how he gets about, etc., he will improve a lot. I am devoted to him.

What he really meant was that he was brutally unkind to Mr Tammer who was a sort of whipping boy. How he put up with the frequent bullying I will never know. Tammer always had troubles on his hands, not least keeping André's fingers out of the petty cash tin.

The office was in a permanent state of turmoil and I was beginning to realise that André was looking for weaknesses in me. He found them fairly quickly. He noticed, for instance, that during the summer months I would play cricket on Saturdays. Saturday was also a day when we were expected to come into the office in the morning for no reason at all other than pretending to be busy. He started off with several jibes about wanting to examine my cricket bag and snide remarks about English public school boys. This got so bad that I noticed him deliberately delaying a break-up of the Saturday morning meeting because he knew that I usually had to get to the grounds by 11.30am. It all came to a head one Saturday when I was captaining my side (The Honourable Artillery Company) against the MCC at Armoury House* – a fairly prestigious match. It was obvious by 11.10 that I wasn't going to get to the ground in time for the 'toss the coin' with my fellow captain.

I made an excuse in the middle of the meeting and rushed downstairs and telephoned Armoury House and explained to the MCC captain the dilemma in which I found myself. Being an amiable man and of course a member of the MCC, he said: 'Well why don't we toss now on the telephone,' so he tossed and thank God I won while standing in the André Deutsch telephone exchange. I was now in a terrible dilemma because I was still technically in a meeting. I elected

---

* The ground at the HAC is that on which the first recorded cricket match ever was played.

for my side to go in to bat. That was my cautious choice. Finally at about 11.30 plus, André, who knew quite well where I had been, gave the signal for the meeting to break up and I found a taxi which got me to the ground just as our sixth batsman was walking to the wicket and the HAC were something like 55 for 5. It was humiliating and I never forgave him for that. This may seem trivial and I should have known better than to expect to enjoy myself at a weekend. I bet it was the first time the MCC had benefited from a tossed coin in a telephone exchange.*

Some time before I worked for André I was asked to play in the Publishers v Authors match at Vincent Square in Westminster. This was organised by the National Book League, as it was then called, and was a fairly swish do which attracted a great many famous cricketers. When I say great I mean great. I was playing for the publishers (National Book League) and they had put together a pretty useful side. In fact there were eleven English players between the sides, not to mention others from abroad. To my amazement, when I had to go out to bat I found that I was facing Ray Lindwall from one end and Keith Miller from the other. While proud to recall this episode, I am not particularly proud of the subsequent disaster which befell me. The famous Middlesex left arm bowler Jack Young came on to bowl and in my head I'd already destroyed myself. I've never been able to play at left-handers and it wasn't long before I'd come half way down the wicket, missed the ball and been stumped by Anthony Kamm, the ex-Oxford and Middlesex wicket keeper.

I got my revenge, though, in another charity match when I was faced with the bowling of Denis Compton, the ex-England hero. In this case, on one of his rare appearances as a bowler, he flighted the ball carefully and it landed just outside my off stump. Fortunately this time I made contact. Unfortunately the ball, which I hit over long on, travelled like an Exocet and ended by hitting a paraplegic in a wheelchair who was then appearing as one of the beneficiaries of this fund-raising cricket match, Saints v Sinners. Unfortunately the ball did more than hit him. It propelled his wheelchair into the village pond and, had there not been a lot of nurses there, we might have had our first drowning on the cricket field.**

* I captained the Honourable Artillery Club at Rugby and Cricket – the only person to have done so.
** I heard of a recent event the other day when a fish fell out of the sky onto the pitch at Clifton College and play was held up. It turned out that two herring gulls were having a dispute. No wonder there was a breathless fish in the Close that day.

A lot of André's time, when not dealing with publishing, was spent in an effort to get visas for his ageing parents to come and live in England. This caused him a great deal of angst and trouble, but he finally achieved his object. The tragedy was that, after three months, the parents said they couldn't stand living in England, so after all the effort he had made he then had to try and ship them back, which wasn't easy either. This didn't improve his temper, so he took it out on us. He often did things and said things that were very funny in retrospect.

One day when we were driving up to some business meeting Ted Collins, the company sales director who was a source of joy to me and an ally, was sitting in the back of the car. André was in the front and I was driving. It was André's car, an Alfa Romeo. After we had been going for about half an hour André fell asleep and in his sleep fell across with his head on my shoulder obscuring the gear box. Ted Collins lent over between us and whispered in my ear: 'Now's the time to cut his fuckin' froat. You could save the nation.'

On another occasion we were spending our time at the Booksellers' Conference. This is a sort of public relations exercise held every year by the Booksellers Association when publishers and booksellers get together to bury the hatchet and get drunk. This time it was being held in Lytham St Anne's in Lancashire. Since this was not far from where my family lived in Yorkshire just over the Trough of Boland, I asked André and a friend of his and one or two other people whom I liked to come over to our house in the Yorkshire Dales and have lunch on the Sunday when there were no meetings. My mother, realising that this was a career move, did everything she could to prepare an absolutely superb lunch. Sunday morning dawned and the time of arrival that André had given us passed, so we had a few drinks. Forty-five minutes later there was still no sign of him. It was before the days of mobile phones. I could see my father beginning to foam at the mouth and my mother, who was desperately anxious that things should go well, was in a panic. Finally there was a roar of an Alfa Romeo engine and his little blue car sneaked to a halt outside our old Yorkshire house. I heard my father say: 'That must be the little bastard now'.

The relief of his arrival was soon eradicated by his extraordinary behaviour. After being introduced, he ignored my parents completely and started to walk around the house looking in all the rooms and then produced a notebook from his pocket and started to value all the furniture. My father, by this time, had exploded and was smoking his pipe in the garden and my mother, sensing that I might have to sell the furniture to keep my job, was looking more and more distressed.

Anyway we finally got down to lunch at about 2.30 and I think that was the beginning of my realisation that time was not on my side and I had better start thinking about something new.

On another occasion the Booksellers' Conference was held in Harrogate. Again this was quite near our house so Jilly* and I thought we'd give a party and asked twenty or thirty people from the conference over for a buffet lunch**. This went well and it was a lovely sunny day although it had been raining. Among the guests was Lord Horder who at that time ran Duckworths. He was well known as an eccentric but this did not detract from his charm. There was an incident, though, which caused a great deal of amusement. My father was, among other things, the church organist in the village and Lord Horder was also an accomplished organist. For some extraordinary reason he always wore high-heeled boots. My father, on the other hand, played the organ in bedroom slippers because it gave him a better feeling when using the foot pedals. I am not suggesting that Lord Horder played the organ in high heels, but on this particular day, standing on the lawn in our garden discussing organ playing, I watched with horror as his high heels gradually sank into the wet grass and he realised that he couldn't move. I couldn't stop laughing, but we eventually managed to prise him out of the lawn and he continued his conversation about organ playing with my father in our kitchen.

However, I was soon to cross swords with André on a technical front which involved honesty or rather a lack of it. I have already said that we were at the beginning of the age of the paperback. One of my jobs with André was to keep the submission ledger going so that every book had a chance to be submitted for paperback rights whilst it was going forward in production. This was quite sensible and there were several sets of rules about paperback rights, but André was not happy with the situation. He was also, as usual, short of money. He devised a scheme whereby Penguin lent him £20,000 cash. For this money he had to give them a guarantee that they would have first refusal on every book that he was to publish in hard cover. My job was to see the contract through and make sure that the advance was paid by Penguin. They had, as I said, the exclusive rights of first offer. This was

* Later to achieve distinction as a journalist and novelist and whom I had recently married.
** Laura Hesketh, the 'urban marmoset' (so called because she looked like one) did the catering.

all very well, but André had exactly the same deal going with May-flower books run by a very jolly, rather drunken, ex-bomber pilot called John Watson. André believed that John had not seen through the plot and was in blissful ignorance of the fact that, although Penguin had first offer, so too did John and Mayflower. My role in this plot was then to ring up Penguin and refer them to the original deal which said that they lent us £20,000 and I was to insist that they now topped that up so that it became £20,000 again because we'd spent say £5,000 on the advance on the book in question. In other words it was blatant dishonesty. This was tempered slightly though by the fact that John Watson was no fool and he took me out to lunch one day and said, 'Don't you worry, Leo, I know exactly what's going on and I can handle it.' But it rankled, or at least it disturbed me, so one day I went to André and said that I didn't like doing his dirty work for him and felt that it was extremely dishonest. He turned from boiled canary to fierce robin within a flash and I got such a ferocious pecking that I didn't dare speak to him for the next few weeks and indeed it was that particular incident, I think, which led to my deciding that I wasn't going to make a success of the job, a decision which in fact had already been made by André himself. Diana Athill and Nicolas Bentley tried to calm the waters, but trouble was brewing.

One of André's other tricks, because he very seldom read the books he published, was to send me to see 'difficult' authors as he called them. These were either people whose book he had not been able to read or those with whom he felt intellectually unequal in their presence. For instance he sent me to have tea with J K Galbraith at the Ritz. Since neither André nor I had read his book and I didn't know much about him, I was in rather a dilemma. The situation was defused, thank God, by Galbraith himself who, by the time I had finished my tea, I had warmed to. He just said, 'I know why André sent you. I know he hasn't read my book. I know you haven't read it either but mark my words it is a very good one.' I was able to read it after that.

André also put me in to look after Crick and Watson, the two authors who discovered DNA; at least I think that is what they discovered. Since all scientists have the reputation of being mad all I can say is that these two were uncommonly normal and absolutely charming, although we never got round to talking about their book or its subject. That would have been presumptuous of me.

There were one or two other authors who were given to me for entertainment purposes, because André was quite generous when it was necessary. One of them in particular, David Caute, a novelist, was rather difficult and cantankerous but was much loved in the office not least because he made a lot of money for the imprint. A number of military titles served to keep my interest going and I particularly enjoyed promoting *The Gardeners of Salonika*. I hadn't lost sight of the military angle, but I suppose, quite naturally, it wasn't really one of André's fortes.

One morning I was sitting in my office wondering what to do next when my telephone rang. I instantly recognised the voice of a renowned book trade journalist called Eric Hiscock, who summoned me to see him. He was chiefly famous for a column he wrote in a magazine called *Smith's Trade News* under the name of 'Whitefriar' and he was well respected in the book trade because he was often able to get advance information about forthcoming publications in his role as the man who sold advertising on the book pages of the *Evening Standard*. He was a good journalist too. Tall and aquiline and very hospitable, he had a beady eye. He never missed a trick. He gradually developed his job as a space seller into something far more relevant and interesting to us promotion people on the trade side. I am not saying he could make or break a book, but his attention could seriously influence the way people looked at forthcoming publications and as a tip-off man I knew few better at the time. In fact he even wrote his own book called *The Bells of Hell* about his service in the First World War when, among other things, he had been wounded in the foot – some said not by accident, but this was unfair. He was always enormously kind to me and to Jilly and he had a tremendous following among the more cheerful and bibulous members of the trade publicity departments.

It wasn't exactly to do with book promotion though that he was ringing me. Without any small talk at all he said, 'Leo, there is a very good job going in the publicity department of Hamish Hamilton. I think you should take it.' This was not the first inkling I had that André was gunning for me and it sank in very quickly. We had a few drinks* and with Eric's encouragement I rang up and secured an interview at Hamish Hamilton. This event was to prove even more taxing than my employment by André, but he, cunning sod that he was, had not the decency to sack me directly and employed someone else, i.e. Eric, to do his dirty work. In mitigation I myself once tried to sack a man who, after three days of interview, thought he had been promoted. I didn't really mind this proxy sacking because I was wondering how on earth I was going to get out of the situation, but it was typical of the man. It was gutless. I was not put in a position to defend myself nor indeed did I wish to. Instead I realised that the writing was on the wall. I don't remember what I said to André when I got back but I moved very fast.

This was not particularly difficult because the Hamish Hamilton office was a few hundred yards down the road in Great Russell Street. I made an appointment to see 'Jamie', as he was known in the trade, with some degree of apprehension, because, if I didn't get this job, I was in trouble.

Although my employment by Deutsch ended in disaster, there is no doubt that my time there was very useful to me, perhaps not so much in learning about publishing, but certainly learning how not to treat staff. The atmosphere in the office was one of deep unease and mistrust. Also, I am happy to say that I did remain on good terms with André after I'd left and subsequent to my becoming a member of the Garrick Club I often used to see him for a chat either in the Club or sometimes in his office. What the episode really taught me, and I keep reflecting on this, was that I thought I knew it all when in fact I knew nothing. I'd been so much on the fringe of the publishing process that a lot of the more technical aspects had not sunk in. I wouldn't like this book to reflect badly on André, or indeed anybody else for that matter, since it is all about me, well nearly all of it. For example, to accuse Hamish Hamilton of arrogance is to add insult to injury. Indeed it was I who was arrogant much of the time and I have nobody to blame except myself. I did learn quickly at Andre's knee though. I learnt about myself and in the long run I have to admire him because he was a man of great courage and in the end I became quite fond of him. He will mainly be remembered for publishing George Mikes' book *How to be an Alien* and for *The Rise and Fall of Nazi Germany* by T L Jarman.

* Eric's watering hole was El Vino's where he and the delightful Philip Hope-Wallace held court.

# CHAPTER IV

## *Jamie*

*When the military man approaches, the world locks up its spoons and packs off its womankind.*

Bernard Shaw, *Man and Superman*

*. . . there is nothing more difficult to carry out, nor more doubtful of success, nor more dangerous to handle, than to initiate a new order of things. For the reformer has enemies in all those who profit by the old order, and only lukewarm defenders in all those who would profit by the new order, this lukewarmness arising partly from fear of their adversaries . . . and partly from the incredulity of mankind, who do not truly believe in anything new until they have had the actual experience of it.*

Macchiavelli, *The Prince*

Thus I breached the portals of Hamish Hamilton and was about to enter a phase in my life which, although taxing, gave rise to many very funny situations, often unintentional. Some of the events that took place were unusual to say the least. However, Hamish Hamilton did have a brilliant list and Jamie was, like André, a brilliant publisher. Also like André he didn't suffer fools gladly either and the way he treated a lot of his staff left a great deal to be desired. I knocked on the door of his office, having been kept waiting twenty minutes and he gestured me towards a seat and the interrogation began.

Jamie was a tall, well dressed, handsome man with an incredibly arrogant manner. He was a crashing snob of the very worst kind, but he knew a book when he saw one and, unlike André, he was very

39

much a drawing-room publisher. He went for names such as Nancy Mitford, Sir Malcolm Sargent, Simenon and Truman Capote, Selina Hastings and Alan Moorhead He published a wide range of fiction and was interested in history in the most general sense of the word. He was also interested in educational books and in a children's list which was run by one Julia MacRae. It could be said of him, I think, that he was one of the more successful post-war publishers, and although half-American was generally regarded as one of the senior members of the English publishing scene.

After he had seen me and we had discussed publishing generally, he asked a lot of questions about my private life which I endeavoured to answer with a degree of truth and then he said: 'I am going to hand you over to one of my colleagues who has been groomed for stardom. I want you to meet Christopher Sinclair-Stevenson'. Since I knew Christopher vaguely anyway, this was no burden and we went out and had a cup of coffee and discussed the whole situation. Christopher was a tall, languid, well read Etonian. He was a brilliant editor, but not, as it turned out later in his career, a brilliant publisher. He told me a lot about the running of Hamish Hamilton and warned me to beware of Jamie and his mercurial behaviour. He mentioned that there was a son called Alistair who was also being groomed for stardom and would eventually take over the firm. Events were to prove entirely different and they had a twist in them which I will mention later. Within the next few days I was given the job in a handwritten note by Jamie offering me the princely sum of £1,750 a year which was £250 less than I was getting from Deutsch. But at least it was a job and I was able to start within two or three weeks since I didn't feel any loyalty to André any longer. Thus the scene was set for two terrible years of ups and downs and certainly a number of situations that make me laugh to this day and some that make me cry.

I said that Jamie was a mercurial person and a snob, but he was much liked by his warehouse staff who seemed to thrive on his autocracy. In the warehouse there was a large oar on the wall from some rowing eight that he'd been a member of and which had rowed at Henley. He also had a private pilot's licence and his face looked as if he should have had one from the British Boxing Board of Control, so squashed was his nose. He dressed nattily and kept very strict hours. He was loathed by a lot of his office staff who were always trying to find out whether they were held in good regard or not. One of the main people I latched on to was the production director, Max Martyn. There was also an ex-fighter pilot called Dick Hough, who was a brilliant children's editor and an author in his own right. Dick

**HAMISH HAMILTON LTD**
90 GREAT RUSSELL STREET
LONDON WC1
LANGHAM 4621

FROM THE MANAGING DIRECTOR

July 1 1966

Dear Leo,

This will confirm that you will join us on August 1, at a commencing salary of £1750 p.a.

I hope you will be happy with us.

Sincerely.

Hamish Hamilton

Office hours are 9 till 5. H.H.

and Max took me out for a drink soon after I arrived to find out whether Jamie had said anything to me about the succession when Jamie relinquished command of the firm. I realised that I was being courted and placed in a political situation which was, as far as they were concerned, likely to benefit them not me. Certainly the struggle for power within the firm was varying and not without its dramatic moments.

First of all a few words about how Jamie treated his staff. There was one lady, who'd better remain anonymous, who was in charge of the publicity and advertising department. I think I had been brought in to fill the gap that she was about to create. Anyway, she was hugely addicted to the bottle, not least in the mornings. One day she passed out on the stairs of Great Russell Street clutching a bottle of sherry, half consumed. As my partner to be, Tom Hartman, of whom more later, was coming in at the time he saw Jamie drifting gracefully down the stairs on his way for his morning cup of coffee across the road. Without batting an eyelid, Jamie stepped over the corpse on the stairs which had now let go of the bottle which seeped cheap English sherry all down the stair carpet. Jamie took one look at the corpse and said, 'Good morning Tom'. That was the end of the affair, not least for the lady with the bottle.

Another encounter that took place on that hallowed staircase was when the sales manager suddenly came face to face with Jamie who was again on his way for his morning cup of coffee and the sales manager was about an hour late coming into work. Attack being the best method of defence, he said, 'Oh Mr Hamilton, good morning. I am sorry I am late but unfortunately my wife has had to go to hospital and I had to take the children to school'. Jamie looked him straight in the face and said 'Couldn't the maid have done that?'

There were two or three powerful people in the Hamish Hamilton organisation with whom it was best to keep on good terms. One of them was the financial director, James Eastwell; a man who I suspect had never read a book in his life but had a cool and suspicious attitude to the business of publishing. He was the man who held the purse strings and Jamie and he frequently had arguments about cash flow. Not that this was an unusual situation in publishing. Eastwell didn't like me and I didn't like him much either. Among other things he would fawn on Jamie and always took his side when he was in dispute with members of the staff. At one stage in their career Jamie decided to take up golf and asked James Eastwell to give him golf lessons in the back garden of Jamie's house in Hamilton Terrace, St John's Wood. One evening I was round there having drinks when Mr Eastwell came to give him a lesson and I had to watch solemnly as he drove a plastic golf ball with holes in it all over the back garden and eventually, thank God, over the fence into next door's garden. Eastwell, like many others, did dance to Jamie's tune and kept an eagle eye on people's expenses and expenditure. I think it would be fair to say that he was responsible for keeping the ship on a steady keel. He did this by manipulating Jamie very cleverly, and although we were always short of money, there was a fairly satisfactory financial situation, but eventually Hamish Hamilton lost its battle to preserve its independence and the imprint was subsumed by Lord Thomson and Jamie began to see his leadership slip away, but that's a different story.

Another important figure was an absolutely charming man, an editor called Roger Machel. He, like Nicolas Bentley at Deutsch, was a gentleman and was also used to calm the waters when Jamie lost his temper with anybody or when there had been unfortunate incidents in the editorial department. Roger was a saint and kindly kept an eye on me and helped me out of a number of ghastly situations with skill and generosity. Certainly he goes down in my book as one of the good and great post-war editors. He lived in Albany on his own and frequently asked me back to his flat there to pour a large drink on troubled waters. I have never forgotten him. Towards the end of my tenure I received a telephone call in the middle of the day from Jamie asking me to go up and see him. I frequently received calls of this nature when he had nothing better to do but this one took me rather by surprise. He didn't ask me to sit down, he just said, 'I've decided to get rid of _____*'. I was shocked and horrified. I couldn't think why he should have chosen me to be the recipient of this startling news. I was frankly embarrassed by it because I had got to know the person he named very well and we got on easily together. I said to Jamie, 'Why are you telling me this and why at this strange time? I don't really think I ought to have anything to do with this and I feel that it is none of my business.' 'I don't mind,' said Jamie, 'but I am going to get rid of him.' I said, 'Well look, Sir,' (I called him sir this time) 'it's not really for me to make any comment but may I ask why?', inwardly thinking thank God it wasn't me. 'I'll tell you why,' said Jamie, 'I can't stand his wife.' I said to him, 'Well really I honestly don't think that's my business and I'd prefer to forget about it, Sir.' He never actually went through with his threat but I was placed in a dilemma as to whether I ought to mention the fact to the man in question. I decided not to say a word. Nor was he ever removed, but some five or six years later, when I met him one

---

* One of the senior editors.

evening, I can't remember where, I said to him that there was something that I thought he ought know and described the episode to him. In retrospect this was probably rather tactless because he never spoke to me again.

It was around this time that a curious episode happened which was either hilarious or tragic depending on your point of view. I was in the office at about half past eight one morning when the telephone rang and a rather weak voice said, 'Is Jamie there?' I said, 'Who's calling?' and the voice replied, 'It's Sir Malcolm Sargent here. Can I speak to Jamie?' I said, 'Well of course you can, Sir, I think he is in the office because I heard his voice.' 'Well, will you tell him that this is Malcolm Sargent and will you also tell him that I am slipping away quietly.' I was so shocked by this news I nearly dropped the telephone. I said to him, 'Hang on a minute, Sir'. I went down the stairs from my office, across the corridor and up the stairs to Mr Hamilton's office. I knocked on the door and heard a voice say, 'Come in'. I opened the door to find Jamie was on the telephone. As soon as he saw it was me he shouted, 'Get out.' I shut the door and went back to my telephone and said, 'I am very sorry, Sir Malcolm, but Mr Hamilton is on the telephone and is too busy to talk at the moment, I think.' Malcolm Sargent said, 'Oh dear, well will you try and get his attention for I need to have a word with him.'

So I put the phone down, went down the stairs, across the corridor and up the stairs and knocked on Jamie's door again. No sooner had I put my head round the door than he shouted to me, 'Get out'. I got out. This happened once more and I finally said to the telephone with the ailing Sir Malcolm on the other end, 'I'm very sorry, sir, but he can't speak to you now and I will get him to ring you back.' All I heard from the other end was a deep sigh and a voice saying, 'Oh dear.' I replaced the telephone. There was silence in the office for about ten minutes and then the telephone rang again. I picked it up and it was Sir Malcolm Sargent's secretary. She said, 'Could I speak to Mr Hamilton?' I said, 'I'm afraid he is busy on the telephone but I will try and get hold of him.' Off I went again and knocked on Jamie's door, going straight in. He was about to shout 'Get out' when I stopped him by saying in a loud voice, 'Sir, Sir Malcolm Sargent has been trying to get hold of you for the last half hour. I think he's dying.' Jamie said, 'Why the devil didn't you tell me?' I said, 'I tried to, Sir,' and he said, 'Well what are we going to do about it?' and I said, 'Well Sir, the secretary is on the telephone to ask me to tell you that Sir Malcolm Sargent has just died. There is not a lot you can do.' There was a horrible silence and I saw

Jamie's face begin to break up. I closed the door and left. I suppose I can claim to be the last person to speak to Sir Malcolm Sargent. I never found out what Jamie made of that episode.

Round about this time Jamie began to listen to those who suggested that our advertising in the newspapers was really rather second rate, and Max Martyn, in his role as production director, suggested to Jamie that we employ a really top class designer to redesign the Hamish Hamilton logo and the borders that we used in the papers for book advertising. This was approved in principle by Jamie, and Max approached a very well known graphic designer called Herbert Spencer to ask him to design a new house style, etc. He was a very fine designer and you can see his work almost every time you take to the road in this country because he redesigned all the road signs – to great effect, I think. Anyway he took one look at our previous advertising and produced a radical new style incorporating the letters HH and weaving them cleverly into a very powerful border. Needless to say Jamie Hamilton had paid little attention to the implementation of this house style. When he saw it he hit the roof and demanded his old colophon and border type back again. He was heard asking who on earth had sanctioned this particular piece of extravagance, because Herbert Spencer was quite expensive. Max Martyn, being the snake that he was, pointed the finger of blame at me and there was another black mark against me to add to the growing thundercloud.

After I had been with the firm for about a year it seemed that Jamie was moderately satisfied with the way I was working out and he began to take a beady interest in Jilly's career which was just taking off at the *Sunday Times*. Her first article had been published to an ecstatic reception which was the beginning of her literary fame. In fact most of her early written work was scribbled on the back of press handouts whilst attending publicity meetings at Collins where she worked. Jamie began to shower us with invitations to dinner. These were fairly formal occasions to which people like the poet, Kathleen Raine, would be invited. They weren't always easy because Jamie wasn't an easy host but there was always plenty to drink. One manifestation of Jamie's snobbery I became aware of was that he would change the photographs on the piano from week to week depending on who was coming to dinner. You would know where you were if there was somebody from the music world because one would find Joan Sutherland, Sir Malcolm Sargent and Kathleen Ferrier. Another time it would be photographs of Nancy Mitford, Kathleen Raine or some other literary figure jostling for space. Once we got invited to dinner twice in three weeks. The second time round all the photographs on

# Publisher's new house style

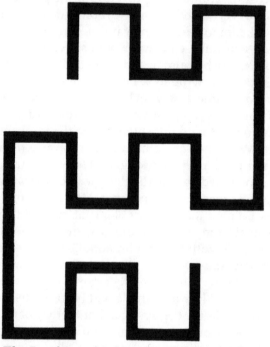

*The London publishers, Hamish Hamilton and Co, have a new colophon as part of a new house style. Designed by Herbert Spencer, the new black and white design is composed of a single continuous line which forms the outline of two bold capital letters 'H', one above the other. The design has the advantage of forming a very strong repeat pattern and is being used in that form on items such as the company's sealing tape and wrapping paper and catalogue covers. It is also appearing on vans, letterheads, display materials and advertisements.*

the piano and on the mantelpiece had been changed for another set of celebrities. This was a fairly common practice.

However, things began to become rather precarious when I discovered that Jamie was busy ringing up Jilly at various times of the day to see if she'd come and have lunch with him. At least that's what he said. One day I had returned early from a visit to promote some books in Glasgow. Instead of calling in at the office after the train arrived in London I went home and arrived about 5 o'clock. I was just telling Jilly about my trip when the doorbell rang. I went to the door and to my horror was confronted by Jamie wearing a pair of co-respondent shoes (brown and white) and under his arm two bottles of champagne. His face fell a mile when he saw me so I thought I'd get my oar in first. I said, 'I've just got back from Glasgow, Mr Hamilton, and I've only been in the house a few minutes so forgive me if I am not very well organised.' I then said that he'd better come in.

Poor Jilly was frozen in the drawing room and told me later that she didn't know what to do. I decided the only way was to plough on, so I got some glasses. It was plain the champagne was intended for Jilly but I shared out the bottles between the three of us. It happened that we had asked one or two people for drinks that evening. They arrived, soon a party was in full swing and Jamie was somewhat lost in the middle of it.

During the course of the evening I had a private talk with him and he asked me what I would really like to have done if I wasn't in publishing and I suppose this is where it all went wrong. I replied that I really wanted to be a game warden at one stage in my life and very nearly became one. After about an hour and a half Jamie disappeared into the street empty-handed in all senses of the word. I was not, however, to hear the end of this story. The following Monday I learnt that Jamie had gone to see Roger Machel and said we must get rid of Leo Cooper because he is not remotely interested in publishing and wants to be a game warden. This incident and one other about expenses contributed to my downfall and I don't think he ever took my interest in publishing seriously after that. The other episode arose from the fact that my expenses were deemed to be out of control. In a year I had spent over £333. I remember the figure exactly because I recalled a photograph of Sutcliffe and Holmes taken years before in front of the scoreboard in Essex showing the figure 555. It was so mean. I don't need to say that the one accusing me was James Eastwell, who said that my spending was outrageous. The sands of time were racing out.

I mentioned that Jamie had a private pilot's licence. One day before the war he offered the editor of *The Bookseller*, an enigmatic little man called Edmond Seagrave, a lift in his aeroplane to the Booksellers' Conference, which was being held in Scarborough. Jamie regarded *The Bookseller*, the organ of the book trade, as a vital tool in his armoury and made sure that he got plenty of mentions by buttering up Seagrave who in turn was flattered by the attention of such an eminent figure. Anyway they took off and flew without incident to Scarborough where they sat through the tedium of two days. On the third day Jamie said that he was bored, so they got into the aeroplane and flew down towards London. Halfway down Jamie appeared to be indulging in some aerobatics and they zoomed all over various parts of Hertford-shire. It was not apparent to Edmond Seagrave what was happening. When they landed at Denham Jamie went round to the second cockpit and opened the lid to be confronted with a white-faced Seagrave, semi-conscious and covered in vomit. What had happened was that the intercommunication cable between the pilot and passenger had come unplugged and, while the aerobatics were going on Mr Seagrave, not party to the event, was convinced they were going to crash, although he was quite safe. Jamie was so embarrassed he walked away leaving Seagrave in the cockpit. They did not speak to each other again until after the Second World War.

It was about this time that I first got to know Tom Hartman well. He was working in the educational side of Hamish Hamilton. I happened to be in my office clearing up a mess made by a sparrow which had got into the ventilating system and was mincing itself all over my desk. Tom appeared at the top of the stairs, saw the mess, saw me and said to his companion 'Who's that?' We were introduced at the top of the famous Hamilton stairs and that was the beginning of a beautiful friendship. It blossomed slowly and we became bosom pals. It was I who suggested that perhaps he might like to take a job 'on offer to him' working for Randolph Churchill who was involved in writing his father's biography. Tom's time at Hamish Hamilton had passed and he wanted a new job desperately. From that day onwards, which would have been some time in 1968, we became closer and Tom ended up working alongside me for nearly thirty-five years.

Among many well known books that Jamie published in this period was Emlyn Williams' about the Moors Murders called *Beyond Belief*. Whilst I found the book absolutely fascinating I was somewhat shattered to learn that Jamie was intending to reprint the famous tapes or rather a transcript of them which made the story so macabre. I got to hear of this and was surprised that even Roger Machel couldn't see why this would be an unfortunate piece of publishing. I felt so strongly about it that I said to Jamie that if they did print the transcriptions (and I'd heard them as well on a tape) I would immediately resign. This was rather a rash thing to do in my circumstances, but some notice seemed to have been taken of what I'd said and one or two other members of staff concurred and the book was published without the transcriptions, which I think was a good thing. I am not sure it did me any good though.

The most frightening author I had to deal with was L P Hartley. He suffered from a number of phobias and one of them was of fire. When I went to visit him in his flat in Rutland Gate I was surprised to see that all the wastepaper baskets were sellotaped to the under side of tables. This, he explained, when he saw me looking at them, was to make sure nobody threw cigarette ends into the bins and thereby set fire to the house. He also had a gentleman's gentleman looking after us who was very sinister and served us drinks on a silver tray while wearing black leather gloves. I was rather alarmed by this.

We got on to the subject of *The Go Between* and I was able to tell him that I'd had some small part to play in the success of the film. The casting director, one Boatie Baker*, came to see me and Jilly one day and poured out her heart about the fact that she wasn't able to get hold of any young English boys who were capable of speaking the Queen's English. All the products of the drama schools were unable to produce a decent English accent. I told her, half-heartedly, that she ought to go and ring up the Warden of Radley because Radley had a fine tradition of actors and spoken English generally. It might be that they had a boy who fitted the bill. Much to my joy and surprise this is exactly what happened. The part was played by young Dominic Guard who was a current Radleian with a beautiful voice. He got the part as a result of my suggestion, but I have been unable to ascertain whether he went on to become a star or not. I doubt it because I have seen no record of him, but then I don't go to the pictures much.

Long after I'd left Hamish Hamilton, Tom and I were in the nearby pub having a drink when we saw Christopher Sinclair-Stevenson, Brian Stone and Gillon Aitken heading on their way probably to the Garrick Club or at least to some west end restaurant. They were all over 6ft 4in

---

* It allegedly was her husband who was dining with Jeffrey Archer on the fateful night when he handed over the cash to the tart.

tall and the trio, as they sped past the pub window, resembled three tall galleons sailing up the channel. Somebody said, and I'm not sure if it was me, 'There go the unpopulars,' because both Brian Stone and Gillon Aitken were current candidates for taking over from Jamie, as indeed had Christopher been at one stage, as well as Jamie's son Alistair and myself. The succession to the throne never took place. Gillon Aitken started a literary agency with Brian Stone and Christopher briefly became a publishing imprint himself ensuring, alas, one of the shortest active lives of any publishing imprint in the 20th century.

I had already seen how Jamie Hamilton was averse to progress. Whilst he marched forward looking behind him all the time, there were changes afoot and one of these affected a vital part of his week. There was a ledger, or rather a volume, called the 'grey book' in which was recorded in longhand the sale of every book at the end of each week. Jamie's first act on getting into the office on a Monday would be to ring Mrs Rumney, whose job it was to maintain the grey book, which she did meticulously and there is no better system and never was (even I would admit this) than hand operated checking for sales figures. At least that was something we agreed on. Anyway progress was afoot, although Jamie didn't know it, but of course he had obviously given his permission for it to happen. We were to be computerised.

Came the day when the whole set up was ready to roll and Jamie arrived at the office at the usual time and rang the bell for Mrs Rumney. There was no reply, so, having rabbitted around various telephones he finally located somebody down in the sales department and asked where was Mrs Rumney and the grey book? 'Oh Mr Hamilton, Mrs Rumney has now been made redundant and the sales figures are done by a commuter.' There was an audible silence at the end of the line. 'What do you mean the sales are done by a commuter?' asked Jamie. 'No Mr Hamilton, that is why they can't show you the grey book.' 'Do you mean that bloody fool Depotex in the sales department?' (George Depotex lived in Henley on Thames and therefore commuted.) 'No sir, the whole of our invoicing system has been commuterised'. The person who was imparting this information realised that he was not getting anywhere. Within half an hour Mrs Rumney had been sent for from her graceful retirement and the grey book was filled in by hand and continued to be so with all the information taken off the computer forever after. Such is progress.

I should mention that while I was working for André we went through the same birth pangs as did Jamie Hamilton with regard to computerisation. The irony of this was that George Depotex, who had been the sales manager at Deutsch and therefore responsible for putting the computerisation into action there had also moved on and was working for Hamish Hamilton at the same time as I. Therefore he was able to point out all the pitfalls of the system which he'd learnt at Deutsch. In my experience very few people at the editorial end in publishing houses bother to consult their printouts. If they did they'd be aware of vast acres of information which could be of use to them, but very few people mention a computer now, except to blame it for breakdowns.

For the time being I continued to propose a small military history list. I was full of ideas and so I did a lot of research and prepared some detailed proposals for Jamie.

Thus 1969 saw the birth of the Famous Regiment series of which the early titles were published under the aegis of Hamish Hamilton who, as I have said, gave me much encouragement as I was currently in Jamie's good books. By the time I'd summoned up my courage and left the company there were several other military titles in production, or about to go under contract, which meant that I could take them with me as long as I paid back the small advances we had offered. It was too much to expect that all the colonels-in-chief of all the regiments would march off parade grounds in high dudgeon carrying copies of their regimental histories, but the word got round and over the next few years regular batches of Famous Regiments were commissioned and in the end, before they were priced out of the market, we had done nearly sixty volumes.

My idea for the Famous Regiment series had come from reading a piece in the newspaper about the Manchester Regiment being disbanded and the contents of the Regimental Museum distributed to various members and old comrades. I thought that if this could happen so easily, many marvellous sources of history would become unavailable before we could get at the raw material. My original intention had been to cover the whole of the British Army, but I was thwarted by production costs and by a falling demand. Later, in the early days in the basement (and subsequently), it was quite obvious that the market was not enamoured of military history. Quite a lot of military history books had been doing the rounds and not finding homes. Fortunately, and eventually, the Famous Regiment series got my publishing imprint very well known because the old boy net was very hard at work behind the scenes. In due course lots of regiments actually got in touch and asked to be included. Apart from the sheer fascination of visiting probably more regimental headquarters in the British Isles than any other person, there was the knowledge that, by trailing my cloak with these single-volume, well-produced little histories, I might attract bigger fish. In other words we might be able to capture the market for the lucrative official Regimental Histories, together with all their colour printing, expensive jackets and publish them as a memorial for posterity.

There aren't that many regiments today who have not been covered by an official history. One or two have bravely taken up the cudgel and done their post-war or post-disbandment volume, but on the whole momentum in this field only began to take off when we proved how beautiful such books could be. We were able to produce them well because of the bountiful nature of regimental committees who were absolutely determined not to let their regiments slide into obscurity. Hence there were Regimental Trusts, many of them set up especially, and donations and legacies which provided solid finance for many of these splendid official histories which we published over thirty years*. There is a list of them all in Appendix II. Some of them were beautiful pieces of military history writing, not least the late Michael Glover's history of The Royal Welch Fusiliers entitled *That Astonishing Infantry*. There was also a marvellous history of the *Scarlet Lancers* by James Lunt and the best of them all *The Light Dragoons* by Allan Mallinson which, apart from anything else, enabled him to crack his teeth on military history writing and to make a name for himself as a novelist in the military history field for Transworld. His recently published novels on the Peninsular War, the Crimea and the Mutiny (all in fictional form) need little introduction now because they have found a happy place in the market. I had been searching for this kind of publishing all along and up to a point reached it, having cornered virtually the whole of the official non-fiction Regimental History publishing before I retired, but I never attempted to crack the fiction market. In retrospect this was a mistake.

My object in founding the series was to save the history of all the regiments in the British army, about 109, and with one or two peripheral titles as well. I had been enchanted by Lieutenant-General Sir Brian Horrocks' programme on Welsh television about British battles and had decided to approach him to see if he would act as general editor for my proposed series. Famous Regiments represented the go ahead, which I was given, that led to the formation of my first

---

* The official histories should not be confused with the Famous Regiment series; see Appendix I.

list but the first four titles in the series were published under the Hamish Hamilton imprint. I also put up a proposal for a specialist list to be developed in military history.

At first all went very well and there was a magnificent launch party for the series at the Royal Hospital Chelsea. Jamie of course was much enamoured of General Horrocks and the General didn't let us down. However, when my time came to be sacked I realised that if I did not act fast I might have to leave my babies at home. The nature of my dismissal I'm reminded was rather unusual. Jamie asked me out for the usual drink at The Plough and made his usual remark when seeing me drink a pint of beer, which was, 'I can't think how you can find enough room for all that.' He then said that he wanted to dispense with my services and, knowing what I did, I agreed without much comment. Jamie left in a somewhat flustered state to go back to the office. I walked over to two friends of mine, the inevitable John Watson and another friend who was a literary agent, novelist and journalist called Victor Briggs, of whom you will hear more. John bought me a drink and one for Victor and said, 'How nice to see you getting on so well with Jamie Hamilton, ' to which I replied, 'Actually the bugger's just sacked me.' This of course had given me the green light. I approached the accountant, no longer Mr Eastwell, and suggested to him that I would like to make a bid for the series. This was agreed and at the same time I got my oar in with Hamilton by telling him that, although he'd tried to sack me the week before, I had already formulated my plans to start my own imprint and so I was resigning anyway and might I buy the rights to all the books that had been published so far under my control. I was on one month's notice. A week before I left Jamie called me in and tried to re-employ me. I said no and this was the beginning of Leo Cooper Ltd.

# CHAPTER V

## *Basement Days*

> *On the way to the branch office one day I walked down the ginnel and there on the wall somebody had written, in large magic marker, 'Leo Cooper Rules'. Underneath somebody had written 'Don't be ridiculous he can't even draw a straight line'.*

And so out of Great Russell Street I went my solitary way. It was 1968. I did not have to go very far – 800 yards I would say. It so happened that my bibulous Scots pilot friend John Watson (who had by now been sacked by Mayflower) was renting the basement of a building in Museum Street. John was paying £2 a week to the Turkish café owner who ran his business from the ground floor. The accommodation consisted of two damp rooms and a lavatory with the drain filled in. He very kindly offered me one of the rooms at the princely sum of £1 per week in cash. It was a good address to have providing that nobody too important descended into the bowels of the earth to visit us. I was a little bit worried about what authors might think of the accommodation. It so happened, though, that General Horrocks was the first visitor we had and if he approved of it, which he did, my worries would be at an end. I had also been able to persuade my secretary from Hamish Hamilton to desert and Liz Drinnan joined me as the first member of staff to be followed shortly by one Toby Buchan*, aged 19, who, Tim Jaques, a friend from the Longman days, had told me, was at a very loose end indeed. So it proved but he was employed as a packer and a gofer. He was later to found his own publishing firm called Buchan & Enright which ended up eventually rather like my own, but while he was working for me he was a constant source of amusement. He entered into the spirit of things. He was very clever

---

* And Bertie his dog.

*My Pen and Sword colophon, designed by Tim Jaques.*

and very funny and all too often precocious, but this did us no harm. He was very much the young iconoclast. Tim Jaques was of enormous help in the early years. He designed my colophon. He had produced some brilliant graphics for Longmans including the jacket for the new *Roget's Thesaurus* and the new edition of *Gray's Anatomy*. He was not only an accomplished graphic designer but was responsible for the ship colophon used, until recently, by Longmans. He was also a painter of considerable talent and in his earlier days a very wild fast bowler of less talent. Another part of his track record was doing all the illustrations for Jilly's books over a period of years. He illustrated for a lot of other publishers, and was also responsible for three children's books with Jilly which to this day are highly regarded. I was his best man at both his weddings and his late second wife was briefly my secretary at Deutsch.

A well-placed piece of gossip in the *Sunday Times* was soon arranged with one Michael Bateman and the show was on the road. He did a piece about my departure from Hamish Hamilton and my setting up on my own, headed *Soldiering On*. My accountant, whom I consulted perhaps rather late in the day, realised that I was naïve about business but promised to take me to his bank manager in Covent Garden who knew even less about publishing than I did. I managed to squeeze a £1,500 facility out of him and I also acquired two punters. One of them was called Tim Carew who had won 'a good MC' at Imphal and was a regular contributor to the *Daily Express*. He had written several military books and he came into a modest legacy which gave him a small private income payable through me. They were quite rightly under the impression that, had he been given all the legacy in one go it would have gone down his throat in no time, so I was really his paymaster. Tim was very close to the bottle but he was a very funny man and was related to Fortescue, the great historian of the British Army. The comparison ends there. I can't remember exactly how much I paid Tim out of his legacy per month but it soon vanished even though it was issued in small measures or, you might say, large ones.

The lawyers were under the impression that Tim was an active member of the editorial staff. In fact we were responsible for paying him once a week, most of which was spent on his train fares to come and collect it. It didn't last very long, but then nor did Tim, who was killed when falling down the stairs in his house in Bracknell, an ignominious end for a brave man. It is just as well that Tim had died the way he did. As we came out of the crematorium Mrs Carew, a formidable player, and various other funeral attendees made a bee line for the pile of wreaths which were left outside on the pavement. Mrs Carew began to pick through them, reading out the inscriptions thereon. John Watson whispered very noisily into my ear as she was leafing through one from somebody he knew, 'Wait until she finds out that Tim has mortgaged the house twice already.'

The other punter was one Henry Nelson from Nelson in Lancashire. He owned a museum called The British in India which was set up in a redundant mill. His sister was currently married to Lord Bathurst. Henry Nelson was not an ideal partner because he knew very little about publishing, but he had that vital thing – access to money – and he put up some two or three thousand pounds which he got back in the end, lucky man. I think he found the publishing world a bit eccentric, so he didn't last very long, but we parted on good terms. Henry's nickname in the office was Ham Tea Nelson. This nickname was entirely due to Tim Carew who had once come with me to call on Henry in his museum. Tim could not get over the fact that at 4 o'clock in the afternoon we were given a full tea with bacon, eggs, sausages and ham. I don't know that Henry ever knew that he was called Ham Tea Nelson but the name lasted for a long time.

So there we were with a small staff and, best of all, the piece in the newspaper had produced a number of manuscripts which surprisingly were of the highest quality. There was some rubbish as well but a number of the submissions made were surprisingly good and there were at least five books which I took on straight away. This may have been a burst of over-enthusiasm but they are remembered to this day and one of them is a classic of World War Two by Alex Bowlby*, *The Recollections of Rifleman Bowlby*, one of the funniest memoirs of that war.

Another book which shone like a star was *Songs & Music of the Redcoats* by Lewis Winstock. He knew nothing about music at all but he was a brilliant historian and we produced what is still one of my favourite books. It contains fifty-six fully scored musical items which were transcribed for the piano by a very beautiful girl called Tammy Broughton. (I once discovered copies of this book in the costume department of Foyles.) Then there was *Mutiny for the Cause* by Sam Pollock, the story of the Connaught Rangers' mutiny in India in the 1920s. That went on to enjoy two film options, but no film was ever made. It is interesting that the same situation arose when a more up-to-date account of the same event appeared called *The Devil's to Pay* published by Buchan & Enright. The book was by the late Judge Anthony Babington who later wrote a classic for me called *For the Sake of Example* about the execution of British soldiers in World War One. I must say in the early days I would gaze at these manuscripts and marvel that I had an opportunity to put them into print and always at the back of my mind was the nagging feeling that I was taking a huge great risk with other people's money and I realised that I knew even less about publishing than did the bank manager in Covent Garden.

It is interesting to note in the light of what I said earlier about production techniques that Sam Pollock's book and that by Lewis Winstock were both on the cusp so to speak. Sam Pollock's *Mutiny for the Cause* was set in hot metal (the last title to be so) by Clark, Doble & Brendon whilst *Songs & Music of the Redcoats* was produced by litho at Lowe & Brydon – the first of many.

* There is more about Alex in thumbnail sketches at the end of this book.

One of my landlord's talents, apart from writing second rate spaghetti westerns, was writing category fiction and he was also the author of a book called *Johnny Kinsman*, the only book I know about Bomber Command which was published in a fictional form, apart from Len Deighton's *Bomber*. At the time of writing I believe I am right in saying that the book has never been out of print. It is an extremely clever atmospheric account of what it was like to be a bomber pilot. No wonder the experience drove John, and many others, to drink. 57,000 RAF aircrew were killed in World War Two. I emphasise *killed* and roughly the same number from the US air force. In the end he died in the shower. He had survived forty-two missions.

The first book I actually published under my own imprint, apart from a reprint of Gleig's *The Subaltern*, was in the Famous Regiment series and was a history of *The York & Lancaster Regiment*, whose cap badge rejoiced in the name of the cat and cabbage – a representation of a lion and an English rose. The book was by one Hugh Creighton-Williamson. It had a curious history. The Colonel of the regiment, General Harman, was so angry that the York & Lancasters, of which he was Colonel in Chief, were to be disbanded that he issued an order that they would buy 1,500 copies of the book. These were then distributed to the regiment, soldier by soldier, on the final disbandment parade. The General was determined that no financial resources left behind by the disbandment would get anywhere near the charity commissioners to which surplus funds were usually directed. To know that the first book I published was guaranteed to sell 1,500 copies kept me confident for a few days and the regiment quite rightly took their place as an early title in the Famous Regiment list referred to earlier. Copies are now changing hands, as I said earlier, at about £40 in the second-hand market and I think of General Harman very often with gratitude. I always like the image of a battalion of infantryman marching off a parade with rifle in one hand and a book in the other. The pen being mightier than the rifle in this case!

I have already mentioned that John Watson, my bomber pilot friend, had kindly offered me the opportunity of sharing his palatial basement in Museum Street and, recalling those days, I am reminded of three episodes in John's life which have always made me laugh.

In his days of running Mayflower Books he frequently had to visit the Frankfurt Book Fair held annually in October. One year he and Helen, his wife, decided to drive there This was round about the time that the whole of Frankfurt was being dug up and the rubble redistributed after it had been bombed to pieces in the war. John and Helen were driving round getting more and more frustrated in a city which was all one-way streets, potholes and ruins. Eventually they came to such a site surrounded by corrugated iron and on the edge of a busy road. Despairing of finding anywhere to park, Watson drove his car on to the bombed site, whereupon an extremely stroppy German in a peaked hat came rushing towards them shouting something like 'Verboten'. After making it plain that he didn't actually understand German but knew exactly what the man was saying, John leant out of the window and said, 'I made this bloody hole.'

On another occasion, in the Ivanhoe Hotel in Bloomsbury, John was pouring some amber liquid down his throat when an increasingly boastful German sitting at the bar next to him started sounding off about life in general and how awful it was in England. John, a Scotsman, could not let this go by and turned at him and said in a stentorian voice, 'How the hell did I ever miss you?' This story was told to me by my friend Victor Briggs, who was a leading player in the Lower Bloomsbury Steady Drinking Club which all too plainly was keeping a lot of people busy. Victor ran the literary agency Scott Meredith for a while. It was a very odd agency and the two pro-tagonists who started it were eccentric to say the least and treated Victor in the most appalling manner. Fortunately they didn't last long and Victor himself, who was the writer of quite a lot of pulp fiction, was usually around in The Plough or The Museum Tavern at lunchtime and was ever one for a quick anecdote. He was a marvellous drinking companion. He and Watson used to go everywhere together and if ever one was at a loose end Victor could always be guaranteed to cheer you up. There is more of him later.

It fell to me, at Helen Watson's request, to give the address at John's memorial service which, alas, came all too soon. He was such a valued friend. I told the congregation of a unique occasion when John had arranged to have some books printed by a printer in Glasgow whose main work was for the Jewish community and who was involved with a whole lot of Hebrew publishing. John had a row with his printer/binder and threatened to take the sheets of one printed book off to another binder. In the end the dispute very nearly led to blows and John was forced at the dead of night to remove the sheets from the printer and send them to another firm who duly bound them up. It was only after he had had the books in the warehouse for some weeks that John bothered to open one of them. To his horror he found the last section printed entirely in Hebrew which sat uneasily on a chapter of the Western type story which was the main text. What had happened was that in picking the sheets off the pallet the forklift truck had inadvertently loaded the sheets of another publication altogether in Hebrew and the binder had not noticed. The book reached the shops with two-thirds in English and one-third in Hebrew. It is of interest to note that not one single complaint was ever received. I am told that I ended my address with the remark, 'As it is now 11 o'clock no doubt John would have required us to be in the nearest pub, so let us go there now.'

John occasionally had violent rows with Helen. On one occasion they were quarrelling so much over something that Helen had said about John not being a provider that he picked up a leg of lamb and threw it at Helen in the kitchen. Unfortunately (or fortunately!) it missed her and went straight through the window of their Bedford Court Mansions flat and landed in the gutter outside the front door. John, having seen what had happened, told his wife to go downstairs and see if she could rescue the leg of lamb which was lying in the gutter among a pile of broken glass. This she did, but, to add insult to injury, John refused to let her back in when she rang the buzzer and she stood outside Bedford Court Mansions with a leg of lamb full of shards of glass wearing only a dressing gown and in bare feet to be greeted by the street sweeper who very kindly showed Helen how to get in by the back door. That evening an actress called Maureen Prior was given roast lamb for dinner. History does not relate whether she managed to leave the pieces of glass on the edge of her plate. She died shortly afterwards.

I mentioned earlier that John wrote category fiction. This genre is difficult to explain, other than to say that you write a series of books featuring the same characters in different situations. Hornblower and Sharp are good examples. John used to write in the basement and usually managed to do a day's work before the pubs opened. One day he went off to the pub leaving an uncompleted page of a manuscript in his typewriter. I couldn't resist the temptation and, without reading what the book was about from the previous pages, I typed a page of gobbledygook and left it in the machine. He never noticed and nor did anyone else. To this day that same book is on my shelf complete with rogue page.

We were not the only publisher housed in 47 Museum Street. On the very top two floors there was an extraordinary man called Howard (Bill) Baker. He was a sort of publisher, but he specialised in reprints of comics, not least the famous Greyfriars Billy Bunter series. He administered this operation with a number of eccentric staff but none was more eccentric than Bill himself. He kept a massive drinks cabinet in his office which had to be replenished from day to day and by noon he was usually sloshed out of his mind. He would then resort to The Plough or The Museum Tavern; the two were equidistant, where he would spend the rest of the lunch hour topping himself up. Thereafter he would stagger back to the office and sleep all afternoon. One day he hadn't gone to sleep quite as quickly as usual. He was currently employing a pair of identical twins called the Freeman brothers, Ken and Jeff, as graphic designers. One of the brothers met Howard, who wasn't seeing quite straight, in the street. Howard was heard to greet him saying 'Hello boys'. He really was seeing double.

I can't do better than borrow the words of Victor Briggs when talking about Howard Baker. The whole passage which I quote is with Victor's kind permission because he knew Baker so much better than I did and I think what he wrote sums up the attitude around WC2 which operated between The Museum Tavern and The Plough and in the bottom end of Bloomsbury. Victor takes up the story:

> Bill Baker as I knew him could rightly claim to provide almost any book to order. I doubt the veracity of his claim to be the author of all the books which bore his name but I never knew him fail to deliver a manuscript on time and in pristine condition, beautifully typed by his assistant Ross Storey, an authoress herself and a former wife of the eccentric author and journalist Jack Trevor Storey who made and spent fortunes from such books as *Live Now, Pay Later*.
>
> Bill Baker was a Cork-born Irishman and was not an easy man to dislike yet the stories one hears about him should have been enough to make me steer clear of him. He was a parody of a man trying to project an air of power and wildness and yet his manner was largely bluff and bluster. When I first met him he spilled over with friendliness and chuckles and I found him good company with a wide-ranging sense of humour. He had the bulk for an authoritative stance but it was negated by his pencil-thin moustache and trilby hat which were probably inspired by his seeing Alan Ladd in 'This Gun for Hire.'
>
> His background was something of a mystery to me, but I recall he told me he'd been as far as Australia, had been to Egypt and been editor there of an English language newspaper. He had later fetched up at Panther Books which was by then defunct and Fleetway Publications also defunct in Faringdon Street as part of the giant international IPC. His job there was as an editor working

on the Sexton Blake Library, a series of popular soft cover 40–50,000 word books issued monthly. It was from this position that he was able to sow the seeds of a successful future business which was to become known as Press Editorial Services.

The desire to get words into print was no less than it is today though the opportunity to exploit that desire has been considerably reduced over the intervening years. Bill Baker was smart enough to recognise a chance of making reasonably easy money in those days at Fleetway and he took full advantage of it.

As I and a number of other people understood it the opportunity presented itself and he realised that, if not a gold mine then a copper mine, was being dumped on his desk every week. Manuscripts from aspiring authors of Sexton Blake novels came in from the provinces like arrows at Crécy. Most of them of course failed to come up to the required standard but some were competent efforts and it was those which were to become the foundation on which Bill, alongside Greyfriars, built his future.

How often Bill pulled the stroke I don't know but I subsequently met a number of authors who fell for his dubious appraisal of their work. Loosely the idea was to tell them that their work was not suitable for publication but then generously suggest an offer of, say £50, for the rights of what was basically a good idea which he or another editor could knock into shape for the Sexton Blake series.

The prospect of having even part of their work published was so overwhelming to most of the previously unpublished authors that many of them jumped at the chance. They would then sign a contract disposing of all their rights in the book and Bill would have himself a property.

To what degree the books were edited I don't know but I had it on reasonable authority that it was minimal and Bill was able to resell the books to Fleetway Sexton Blake Library Series for much more than he paid for them. Years later these books some with rearrangement would reappear again in another guise long after Bill had departed from Fleetway. I know because I unwittingly published some of them under the Consul imprint. So too did Mayflower Books and in one case Sexton Blake made an unscheduled appearance in the middle of a book which had as its hero a character called Quintain (né Sexton Blake).

In retrospect shady as these practices might have been, I doubt if they did much harm. Many of the people who wrote for Sexton Blake Library might otherwise never have seen their work in print and Bill did tidy up their manuscripts and also presented them in a professional condition ready for printers so he wasn't all bad.

I am very grateful to Victor for allowing me to use his words here as this eccentric side of publishing never really gets a look in. Yet there is often an undercurrent of dubious publications constantly being churned out by a gang of hacks, or there was in those days.

One of the early successes of our author recruitment operation from Museum Street was a writer called Charles Whiting. Charles was one of the early visitors to the basement and had, at the time, one novel already published. He was a frequent contributor to the *Times Educational Supplement*. He had served in the war in The Reconnaissance Corps, was married to a German lady and he lived at that time on the borders of Belgium, France and Germany; at least I think he did. He had a fascination with the Second World War and the campaigns in North-West Europe. Having served there himself he was well qualified to write about that area of constant battle. What was surprising though was the volume of information he unearthed. So well researched was it that he became a sort of industry in himself.

The first book we published for him was called *Massacre at Malmédy* and from then on he never looked back. He became such a successful writer that there was a stage when I had to advise him to write under other names because nobody could put up with the volume of titles that came from the same author in a year. At one stage I think we estimated that he'd written over two dozen titles in the course of one calendar year. He needed careful editing though, which Tom was able to provide, and he had that great gift which so few writers have – readability. He wrote books under several pseudonyms, and I recall the name Leo Kessler which was a pun on my name and the double S in the title was the SS badge. This was an in-joke.

Leo Kessler is now translated into a dozen different languages from Finnish to Hungarian and still going strong thirty odd years later. As Charles remembers, I suggested that Anthony Cheetham had a project for him. We met in Halle 7 at the Frankfurt Book Fair that year and Anthony said, as it was lunchtime, that we ought to eat something. Being a very canny man with a penny, he didn't invite us to one of the inside places (too expensive). Instead we went outside to one of the booths where he generously ordered Bratwurst and Bier. Then we sat in the freezing cold on a bench, with the early snow falling lightly, enjoying this splendid meal and thought of a name for the new author who would write about the SS (according to Anthony), rather like the good and bad guys in the old westerns! Then came the name. I had already brought up 'Leo' then both Anthony and I remarked that at that time Hassel was cleaning up the market in that kind of war fiction (Hassel had of course been a real SS man). What about something Germanic on that basis? Hassel thus became Kessler ('kettle maker' in German) and the black uniformed monster was born – Leo Kessler the creator of the immortal Sergeant Schulze famed throughout the SS NCO Corps for his talented musical farts.

Charles also rejoiced in the name of K L Kostoff and, for slightly more British things, Duncan Harding. There were others. To say that he was prolific would be putting it mildly, prolix would be better. Certainly he was publishing books with other people while I was just plodding along doing his non-fiction. He used to write series books and in some cases I just let him go ahead and sign six-book contracts with various paperback firms which kept him busy so that he would be writing category fiction on the one hand and non-fiction largely invented by him (faction we called it) on the other. It got to the stage where even he was unable to remember what he had written and what he hadn't and on one occasion we actually caught him plag.arising his own work.

Charles always let you know what he thought about everything. He was straight as a die and was industrious and sympathetic to our cause. He was, and is, the most loyal of authors and he was frequently available to give his views on other people's work and indeed on the publishing scene as a whole. Gradually he began to appear on everyone else's lists under his various names. He was seldom reviewed. When I persuaded him to sign up for the Public Lending Right* he immediately rocketed into the top bracket which, at the time of writing, consisted of only 380 authors. The limit that any one author can earn from the PLR in a single year is, at the moment, £6,000 and he consistently recorded the top figure every year and has done since he signed up.

It was material such as Charles's that helped a small publisher like me get off the ground. He never asked for advances. He was sharp with money but not greedy; he became a great friend of the family and I couldn't have proceeded without him. He supplemented early cash

---

* PLR, as it is called, was primarily achieved after a long battle with the Government. One of the primary lobbyists was my Aunt Lettice and, thanks to her, authors are entitled to a modest sum per library borrowing. The rate at present is 5.26p per borrowing (2005).

flow by his productivity and he was very much the house mascot. We did actually republish some of his fiction paperbacks in hardcover to get the library market, but it was felt generally that we were issuing books in the wrong order by doing this.

Among other things Charles was frequently in touch with members of the former Nazi regime. He knew many Nazis such as Jochen Peiper (real name Joachim but that was biblical and too Jewish), Eisenhower's Public Enemy number one in 1944 and Otto Skorzeny, who had rescued Mussolini from imprisonment in 1943 – even Churchill had been impressed. Then there was Captain Giskes of 'Operation North Pole' fame. Giskes of the German Counter-Intelligence was instrumental in playing the radio game with the British and Dutch for two years netting some fifty unfortunate SOE agents in Holland. Later he went on to work indirectly for the CIA. There was also the Bormann family. Bormann, Hitler's 'Brown Eminence' and the most important man in the Third Reich after the Führer, was supposedly still alive and on the run in the '50s when Charles took up the chase. Charles never found Bormann (he was already long dead) but he did find the last woman to see him alive in the Bunker in 1941 – his secretary Else Krueger – and where did Charles find her thirty years later? Cambridge! But that's another story.

I don't mean to imply that he was a sympathiser, but by living on the borders of Belgium, France and Germany he was fortunate because he was sitting on a gold mine. He exploited this splendidly, as the following story shows. We went down to the branch office one day, which was what we called the pub behind the office, of which more later. All authors ended up there at one time or another in their career because of the dim lighting, friendly bar service and nice little corners to sit in. The Oporto, as it was called, became very much our Shangri-la and all the landlords (and there were many) seemed to be called Dermot. They were also our bank! In this case Charles and I sat down to decide what he was going to write next and I had some idea that it might be worth doing a book about the German parachute regiment whose last sally as actual parachutists ended with a bloody nose at Heraklion in Crete. There was no previous volume on this subject and Charles said he thought he could write one fairly quickly. I didn't see him for six weeks because he went back home to Germany, but the next time he did roll up I met him in the pub and he put a large envelope in my hands and said 'There's your history of the German Parachute Regiment – *Hunters from the Sky*'. Sure enough in six weeks he had written what turned out to be one of the biggest money spinners we ever published. It sold in America immediately, it sold book club rights in the UK and the States and it went into paperback editions on both sides of the Atlantic. I was dealing at the time in the USA with Sol Stein* who had the same feeling about Charles Whiting as I did. That was to publish anything he wrote but in no specific order and at a pace that suited us not him and often under different titles in the USA. This was another reason Charles appeared under so many imprints. Anyway I am still in touch with him and, although I don't have to keep up with him any longer, I am eternally grateful for the way he stuck to his last and we couldn't really have continued to publish without him.

Another author who became very much a house property during the basement days was one A J (Jack) Smithers, a lawyer who had been in the retreat from Dunkirk and was unique in the fact that, having got back from the disaster over the Channel, he realised that some of his men were missing so he found a boat going back, discovered them and led them to safety. He came to writing late in life which was a pity because he wrote some really delightful books. He was erudite, witty and another author utterly loyal to the imprint. He too stuck to his last and never ceased to be kind and understanding, particularly about our limited resources. I think (with only one desertion) we must have published about eight books of his, none of which quite got the treatment they deserved. But, again like Charles Whiting, he was aware that we were a small publishing firm, that our resources were limited and that like us he was taking a risk. The fact that he stuck to the rules was a tremendous morale booster for us as were his visits to the office which always raised our spirits. He could be and was a very long suffering man. Recently he managed to get published a book that he'd been trying to place for years and I had been refusing just as long. It was about the fight for Tangier, during which campaign the British Army really became an entity. It was a beautiful little book but I turned it down on a number of occasions. The fact that it is finally now going to see the light of day is a tribute to Jack's persistence and perhaps my blindness. But I shall always be grateful to him, as all those who worked with me were and are.

And so gradually the word got round that we were a growing business. The daily post began to increase and the word spread that there was a new publisher in the market who was actively engaged in trying to find authors. Information travels fast in our quarter and very soon manuscripts began to arrive unsolicited, as well as letters from

* Sol Stein went bust in due course.

people asking if we'd be interested in certain titles. I was torn between the idea of volume, in other words to publish anything I could lay my hands on to start with and to get the momentum going, and the awareness that lack of finance which persuaded me that caution, where possible, was not a bad idea. I was sorely tempted sometimes by projects which looked promising. A close examination of their potential, however, revealed that they would have broken us if we had taken them on. On only one occasion did we bend the rules seriously and this was with Lord Anglesey's history of the British Cavalry which eventually appeared in eight volumes. This was very much Tom's baby and he became a close friend of the author and Lord Anglesey himself became one of our most loyal supporters. The series eventually won the Templer Medal and the Chesney Gold Medal. The publication of the eight volumes spanned twenty-five years. When the final volume appeared the only casualty was the cartographer, Patrick Leeson, who became very ill and died. The design, production and editing of the books were in the hands of Tom and the designer of the jacket, the printer (changed to litho midway) and the publisher (me) were all the same people who'd been in at the beginning of the act.

One other person who comes out of the Anglesey operation with credit is the author's agent, Diana Baring, who was then working through John Farquarson. Realising that she had a monumental product on her hands and that she would have the greatest difficulty in publishing it at that time because economic conditions weren't too happy, she very kindly contacted me, not the richest of publishers, but she felt the right man and we did a deal where the advance was very modest. In fact I think it was only £2,500 up front per book. The series did not begin knowing quite where it was going, but what had been planned as four volumes eventually turned into eight. The joyful end to all this is that all the volumes have been reprinted in modest quantities and the whole set is still available; the early editions are fetching high prices on the second-hand market. I think that this British Cavalry operation was the apex of our publishing career and it received a marvellous press. When you get publicity like that it brings with it other queries, offers and indeed manuscripts.

One can only stay for so long in one place and it became apparent that we were bursting at the seams at 47 Museum Street. I began to look around to see if I could find accommodation for what was beginning to be an over-staffed organisation and I had a piece of good luck. Somebody mentioned that there was a peculiar firm, somewhat antediluvian, only a few hundred yards down the road, called Seeley Service, who over the years had been particularly famous for the series

**1.** The Graf Zeppelin.

**2.** "It was at least 600 feet up in the sky".

**3.** The lake at Ingleborough Hall where I might have drowned.

**4.** An early example of interest in things military.

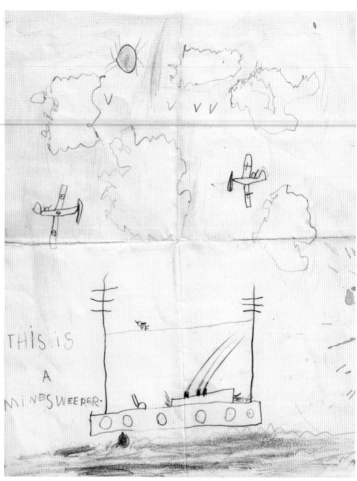

**5.** "Underneath the Arches" – The Settle Home Guard. The bar was not presumably open yet!

**6.** Major L Cooper in all his finery wearing his Minden Rose.

**7.** A little lad, aged 10.

**8.** Cooper *(left)* and Booth *(right)* growing up. 1947.

**9.** The Radley College CCF Band led by their 1st Trumpet.

**10.** Aunt Lettice collects her OBE flanked by my father and Aunt Barbara.

**11.** John Lehman … beware.

**12.** Five Training Battalion Barracks, Aldershot (Blenheim) – 22867795 (Intake photo).

**13.** Nick Smith later of *Are you Being Served* with Ronnie Wax at Willems Barracks, Aldershot – Two Training Battalion.

**14.** Passing out parade – Buller Barracks, Aldershot – 432316 (JUO Cooper).

**15.** Passing out parade. The author, 2nd left and Robin Ray, 4th left.

**16.** Commissioned at last.

**17.** HMT *Empire Windrush*.

**18.** A platoon, 92 Company EAASC, on the way back from Nairobi to Nyeri.

**19.** Baden Powell's grave at Nyeri (Kenya). The circle with the dot in it is the Boy Scout's tracking sign for 'Gone Home'.

**20.** Cricket at Nyeri. 70 East Africa Brigade HQ in the background.

**21.** The author with his driver Otieno Onyango (a member of the Acholi tribe).

**22.** Kipos Soi, my batman, of the Kipsigis tribe.

**23.** In a Lincoln nose turret.

of books called *The Lonsdale Library* and another called *The Badminton Library*. They also published *The Weekend Books* and in naval history they were the publishers of Oscar Parkes' *British Battleships* and *British Destroyers* by Edgar March – magnificent and expensive books, but with a very strong sales record. Getting to hear of this opportunity required no knowledge but it required a lot of subtlety to land the fish which in the end we did do after intense negotiations.

So we said goodbye to 47 Museum Street and left overnight with our pathetic belongings and quite a stock of books which had made the retired lavatory look like a decent storeroom. We were about to change our whole style (wrongly as it turned out). We now controlled our own distribution and above all had access to a lovely old office building in Shaftesbury Avenue which belonged to the Service family. A merger was proposed, an offer made and Seeley Service & Cooper was born. A holding company was formed to publish under the separate imprints of Leo Cooper and Seeley Service. It was 1970.

Our new offices were in Shaftesbury Avenue and came with a four-storey warehouse absolutely crammed with files, books and dead manuscripts, together with young John Service as a trainee and Alistair Service, his cousin, who was currently running The Family Planning Association and once described himself as a man of French letters. John Service left us after a bit to visit the family business in Brazil which was to do with paper manufacture and, although he reappeared in the office from time to time, one could never say that he was actually a full-time member of the staff, any more than was Alistair, but they represented the Service family and were absolutely charming.

There was very little of much interest except the knowledge that the filing from the last hundred years was still there in the warehouse gathering dust and waiting to be sorted. It was an astonishing collection of old files, illustrations, blocks and all the detritus of publishing which had simply been dumped in this warehouse. It was literally enveloped in layers of dust. There was a small packing staff at that time run by a man called Jim who ruled his kingdom with a rod of iron and later also Matt, a blind packer, who was twice as efficient as all the others put together. This meant that we now had an operational warehouse to look after. The rest of the staff were unbelievable. The whole place was a time warp. Mr Brockwell, the manager, turned out to be well into his 80s and had been falsifying his age to enable him to remain in his position for some time. The chief invoice typist, Miss Bathgate, couldn't use a typewriter and two other ladies, Miss Pickard and Mrs Kidman, had been there for many years. I did not enquire too much but I remember one of them, Miss Pickard, told me that during the General Strike when she was still in her youth working at Seeley Service, she was required to walk daily to and from the office. I thought this was very commendable but I didn't know at that time that she lived in Dulwich, or was it Peckham? No sooner had she got to the office then she would have to turn around and walk back.

The office was, as I said, in Shaftesbury Avenue right on the corner of Neal Street and Monmouth Street. It was a splendid place to have an office because it was in a very lively part of London and also the back entrance to the building was a small ginnel* which led directly to the 'branch office', The Oporto. A great deal of my business activity took place in The Oporto and now we had almost direct access. This meant that very often the packing staff were to be found in the branch office rather than the warehouse and vice versa because there wasn't that much volume of publishing going on until we got ourselves sorted out. This we did by having to remove, sadly, a number of ageing retainers from their strangely Dickensian surroundings. In one office we found a clockwork typewriter. In other places were pieces of antique furniture which were far too valuable to have in a London office and these were duly returned to the Service family who still played a small role in the publishing but they had, as a family, lost interest in the business itself. The advantage of an established publishing firm with some staff and distribution was too much for us to miss. There was, with some element of luck, a publishing house full of opportunity with all the facilities in place. But we were to blow this opportunity by a series of mistakes which were almost inevitable. We very nearly broke down early on during the first postal strike when that awful man Mr Jackson, with the twirly moustache, led the Post Office into a totally useless strike. When it was over (I think it lasted six weeks) the volume of orders that had come in from around the country, some by hand and others by courier, caused our extant chief packer to take one look at the pile of work and have a heart attack. This didn't help matters very much. However, we had enough momentum going to enable us to play a practical joke on ourselves which we did with interesting results.

When the Famous Regiments were beginning to take off we, with Toby Buchan's help, decided to publish a spoof of a regimental history** because we were getting so many ill-written submissions and indeed there were some that got published which were so awful we

* A *ginnel* is a passage between two buildings, sometimes referred to as a snicket. There is a famous threat in Lancashire: 'I wouldn't go up there, there's boggats up yon ginnel'.
** See endpapers.

decided that the only thing to do was to imitate one. We got hold of somebody called Andrew Graham who was an eccentric to say the least but also an authority on London clubs and regiments. He had a delightful sense of humour. He had been in the Welsh Guards and fought in the war and was on the verge of Alzheimer's Disease, but it didn't show. We got talking and I suggested to him a spoof regimental history embodying all the clichés that one had been led to expect would be introduced. It didn't take him long to get going and in the meantime I approached Osbert Lancaster to see if he would be interested in doing some line drawings for the book. Then the joke really began to take over. Toby designed the bass drum score for the regimental march which was called *Bobadillo*. We had all the clichés that you'll find in every regimental history and the book was produced in mini format, much the same as a Famous Regiment title might look, although smaller. The book was an instant hit and was celebrated by a launch attended by General Horrocks in the Lebegue Wine Cellars under the Charing Cross railway station. This was all due to a master of wine and a *bon viveur* who was known to me called Pat Grubb. The crowning glory came though when we received a letter of complaint from the Ministry of Defence library who were furious because they had a standing order for the Regimental Histories and they did not take kindly to being supplied with a dozen copies of *The Queen's Malabars* by Andrew Graham because they could find 'no trace of this regiment in the Army list'. And so it sailed into history and is now a very rare book indeed containing many very funny spoofs and it was Toby Buchan who had a large part to play in that.

Colonel Green was an author I acquired almost by mistake. He was an unusual man. He had fought on the first day of the battle of the Somme with the King's Liverpool Regiment and he was also a director of the Army & Navy Stores. He was a military history buff in the days when they were considered to be somewhat eccentric like war-gamers. He was early into the battlefield tour market, had published one book and was planning another rejoicing in the title of *Famous Engagements*. Having always been interested in battlefield tours myself, I saw that this might present a foot in the door and offered to take over *Famous Engagements* in their mid-existence. The Colonel Green School of History was undoubtedly a trail-blazer but in true amateur fashion it very often promised more than it delivered. A typical entry would consist of 1,500 words of Colonel Green's version of a battle accompanied by a photograph of Mrs Colonel Green standing to attention beside a Ford Cortina bang in the middle of Marston Moor or wherever. Thus the battlefields of the United Kingdom were catalogued with the same Mrs Green and the same Cortina in every photograph. I got to know Colonel Green very well. He was a very formal man so it was much to my surprise one day when he came to the office and said 'Look here Cooper, we've known each other for quite a long time now so I suggest we drop the formalities. I will call you Mr Cooper and you may call me Colonel.' And so it was.

I have already said that unsolicited manuscripts were beginning to come through the post. Receiving submissions of this kind meant that at least our name had registered and we were creating quite a slush pile, the expression publishers use for unwanted or unsolicited manuscripts. Mind you not everything was unwanted. One of the finest books I ever published came straight from the slush pile. It was a First World War diary called *Some Desperate Glory* by Edmond Campion Vaughan. I persuaded John Terraine to write an introduction to it and it remains one of the great classics from that conflict. To give you some idea of what the slush pile was like in one of the bigger firms, I was told by a friend of mine who worked for Collins (in the Billy Collins days) that during the course of one year they had received over 15,000 unsolicited manuscripts. Of those only five made it to publication and one of them was an author called Susan Howatch who later went on to become a distinguished novelist. There was one other book which came in on spec but I think I was largely responsible for running it to earth. I had read a piece in *The Spectator* which was an extract from a padre's diary and was an account of his spending the night with a private soldier who was to be shot the following day. It was one of the most moving pieces I have ever read and I followed it up and found that it was an extract from the diaries kept by the mother of six sons – two army padres and four lay brothers. She didn't spare us anything. The diaries themselves were probably five times longer than the book we got out of them, but I still think that it is a necessary book to have when reading about the First World War, not least in its account of the execution of soldiers for cowardice. Bishop Bickersteth, who I was dealing with, had previously been Bishop of Bath and Wells and was a stickler for accuracy, a hard worker and a delightful man. I felt rather strange bossing a bishop about but he took it very kindly. I am glad to say that the book was a great success, went into three editions and is an example of being able to create books out of nothing or rather manipulate a well organised product from very voluminous material. Not something a lot of publishers are prepared to do any longer. The book was called *The Bickersteth Diaries*.

# CHAPTER VI

# *Escapes and Evasions*

*Do not neglect to show hospitality to strangers,*
*for, by doing that some have entertained angels*
*without knowing it.*

I make no excuse at all for devoting a disproportionate chunk of this book to escapes and evasions. The experiences of those breaking out of prisoner of war camps or surviving being shot down or sunk at sea, or indeed imprisoned and escaping are among the most dramatic of all the stories that warfare produces.

Ever since my prep school days I have been fascinated by escape and evasion stories. We used to play games on sports days where several boys would be sent out with pieces of wool tied around their arms and other boys would have to locate them in the grounds of Ingleborough Hall, break the wool and then return with the prisoner. He whose arm band was not broken was declared the winner. After the war ended various accounts of such escape and evasion performances began to appear and were published, many of them too soon, some post-humous and others of little value. They were usually badly written. This meant that they didn't get the audience they deserved. People were fed up with warfare and the old brigade reminiscing, and, although Evans Brothers, William Kimber, Harraps and one or two other imprints took up the challenge, they missed out on the enormous volume of new escape and evasion stories that resurfaced in the mid-70s and 80s, aided and abetted in many cases by television series and various anniversaries. Also, of course, veterans were beginning to drop off their perches. Manuscripts emerged from bottom drawers. As I said, it had always been one of my pet fascinations.

There were two aspects to this fascination. First of all there were the stories of those who had been captured and taken into prisoner of war camps and then attempted to escape, in not many cases succeeding.

There were also the SAS/SOE, behind the enemy lines, spy-type experience which was an equally fascinating topic. Some of the greatest adventure stories I ever read come into this category. One or two titles had already appeared, *The Wooden Horse, Maquis, Ill Met by Moonlight, The White Rabbit,* and so on. My fascination led me to go looking for new material. It was a rich field because by the 60s and 70s many of the SOE agents who'd survived to escape and who at least remembered what a strange war they'd had felt able to start talking about their experiences. Programmes began to appear with regularity on television and eventually so did many memoirs in book form. There were some simply amazing stories.

Although some prisoners of war managed to escape and make 'The Home Run', as it was called, there were thousands who tried and failed. Those who succeeded were party to such astonishing adventures that one began very often to doubt their veracity although they almost all turned out to be true. Probably the greatest of these stories was one which we turned into a book called *The Long Way Round*. It tells the story of a subaltern in the Seaforth Highlanders, one Richard Broad, who, in 1940, found himself separated from his battalion and rapidly running out of ammunition in the middle of a cornfield as the German guns and armour fought through to Dunkirk and later on to St Valéry. Richard, looking round the cornfield where his few remaining men were gathered, ascertained that there were six soldiers all from 13 Platoon apart from himself. Five of them were Seaforth Highlander Infantrymen, but one of them, Private Dodd, was a driver and had tagged along for the ride but with no vehicle. There they sat in the middle of a cornfield being shot over from all angles. Broad, who was 6ft 3in, older than most of his platoon by virtue of the fact that he'd come to the Army late, and a Scotsman to boot, realised that he had to grab the bull by the horns. So he gathered his men together and said, 'Those who want can give themselves up to the enemy but I'm going in the opposite direction. All those who want to go with me raise their hands'. There was a unanimous response in favour of evasion and they set off on an epic journey on foot which ended in them being known throughout the Army as Snow White and the Seven Dwarfs.

Richard Broad managed to lead his men, still wearing British Army uniform and, for the early part of the journey, armed, down the middle of France (via Paris), eventually arriving in Marseille. He was put in a civilian prison by the militia from which he was able to negotiate enough assistance to enable him and his men to cross the Pyrenees and eventually ended up reporting his unit to Headquarters in Scotland eighteen months later with the immortal words: 'Second Battalion

Seaforth Highlanders at your service, sir.' Richard Broad was later to make a name for himself in the fatuous SOE operation in Madagascar, but his leadership of the small group of Seaforth Highlanders was an epic of its kind and he ended the war with a Légion d'Honneur, the MC, the DSO and two Croix de Guerre.

I mentioned one man who was a driver, not an Infantryman. Private Dodd, or Doddy to his friends, is the only man now left alive who took part in this adventure. He was in fact a hairdresser in Chester and ran his own salon after the war. He is a very active Seaforth. He still attends their annual dinners. He is a most remarkable man. His recollection of the journey varies from time to time (he is into gallons of Bells whisky as the illustration in this book will show) and is a little hazy, but he surely has to be one of the great unsung war heroes and he is also an enchanting man to have around. All efforts to track down his fellow escapees failed and Richard Broad, alas, died only the other day. A remarkable man. At one post-war stage, which I found rather ironic, he was the lawyer in charge of the Enid Blyton estate, which, I read recently, was very much a battlefield of its own in terms of who owned the copyrights. I know that he resigned in despair saying that the fighting in boardrooms and accountants' offices was twice as difficult as it was negotiating the journey on foot in battledress down the backbone of rural France.

Another escape story always fascinated me. In this case the escapee was one Joseph Orna. He was of Italian extraction and had been in times past an altar boy in a Soho church and worked in the week as a waiter. He was a private in an ordinary regiment and was captured in the desert with his platoon. Like so many of those captured in the North African campaign in 1943, he was dispatched to Italy where the Germans had built a string of prisoner of war camps. It was from one of these camps that Joe Orna decided to escape. He cunningly worked on one of the friars from the local monastery, persuading the friar who was on a pastoral visit to the camp to lend him (Orna) his monk's habit. Over a period of months he managed to tailor his hair into a rough form of tonsure and came the day that he swapped clothes with the friar, he found himself, having been nodded through the camp gates, alone in the middle of Italy dressed as planned. What had not occurred to him was the fact that, as he was obviously a man of the cloth, every time he walked through a village or town it was necessary to play the game and pretend to be a priest. To be fair he'd had experience as an altar boy, but that was about as far as it went.

He travelled several hundred miles on foot over a period of months and eventually came to a village where the resident priest was very ill.

Seizing on this new recruit, he turned to Joe and said (in Italian of course), 'Will you please take mass for me this morning? I'm not up to it', or words to that effect. Joe, who had had various adventures on the way down, some of them far-fetched and most of them involving women or explosives, was forced into a corner and said that he would help as long as the priest himself also attended the mass. The service duly took place and at a critical moment when the host was being exposed, or whatever happens, the priest, who was by now slightly recovered, whispered out of the side of his mouth to Joe that he knew exactly who he was, that he needn't worry and that he would help him on his way. Joe did eventually make his way back to the United Kingdom and, although much of his story is not remembered by him, it nevertheless constitutes one of the great escapes and his account of it in the book called *The Escaping Habit* is another one of those which I treasure having had the opportunity to publish.

Equally imaginative as escapes go was the adventure of a trio of British officers who, like Joseph Orna, had been captured in the desert and shipped back to Italy. There was a brief period after the Italians had surrendered when the Germans took over the prisoner of war camps, but only after a short delay. By this time a great many prisoners had gone on the run and the Germans spent an enormous amount of time, money and frustration recapturing them. Among this floating population of escapees was a trio consisting of Tony Davies (a trainee doctor), Michael Gilbert (later to become one of the best crime writers in England) and Toby Graham. With them later on was Eric Newby who, among other things, wrote that famous book *Love and War in the Apennines*. These four teamed up with Italian resistance groups. Newby, who had a broken ankle, ended up in hospital and Graham went his own way, but Tony Davies and Michael Gilbert continued walking. Tony managed 800 miles on foot all the way down from northern Italy heading for the British lines which were moving up from Sicily and Salerno. At about 150 yards from the British positions he was spotted by a German sentry, shot in the foot and recaptured. Tony remained a prisoner for the rest of the war, but his escape was a magnificent example of fortitude and imagination. Newby's book is, of course, one of the great epics of World War Two and is only first past the post by a few inches from Tony Davies' brilliant account of his adventure called *When the Moon Rises*\*.

I am reminded of another title which I never actually published. It

---

\* This is what the Italian peasants used to say to the escapees before they set out from their hideouts at dusk: 'When the moon rises you must go.'

was by a South African who was on the run like others I have described and who wrote a marvellously fine synopsis, but never the book, of his escape which would have been called *The Fugitive Days*. I met this South African at a game camp in Tsavo, Kenya on one of my later visits. It was to lead to an astonishing encounter with one of the legends of World War Two. We were sitting round the camp fire at night after dinner, talking generally, and there was a very distinguished but quiet woman among us. I noticed one thing about her. She was wearing bedroom slippers which seemed incongruous out in the Kenya bush. Eventually she retired to bed, as did the other people around the fire, and I was left with this game warden. He said to me, 'Do you know who that was?' I said, 'No' and he said, 'Well that is Diana Churchill, the famous SOE agent who was captured by the Gestapo. Did you notice,' he added, 'that she was wearing bedroom slippers? Remember, they pulled all her toenails out.'

All in all I published something like twenty escape stories. They almost all had their own particular flavour, i.e. no two escapes were ever quite the same and I never cease to marvel at the fortitude and inventiveness of those who had been incarcerated in prisoner of war camps and tried to break out. This also led me to study the stories of those aircraft crew who were shot down and survived uninjured. The attempts by air crew to escape were doubly worthwhile, partly because a bomber pilot, or indeed an aircrew member, was of slightly more value to the country than, for the sake of argument, an ordinary rifleman. These air crew escapes were miraculous and full of adventure.

To mention some more exciting escapes, few men had such an extraordinary series of adventures as John Goldsmith, who was caught up at the beginning of the war in Paris, where he worked among the horse racing fraternity. He was as highly decorated, if not more so, as anybody else who became, as he did, accidentally an agent for SOE. He ended the war with a Légion d'Honneur, three Croix de Guerre, the DSO and the MC. You can't do much better than that. According to M R D Foot, it was John's book *Accidental Agent* that opened the floodgates of SOE memoirs. He was first of all sent to SOE, having returned to England for briefing and among his adventures was rescuing a French General, Chambe, walking him over the Pyrenees in a lounge suit posing as a black marketeer, and later parachuting into enemy territory and being arrested by the Gestapo for the second time. He had actually escaped earlier from the Gestapo and his adventure was relived for me when I took him and a journalist from the *Evening Standard*, Paul Callan, back to Paris to celebrate the publication of

John's memoirs. There was a very unusual incident that took place in our visit and, though it is a story against me, I can't resist repeating it here.

John took us to the Inter-Continental Hotel where he had been incarcerated after being captured. The hotel had been co-opted by the Gestapo as one of their headquarters and John was locked in a room on the fourth floor while they decided what to do with him. He, Paul Callan and I went to the hotel and asked the manager if we could go and find the room in which John had been locked. This we did. It was a small room now used as a laundry on one of the corridors and it had been divided by a false partition. John showed us how he climbed out of the window and took his shoes off (his laces had been taken away) and with one hand edged his way along the window sill until he came to the next room where he hastily ducked down because there was a German busy on the telephone. The next window but one he found, fortunately, opened. He pushed up the sash and, clutching his shoes, carefully got into the room and very quickly walked out into the corridor hiding his shoes under his coat. He had four floors of stairway to negotiate in stockinged feet. Believing that bravado was the only thing that would get him through, he eventually reached the foyer and tiptoed straight through, down the steps and into the street where he hid behind a newspaper hoarding, replaced his shoes and belted it.

After we had seen where all this happened we went and had lunch. It was the day of the arrival of the new Beaujolais and since Paul and I had had several drinks on the aeroplane we somewhat unwisely set about celebrating the arrival of the Beaujolais Nouveau. Lunch having finished, we went back to Paul's hotel, where he had booked in for the night, and I went and sat in the room while he had a shower. I rang for room service and rashly ordered a bottle of champagne. We were to have a party later that evening to celebrate the publication of the book and I was determined to be in a reasonable condition so I sat quietly in the chair while I could hear Paul singing away in the shower. Suddenly there was a short cry and a thud at the same time as there was a knock on the door. A waiter entered carrying a bottle of champagne and two glasses and I saw to my horror that Paul was lying on the floor with blood pouring from a cut on his head and the shower was all over the place. I went over to see if he was all right and noticed that the room service man had looked aghast at this scenario – a bleeding journalist and a somewhat cheerful but damp Englishman. He disappeared from the room before I could even tip him. What had happened was that Paul had trodden on a bar of soap, slipped and temporarily knocked himself out. With the skilful training of a boy scout, which was my only experience of difficult situations, I decided there was trouble brewing and I let myself out of the room and headed towards the lift which was at the end of the corridor. I was just in time to slip into the lift when I heard the next one open and voluble conversation in French emerging from a group who were heading in the direction of Paul's room. With a huge sigh of relief I managed to get out into the street and made myself very scarce until the party at about 6 o'clock, but we had made a significant mistake. We had forgotten to tell Sam White, the famous journalist for the *Evening Standard* whose patch was Paris, that we were in town, particularly as Paul Callan was writing for the same paper. We learnt subsequently that Sam, furious at our not reporting to him, had killed any story there was likely to be. The highlight of the evening was that in the middle of it all in walked the mysterious French General Chambe whom John had accompanied over the Pyrenees in what was one of the most famous escapes by a senior French officer. Nobody had known that he was coming and his arrival caused a sensation. There is a photograph of various people in the book, most of them former members of the Resistance, who attended the party.

The book *Accidental Agent* became a great success and John was lionised. He was one of the first SOE people to come out into the open after the war when, unfortunately, he had a sad career. He got the job of looking after the racing fraternity in Hong Kong and died of a heart attack when he'd only just taken it up. I'll never forget the episode in the bedroom and nor will I forget the feeling I had when I opened the window of the room from which he'd escaped in the hotel and saw the narrow ledge along which he had climbed. At the time the book was published I managed to get in to the press the fact that 'John Goldsmith's book made James Bond seem like Noddy'. This could equally apply to Richard Broad's book!

There were not that many escapes from the Far East. It was too far for anybody to make it home, but one man did manage it. His name was William Doyle and he was in the Royal Marines with whom he was serving in Burma. James Leasor wrote up his story under the title *The Marine from Mandalay*. Doyle interpreted his commanding officer's instructions literally. These were quite simply 'Doyle, make your way back to headquarters under your own steam'. Doyle, considering this to be an order, then set out on an incredible journey which took him something like eighteen months, until the day when he eventually managed to turn up at Royal Marine Headquarters in Plymouth. He reported to the Guard Room and then to the local Commanding Officer, saying, 'Marine Doyle at your service, sir' and was promptly clapped in irons as a suspected deserter. It took a lot of negotiating to persuade the HQ of Royal Marines that he had actually walked, to all intents and purposes, all the way back from Mandalay.

One of the more bizarre escape episodes from Singapore involved somebody called Lord Langford*. Not Lord Longford but Lord Langford. He and a number of others had stayed on until the last minute at Singapore and, having got together almost unofficially, they commandeered a boat rejoicing in the name of *Sederhana Johannis*. There were some soldiers and some naval officers on board – about eighteen people. Theirs was probably one of the last boats to escape the Japanese. How they got the boat going dazzles the mind. The other most unusual aspect of this escape was that they had a camera with them and they were able to record all the events of their voyage which eventually ended with them being picked up by a steamer off the coast of Ceylon, having travelled 1,600 miles. There are some very moving photographs taken on the voyage but none quite so moving as when, having boarded the steamer, the captain ordered his ship to turn its guns on the gallant little boat, *Sederhana Johannis,* and we see pictures of the boat slowly sinking, having delivered to safety people vital for the war effort.

I also published a book called *Singapore, Too Little Too Late* by Brigadier Ivan Simpson RE. He was sent out to examine the defences of Singapore and reported in to his local Commander that the defensive positions and the way they were manned and constructed was a total shambles. His words fell on deaf ears, but his contribution to military history was borne out as being more valuable than many of the subsequent accounts, because, being an engineer, he understood what he was meant to be looking for but couldn't find. I heard about the book from Sir Basil Liddell Hart, who tipped me off about its existence and told me that I'd get a very good book out of it. I did indeed and the sad thing was that on the day I had a thank-you letter from Sir Basil, who had been staying with Field Marshal Montgomery at a hotel in Bournemouth, I found out that he had posted his letter to me from there and that was the last letter he ever wrote. I treasure it to this day.

There can be very few escapes recorded of those who managed to get away from the railway of death. One man was Corporal Roy Pagani and his extraordinary account of escape from the Burma/Siam Railway, where thousands of allied prisoners of war died, makes remarkable reading. Disguised as an Indian, barefooted Pagani walked 200 miles to the Karen Hills where he joined a guerrilla band

---

* Geoffrey Rowley-Conwy describes the adventure in *Escape from the Rising Sun*.

led by the legendary Major Seagrim GC. Setting out again for India he had to avoid repeated attempts by the Burmese to capture him. Safety seemed close but he almost drowned in the Irrawaddy river, then the Burmese captured him and handed him over almost dead to the Japanese but he lived to tell the tale. The book, *The Flame of Freedom*, was by Robert Hamond who himself had been incarcerated by the Japanese.

One of the most extraordinary books to come my way during the mid-1970s was *The Frolik Defection* by one Joseph Frolik, a Czechoslovakian security man who defected to the West. The book arrived in a roundabout way and I am almost certain it was planted on me by M15 or M16 or one of the spook organisations who were looking for trouble which they could control. They wanted to have it published and I suspect that my contact knew that I might be prepared to take a risk and so the manuscript eventually found me via my contact, whom I can't name. It was an extraordinary story and it happened round about the time that a cabinet minister, John Stonehouse, a member of the Wilson cabinet, did a vanishing trick. At one stage the Czechs had been on to Stonehouse because he had apparently been one of the few people ever to sit in the cockpit of the TSR2, an incipient fighter aircraft of which only two marques were manufactured. Frolik himself had a main job which was to infiltrate the trade unions in the country and the account of how the security people in England handled a defector was frankly bizarre.

I got to know Joe quite well, even to the extent of flying to meet him in Washington together with Richard Stott who was on the *Sunday People* at the time and had been given an exclusive on the Frolik story. Unfortunately, as we were high over the Atlantic another story emerged back home which took the spotlight; unfortunately I can't remember what it was, so we never made the headlines. Charles Whiting came with me on this trip as a contact man and we met Frolik near our hotel in Washington in a thoroughly furtive sort of atmosphere. Later Joe was released to come to England and made contact with us. There again ensued a series of clandestine meetings in pubs and clubs in and around London. Gradually we got the book out of him which Charles Whiting wrote for us and its publication created quite a lot of fuss. Joe himself would communicate with us through a strange third party in the States who rejoiced in the name of Olga Malina. I am sure that this wasn't a real person but for a while correspondence ensued between us and that was the addressee that Frolik gave us.

He had the look of a hunted man and in those days before the East/ West détente he was a man with a price on his head. There was one curious occasion when I introduced him to a friend of mine, none other than the bomber pilot John Watson who bought him a drink in the Ivanhoe Hotel. Later that evening John came down to see me at my branch office and we were having a chat when in through the far door came Frolik himself and was immediately greeted by Watson with 'Hello Joe, how are you?' Frolik didn't immediately recognise John and he went a deathly shade of green, amber and then red. He thought he'd been rumbled. We put his mind at rest and duly published the book, but I can't say that it was as good as it should have been as we had to leave out a lot of names. The only real information that I ever got out of it was the fact that he needed at least three pairs of shoes a year because of the amount of following he was required to do when targeting people who left the MOD offices and went for a drink in the evenings after work. He would have to do this on foot. The idea was to try and catch somebody *in flagrante delicto* and then blackmail them so he would hang around outside the Ministry of Defence watching the staff leave and follow them just in case they were up to something. This was a way of trapping informers*. As far as I can tell it didn't work and Joe eventually disappeared out of our lives but not before begging us to send him more money. I heard on the old boy net the other day that he is no longer with us but it was a very strange episode and one which brought me into touch with our own security services with whom I was not deeply impressed.

It wasn't long after this episode that the cultural attaché of the Russian Embassy started taking an interest in me and was making what I considered to be rather too many visits to the office. This culminated in an invitation to me and Jilly to go and have drinks at the Embassy. I spoke to this man, whose name I can't remember but it was something like Ivanoff, and said, 'You do realise don't you that my wife is a journalist and I wouldn't like you to find that you've invited the wrong sort of person to the party.' 'I know,' he replied. Anyway we did go and there was an extraordinary gathering of people, only two of whom I recognised – one was the late Maurice Macmillan and the other Sir John Fletcher-Cook. After we'd had a few drinks, I remember it was pouring with rain and I was soaked to the skin. We made an excuse and left but there were two further telephone calls in the next week from this same man and finally I rang

---

* He was also charged with infiltrating the Trade Unions which he did with some success.

up one of my authors who I knew was a retired spook and told him what was happening. He said that I was to keep my mouth shut and he would see what he could do. About a week later a man in a gabardine mackintosh appeared in the office, asked for me and introduced himself by some name that I can't remember, but I am absolutely certain that he was the same man who was later convicted of espionage on behalf of the Russians and he was posing as an M15 agent*.

We notched up one unusual author at about this time on the more historical side. He was Major Ismat Hasan Zulfo and had been a Sudanese army officer; he had written the *fuzzy wuzzy's* version of the Battle of Kerari, as they called it. We, of course, call it Omdurman and it was the battle in which Winston Churchill took part with the 21st Lancers. Major Zulfo was distantly related to the Mahdi (aren't they all?) and the political situation in the Sudan was such that he was not entirely in the best of odour with the current government of that country, hence he moved with some caution, rather like Joe Frolik, round the West End of London. He lived in a degree of luxury in a rented flat or sometimes in a hotel in Oxford Street. He was, I suspect, not up to much good, but he was a delightful man and having his book *Kerari* translated into English had given him a fillip or at least some kudos. It also must be very rare that somebody from the colonial past and ethnic background had written about opposing colonialism. He must be one of the few post-colonial victims who have had the opportunity and the courage to strike back with the pen and not the sword. I don't know where he has gone now. I often wondered whether some of these people we came into contact with were real. I think he was, but he had a large number of rather dubious friends who kept on ringing me up and asking me to supply them with books which after a bit I refused to do because they never paid for them. Anyway I am very proud to have published him. A one off, I think.

Another extraordinary person I got hold off was a woman called Helga Pohl Wannamaker (you can go a long way with a name like that). She came to me one day at the Frankfurt Book Fair. A right-looking number with dyed blonde hair, expensive jewellery, coloured fingernails and make up you could have mistaken for a bacon and egg breakfast. She had a story, which we took with tongue in cheek called *Red Spy at Night*. She claimed to have been Beria's mistress and she

---

* Shortly after all this happened Sir Alec Douglas Home, the then Prime Minister, sacked seventeen agents from the Russian Embassy – my man was one of them.

spoke English not only faultlessly but thoughtfully, and I began to believe her. Every Frankfurt Book Fair she would appear with her son who had one wall eye which I found rather disconcerting. The book didn't do particularly well but I couldn't fail to be fascinated by her attitude. She seemed to be fairly open-minded about whom she went around with, but wouldn't answer any questions about Beria. I don't suppose there was much to him anyway because he didn't last long after Stalin died. There is a picture of Helga in this book which tells you more than I can do in words.

By the mid-70s we had hit the ground running and things were beginning to look quite healthy although we were still short of money. What gave us a tremendous boost was winning the W H Smith Award with Ronald Lewin's book *Slim, the Standard Bearer*. Not only did this achieve the WHS Award but it was widely reviewed and praised. For a small publisher like ourselves it was a tremendous morale booster. Ronald Lewin was the most delightful author to work with. He had been an editor at Hutchinsons and had written one book for me previously, but this was probably the most exciting project we had during the whole of our time as publishers. The fact that Ronald had been a publisher was a tremendous help; working with professionals, one always needed to be well briefed and here was an author who knew exactly what he wanted, how he wanted it and more often than not when he wanted it. He was generous to us and, when we ran into trouble later on, when we were considering doing his biography of Wavell which was eventually published by Hutchinson, we had to withdraw because we didn't have the finances to do it. When the book came out the first and earliest copy off the machine was posted to me with a marvellous inscription by Ronald because he knew how miserable I was at the time.

Another author who was less generous but equally professional was the late John Terraine. A long time before I'd commissioned a book from him called *The Road to Passchendaele* and this took nine years to sell out, but I had had my eye on the general Terraine oeuvre and I decided the only thing to do was to offer to reprint some of his great classics which had gone out of print, including *Haig: The Educated Soldier*. At the same time I commissioned him to do a book rejoicing in the title *Business in Great Waters* which was an account of the submarine war in the Atlantic in both wars. The trouble with John was that I don't think he ever thought he was appreciated enough. He wrote like an angel and I was very much on his side when it came to the loyalty one was required to show to Field Marshal Haig. We republished about seven of his backlist titles. There was one problem and that was that they were all with different publishers which might indicate that he was a difficult author. They were, as well, all in different sizes so it was very difficult for me to try and produce standard editions of his works and we failed to so. John was getting progressively more ill when we parted company. He died in December 2003. He was another author that I am enormously proud to have looked after, despite the difficulties.

While this was going on Tom was beavering away on Anglesey and by 1979 we had got up to Volume III. I am not saying that it took Tom's eye off the ball but the meticulous editing that was needed meant that his skills were not being employed in other areas which made life rather difficult. Anyway, he had that task to keep him fully occupied and he did it impeccably. Anglesey won the Templer Medal and the Chesney Medal and few publishers could have had a more willing or helpful author. On several occasions I was invited to stay at Plas Newydd in Anglesey and to this day I am haunted by the house in which he lived which is now owned by the National Trust and contains the famous Whistler murals. I used to lie in bed at night telling myself that there were rewards in publishing in the end. I would hear the wind howling round the house and up the estuary and the ropes of the flagpole which stood opposite my bedroom window would make a slapping sound all night but I found it comforting. What I didn't find quite so comforting was one day when I was taking an early bath before breakfast and there was a knock on the door and Henry was shouting at me, 'Leo, come out quickly. It's something rather urgent'. I didn't respond immediately and I learnt later that he'd thought I'd passed out in the bath, but what had happened was that I hadn't heard him knock, I just heard a voice. Anyway he extracted me from the bath wrapped in a dressing gown and shoved under my nose the proofs of the title page of Volume III. To my horror there were two major misprints on the first page of the display type and I had some fast talking to do. Unfortunately we had already gone to press but it was a worrying moment, handled, needless to say, impeccably by Henry. We had to do a tip-in* (a technical term!).

Now, from the sublime to the ridiculous, let me tell you the tale of Tommy our local dustman. After talking of escapes and evasions we must be allowed a little light relief. Tommy was very useful to us because he was able to remove unwanted packaging and bits and

---

* This means a manually inserted, printed page replacement.

pieces from the warehouse for a consideration; the dustmen in Camden Borough were very much a law unto themselves in those days and Tommy was no exception. He knew everybody's dustbins like one knows people in the street in a village. He frequently brought me items that he'd recovered, such as old medals thrown away and books and all sort of interesting bits and pieces. He had, and indeed so did some of his fellow dustmen, triumphs of his own, but they all united in one particular scam which was the meat market at Smithfield where you could pick up nice joints of meat if you knew who to ask and it would be brought to you by the dustman on his return trip. It usually came in under the driver's seat of the truck. Many is the good steak I've had from there.

Tommy's great hobby was ballroom dancing. When he'd finished his rounds on several days in the week he would whiz back quickly to his flat, get into a smart suit, grease his hair down with a quiff and could be seen after lunch heading towards the Lyceum Ballroom, dapper as ever, to take part in the *Thé Dansant*. Apparently when asked by his partners where he worked he was completely honest in replying that he worked for the Council.

Tommy is no longer with the dustmen, otherwise I wouldn't be able to write about him like this, but he is responsible for one incident which caused a great deal of mirth. Returning on 24 December one year from a scavenging trip, he had had one too many and was unloading his goods off the truck into a cardboard box prior to taking them round to his customers, but the result of his foraging had involved him imbibing several large potions in various places. Unfortunately he went to sleep in the truck. When he woke up – remember it was Christmas Eve – everybody in the depot had gone off for Christmas. There was only a reception shed which didn't have a telephone and there was no water. First of all he wondered what to do but was too frightened to raise the alarm in case they thought he'd broken in and was trying to steal things. He spent all Christmas Day fast asleep and it is odd that nobody noticed that he'd vanished. On the following day, Boxing Day, he could take it no more, so he went to the wire gates which secured the depot and peered through them and started shouting. Everybody thought he was one of the loonies from Lousy Island* and took absolutely no notice until one chap who had an office nearby which was well serviced by Tommy realised that he was trying to convey some message. The problem was that once it was

* The triangle at the top of Shaftesbury Avenue where the lepers used to sit and where there was a plague pit.

explained what had happened nobody knew who had the key so the day after Boxing Day Tommy existed on further libations poured into a glass through a straw from the other side of the metal gate and eventually a locksmith was secured to undo the lock and his bosses never discovered that he'd spent three days over Christmas in an empty compound. He's never been allowed to forget it. I last heard of him working at the Savoy or near it. He was a splendid man and he joined the Army in the same intake as I did. My number was 22867795 and his was 22867794. Of such things are friendships made.

To get away from escapes and evasions, general military matters and dustmen, I decided to slip a few naval titles into our repertoire. I commissioned several naval books because I felt that the subject would be some help when branching out a bit. I picked up an author called Edwyn Gray who came to us via Curtis Brown, literary agents. Edwyn was in fact an income tax inspector who was then living in High Wycombe. His other activity was glamour photography for his own consumption. He was, however, an expert on submarine warfare and he came to me with several submarine subjects, all of which appeared to be thoroughly well researched and were in the course of time to become successful publishing ventures. Many of the titles reprinted. I remember congratulating Edwyn one day on his research and I said to him I was particularly interested in his remarks about the wartime paint used by the German submarines on their conning tower. 'How clever of you to have found out the actual code number of the paint,' I said. He looked at me quizzically then said in his high whining voice, 'Oh I just made that up'. This made me less confident of his ability as a genuine naval historian, but, like Charles Whiting, he produced books at speed and here again he had lessons to teach people about readability. You could not put an Edwyn Gray book down and he was one of the most loyal authors and, as far as I know, is still going strong.

With Seeley Service's *British Battleships* and *British Destroyers* on the publication schedule waiting to reprint, I began to pay more attention to naval and indeed in some cases aviation subjects. Another naval author we picked up (I can't remember where) proved to be quite a catch. His name was Captain H P K Oram and he was chiefly famous for being one of the three people to escape from the submarine *Thetis* which sank in the Mersey with almost total loss of life in the 1920s. Oram was on board as an observer rather than a member of the crew and he was of a more senior rank than anybody else on the boat. He volunteered to use the escape hatch and he and two others were the only survivors because so primitive were submarine rescue departments in those days, that, although people could see the stern of the ill-fated submarine sticking out of the water, they were unable to reach it and rescue anybody before they had all suffocated. Poor Captain Oram was vilified for the rest of his life because there were those, not least in the press and relatives of those who died in the disaster, who felt that he should not have escaped himself but allowed an ordinary seaman to escape instead. Captain Oram's response to this was courageous and he said that he knew more of the inside of the submarine than anybody else and by getting out early he might have been able to give them enough information to effect a rescue. In fact this didn't happen and the end was disaster but he never lived it down.

His first book was called *Ready for Sea*. He had started his naval career on the tall ships and had sailed to Australia several times on clippers and his reminiscences made marvellous reading. Later in his life he was involved in yet another naval disaster when a group of K class subs ran into each other and sank. Although he was not to blame, there were those who tried to pin the blame on him. I met him towards the end of his life when he was virtually bedridden. The last time I saw him he gave me a vivid account of his service at the battle of Jutland, so he'd seen it all really, from the clippers to Jutland to submarines and three days after I visited him, when I think he was in his mid-90s, he died. I was very flattered to see that when I last called on him he was busy reading one of the books that I had published* although not, happily, by Edwyn Gray.

Among the most distinguished authors in the naval field was Admiral Sir Henry Leach. He was First Sea Lord at the time of the Falklands War. It was he who turned up in the lobby of the House of Commons in full uniform and caught the eye of Mrs Thatcher and who made people realise that the Falklands War was likely to turn very nasty. At that time the Navy was under threat from the possible selling off by Defence Secretary John Nott of half their ships. Admiral Leach and various other naval dignitaries saw this as an opportunity to prove that the Navy was still an effective force (which needed to be done anyway). They were about to have their ships confiscated, so to speak, when Mrs Thatcher, Prime Minister at that time, asked him to her office. The net result of this was that Sir Henry persuaded her that the Navy was capable of mounting a task force in a very short period of time and she, on the strength of his word, had the courage to go ahead

* His autobiography was called *The Rogue's Yarn*.

and tell him to get cracking. It is no place here to go into the history of that campaign but it certainly saved the Navy who took very severe losses but who proved that there was more to them than met the eye. The Royal Marines were also spared cuts.

Henry Leach was an enormously popular man in the Navy, albeit even more after than before the Falklands War. He approached us to see if we would be interested in publishing his autobiography. He had been recently widowed and had been moved by his family to a cottage outside the walls of the 'big house'. He asked me to lunch and I drove down to Hampshire and eventually found his cottage. We had a useful conversation and it was plain that there was a good book to be published. Fortunately it turned out to be twice the success one had hoped. It was very obvious that he had spent a lifetime being looked after rather than doing things himself but he very gallantly gave me a delicious lunch. There was pâté sent down from the 'big house' and we started off with that and then he said, 'I think we'll have some soup'. To my horror he then got out a pack of Cuppasoup which he emptied into an electric kettle and turned it on, having added some water. This novel way of making soup did not allow for the fact that when poured most of the onion, etc. clogged itself in the spout and with a lot of shaking and probing he eventually managed to get two decent mugs of soup out for our lunch. I was so embarrassed by this that when he went to have a pee I quickly went into the kitchen and unclogged the kettle for him and just as he emerged I said, 'I thought I'd just wash up for you, sir.' And he thanked me. It always struck me as rather a touching image, me being given a Cuppasoup by the First Sea Lord. Distinctly Gilbertian.

When we did publish the book I asked him if he had a list of friends and acquaintances to whom we could do a direct mail operation. I was totally unprepared for what happened. He gave me a list of over 800 names and these were all close friends, acquaintances and people he'd served with. To my delight, when we did a special mailing, we sold over 500 copies direct. This sale was another example of how direct mailing can be, and is, used for special projects like autobiographies. The book was entitled *Endure no Makeshifts* which I believe was a quotation from John Buchan although I have never been able to find it. I'd met a really remarkable man and I was very fortunate because he was, without being indiscreet, fairly revealing about some aspects of the Falklands War. I am very proud to have published that book.

While all this was going on I had been tipped off by the egregious John Watson that there was a flat going on the corner of Shaftesbury

Avenue and Monmouth Street. This was owned by the Karamani family who were the landlords for the whole building. I went to see them and so began a friendship between the Karamani family, my firm and indeed my family which exists to this day. They were a wonderful family business. When I knew them a long time ago their upstairs restaurant was a Wimpy bar concession and downstairs it was Greek Cypriot. Gradually things began to change and eventually the Wimpy Bar became The Kantara Taverna and operated out of the ground floor as well as the basement. The family, consisting of Mr and Mrs Karamani and their three sons, John, Panos and Dimitrios, worked seven days a week. They eventually tarted up the ground-floor restaurant and called it The Farmhouse Table, somewhat euphemistically. But this didn't stop a relationship working, as it does to this day. We provided them with a constant stream of customers. We ate or drank daily in one or other of the restaurants and if friendship can really be counted in that sort of business they certainly had a gift for it.

There are several funny stories about goings on in the restaurant, not least when Tom took a couple of Brigadiers out for a Christmas lunch without having been warned that it was the lunchtime belly dancing festival. No one who knew Brigadier Sutton of the Royal Army Service Corps could imagine that he'd be so delighted when this lady came on shaking her tummy all over his dolmades. From that day on we could do no wrong with him. The word got round and the following Christmas hordes of Brigadiers with their tongues hanging out were seen descending the steps into the restaurant. 'Where such depravity is found it only can live underground.'

On another occasion a binder called Ken Webb was doing some business with us upstairs and when we'd finished he said, 'I've got a friend I want to take out to lunch round here. Can you make any recommendations?' Without thinking Tom said, 'You could always try the Ledra Palace Hotel'. This was the nickname which we used for the restaurant because Tom had once had a holiday in Cyprus and had stayed at the Ledra. About a couple of days later Ken Webb came into the office again and said, 'I wonder if I could ask you a question. I can't find the Ledra Palace Hotel anywhere in the London telephone directory'. He hadn't realised that it was a nickname. We often did our entertaining down there and we had a farewell party there when I decided finally to leave London. It was very convenient, though, having the flat above which also doubled up as the office which had been at 196 Shaftesbury Avenue. We were living in Putney then and it was becoming an increasing slog from there to Shaftesbury Avenue on a 22 bus; when we moved out of London to Gloucestershire I was able to do three or four days a week in the London office without having to move which saved me an enormous amount of time and energy. It also meant that the children could use the flat in London at the weekend if they wanted.

I am well aware that I have spent a large amount of time writing about escapes and evasions, but I make no excuse because as I have pointed out the stories of these gallant people never cease to impress me. For everyone I have written about I could treble the number who are waiting in the wings. I did try to do a book called *The Home Run* but it was not a success.

The trouble with escapes is that there are very few records. The only record which claims any authenticity is that kept by the New Zealand government who I think recorded over 600 successful escapes during the course of the war. That sounds rather a lot to me but one's got to remember that particularly during the desert war large numbers of British prisoners were taken. Many of them were shipped over to Italy which then surrendered. A large majority of escapers set off from places in Italy. The Germans, however, were annoyed at the scale of this situation and wasted an enormous amount of their time trying to recapture all the escapees. There is no record of numbers but I imagine, from what I have read, that getting on for 6,000 people escaped and reached freedom of one sort or another. Some for instance holed up in Switzerland. Others managed to smuggle themselves on to boats in places like Norway, Sweden, Denmark and Finland. I have always wanted to get hold of some of the prisoner of war guards. The only one I know of and whose work I have read was the chap in charge of Colditz. But, without wishing to take anything away from those who were incarcerated in Colditz, that was the final straw and very few people actually got home from there. Ironically, one was Airey Neave, Mrs Thatcher's great supporter who was blown up by a car bomb in the House of Commons.

We didn't always eat and drink in the Ledra Palace. Tom and I were both members of the Garrick and many of our authors were members of the Rag*. Entertaining people at one's club was good public relations and, although Tom eventually gave up his membership, he often joined me at other clubs where our authors were members. There was a hilarious episode once at the Athenaeum where we were being lunched by Brigadier 'Honker' Henniker, a Royal Engineer of some

* The Rag is the nickname for the Army & Navy Club.

distinction. The Athenaeum was not renowned for its jollity or indeed its menu or, if it comes to that, its membership, but in recent times it has tried to become a little bit more modern. On this particular day Honker must have been feeling on terrific form because he suddenly picked up a spoon and started singing to an astonished dining room 'I am the very model of a modern Major General'. Tom and I both felt like beggar's dogs as we hung our heads in shame as the Brigadier sang on.

The worst experience I ever had though was at the Cavalry Club which I like and respect very much. I had arranged to meet one of my Famous Regiment authors there. Dicky Brett-Smith he was called and he had written for us a history of the 11th Hussars, his regiment (and Tom's), although it was far too long for the series. We had to cut it heavily which was a pity and it annoyed him. He asked me to lunch at the Cavalry Club. When I got there he was sitting somewhat unsteadily on a tall stool in the back bar. He was bright red in the face and swaying like a pine tree in the wind. As he saw me enter the bar he suddenly fell off his seat and crashed to the ground. Not realising quite how bad his condition was, I rushed to pick him up and restored him to his seat. About ten minutes later he fell off again so I thought the only thing to do was to make a quiet exit. In doing so I ran into the Secretary of the Club who was heading in the direction of the bar. I apologised although it wasn't my fault and indeed I hadn't even had a drink by then and I suggested to the Secretary that I make myself scarce because I was unlikely to get any lunch which proved to be true. Some two months later I was asked to lunch there by Brigadier Frankie Wilson, a well-known character who among other things was responsible for all the drawings in the Stephen Potter books. We managed a few drinks in the bar but I then realised that he was not entirely steady on his feet. Eventually we made it upstairs to the dining room which has one of the most beautiful views out onto Green Park and we sat down by the window, whereupon Frankie Wilson started shouting and gesticulating making a great deal of noise. To be honest he was drunk. Eventually the head waiter, seeing that Brigadier Wilson was not likely to tone down his behaviour, sent for the Secretary. He came into the dining room, took one look at me and said, 'Not you again'. Unfortunately I had to leave Frankie Wilson shouting the odds at his table because they refused to give him any lunch and once again I left the Cavalry Club hungry.

But for every eccentric there were at least ten nice, well-brought-up, funny, good mannered and clever people at hand. One of these was Lieutenant Colonel Val ffrench-Blake who'd commanded the 17th/21st Lancers at the battle of Kasserine. Val was a man of many parts, a fine commanding officer, a brilliant horseman and an expert on dressage. He wrote military history well, played the piano beautifully and was a flautist. He was one of the classic examples of an educated soldier. Among other things he restored paintings and one of his books, *Dressage for Beginners*, which we did publish and sold to Houghton Mifflin in Boston, USA, turned out to be a bestseller and is still in print after fifteen or twenty years. He started a series with me called *Concise Campaigns* in which he acted as the editorial adviser. We managed to publish about five or six titles, but, like so many series, it died just when it was getting interesting. This was not his fault, it was mine, but I think he has to go down in the record as quite the nicest and most professional author we ever had to deal with.

# CHAPTER VII

# *For What We are About to Receive*

> *England is a strong land and a sturdy, and the pleasantest corner of the world . . . England is full of mirth and game, free men of heart and with tongue, but the hand is better and more free than the tongue.*
>
> Bartholomew Anglicus

Once we had established ourselves in Shaftesbury Avenue, it was time to take stock. The ten years to come would be full of incident and the ups and the downs would just about equal each other. We were, however, now secure in a custom-built (albeit Victorian) set of offices together with a warehouse at a very good address in the centre of London. But it is also true to say that we had inherited the liabilities that came with this privilege which was, of course, welcomed by the Service family. Not only that but we had inherited a number of titles, stock of which was still languishing in the warehouse. Some of it should never have got in there in the first place but there were some titles which were likely, if handled properly, to generate a reasonable amount of turnover. For instance, *British Battleships* and *British Destroyers* alone were high-price gems and several of the Lonsdale Library titles were relevant in the current market place.

It was now the 1970s. Occasionally my chronology may be slightly out of order in this account of our life in Shaftesbury Avenue. It is arguable though that many examples of our publishing activity were somewhat unorthodox as far as others were concerned. We didn't really have enough capital and the next ten years were to prove that, despite everything in our favour, we were always to soldier on under pressure. The years following on from that were not easy. I've tried to pick out the more interesting practical details showing what it was like running a small publishing company (any publishing company) from the West End of London with little capital, a great deal of imagination, a few enemies, and above all ability to ride the troughs that Dame Fortune and Dame Britannia create when they are stirring up the waves, so to speak.

What we had to do quickly was to build our own backlist to set alongside the Seeley Service list and to take on more books. This of course was very dangerous because nothing sinks a publisher quicker than overproduction or financial over-commitment, i.e. authors' advances. You have to remember all the time that any fool can create a book by going to a printer with a manuscript, having it set, printed, bound, jacketed and plonked in the warehouse. It then requires a genius to sell it out of that warehouse quickly, and at the same time make sure the turnover created by these sales is converted into cash as soon as possible. Herein lies and lay the snag. Apart from giving booksellers generous discounts, and apart from selling direct, which I always did despite the Net Book Agreement, there is a horrible time gap between invoicing for goods supplied and being paid for those goods by the bookseller. In the meantime, somebody like a paper manufacturer, and some printers as well as the service industries, are clamouring at the door because they have provided their goods at the right time and yet there is a long delay before the actual book produces any revenue.

First of all is usually the paper supply because that's the earliest ingredient to be bought in. You ordered it from paper merchants in bulk and in those days had it shipped to the printer of your choice. The wise publishers got their printers to supply paper of a stock type which enabled them to pay later. Paper merchants' terms were strictly thirty days net because they were having to import the pulp or the paper itself and they were on an equally strict turnaround. This, apart from finance, was one of the biggest problems we had to face. Printers were on the whole more accommodating because it was in their interests to give long-term credit. Nobody could say that we didn't try to pay when we were pressed, but I'm afraid the plain truth is that you can't be a successful publisher unless you're properly capitalised (I know I keep repeating myself – I mean to). And even then, you can make an absolute balls-up of things that you should never have started in the first place. This niggling albatross never left my neck. As far as I know there are many flocks of albatrosses floating round Bloomsbury to this day looking for necks, although of course, the bigger publishing groups now purchase in bulk and are in a position to negotiate favourable deals. The small publisher has only his wits and indeed his unparalleled optimism (some call it ignorance) to enable him to keep his head above the water. A bestseller can kill a small publisher overnight*.

We brought with us, from Museum Street, one other freelance operator who was to prove a godsend in our early years. John Mitchell was a vastly experienced printer's broker and production expert. His father had been a master printer and he was steeped in the practical side of printing, paper, etc. Very early on I threw myself at his feet, partly to compensate for my lack of knowledge of production so easily described in the early parts of this book. John was the still, small voice of calm. We didn't always agree with his suggestions and he never was backward in coming forward when it came down to his opinion of what numbers we should print, and what paper we should buy, or anything like that. To say that he was a pessimist would be putting it mildly, but that's because he knew me and Tom and he was also a self-appointed ball and chain, quite rightly. He would query our desire to go ahead with a Book Club deal, for instance, where in fact we were receiving less than the unit cost of the book. I had to explain to him, although I didn't feel that I was entirely right, that this enabled us to afford to print slightly more copies and therefore the unit cost on the trade titles was more viable with the Book Club run included. Although this was true to a point, it didn't really do anything more than ensure that we broke even and that is really what it was all about. You can keep going, just about, if you break even. You can't keep going very long if you're publishing a book and selling it at less than the unit cost allows. Many is the lunchtime storming session that we had about how to spread our pathetic amount of jam over ever-increasing slices of toast.

Looking back, already I can see that we should never really have survived as long as we did. The seventies were a time for readjustment after the volatility of the sixties and the publishing world was beginning to re-form with large conglomerates lining up to devour the ailing imprints and taking over, in many cases, the production process. They had the clout. We worked really hard during those years and we had our rewards. We also had some disasters. It's ridiculous to try and pretend that they didn't happen. There were funny ones and there were sad ones and there were welcome ones, but one always had to keep one's eye on the ball. We worked on Saturday mornings and one

---

* He will have to find some hard cash to pay for the welcome reprint before the extra revenue arrives.

of our earliest tasks was to see if we could bring the warehouse back into an earning situation so we investigated the possibility of doing distribution for other publishers. We were well-placed in the West End and although our machinery was antediluvian, we were able to provide a good service and this helped to pay the rent.

All this was done in the face of ever-increasing postal costs and the overhead created by the building and warehouse maintenance meant that we were paying a high price for the right address. Also a recession was taking place. One of my jobs was to work out a way of increasing turnover without necessarily increasing expenditure in the shape of advances. The advances to authors are notorious for being the Exocets that eventually sink the ship. The liability to an author or indeed an advance, which is excessive, can very quickly kill a book, or rather kill a firm. I remember once being rung up by John Watson's accountant, who asked me whether it was usual that figures shown in the hospitality expenditure column of the accounts should be twice as high as those in the production section. That one needs no explanation!

On the whole we avoided doing business with those who would finance their own publications. Vanity publishing, as it is called, was not for us although we did experiment once or twice. Money up front was certainly available when publishing regimental histories, but that was a different kettle of fish.

Surrounded constantly by dismal Jimmies and people wanting their books published in a hurry, we nevertheless began to attract attention to the extent that the volume of submissions increased on a regular basis. Sometimes even literary agents (of whom more later) recognised our existence and started sending us things on spec. However, the majority of our publishing in the early years was based on my entre-preneurial abilities and very much on my own personal taste. I went out and invented books. Tom and I frequently disagreed about what we should take on. Sometimes he was right. Sometimes he was very wrong indeed and we occasionally played a draw. Publishing at *our* level is such an idiosyncratic operation that it can only work on a small scale which is why so many publishing houses, particularly since the war, have been ruled by ferocious and inefficient foreign masters who had a way with other people's cash.

I always laugh when I remember that Fred Warburg, who was certainly foreign, wrote a book about publishing called *An Occupation for Gentlemen*. I think I said earlier in this book somewhere that I was unaware of the existence of many gentlemen in the trade. He definitely wasn't one. Certainly there were very few successful Englishmen, or women. Cooper's law of publishing says that you've got to be a foreigner to succeed. In my experience, and I include Scotsmen as foreigners, there are very few, if any, actual *English* publishers, except curiously enough Longmans. It suggests I suppose that English publishers are more likely to be profligate with money. Let me give you an example of the sort of meanness *required* (although I hadn't realised it at the time). It was André who, apart from changing light bulbs, taught me, after the post has been opened, to put the envelopes to one side in a tidy pile and then, when the operation is complete, take every envelope that's been opened and hold it up to the light. More often than not you will find a cheque in it. I saw this proved time and again at the morning post-opening session. And there was always a grin of triumph on André's face. I never ceased to follow his example. He also kept the foreign stamps.

A classic example of how careful you have got to be socially happened to Jilly and myself when we went to dinner with Ilsa Yardley, referred to earlier, with whom I had worked at Deutsch. Among the guests at Ilsa's flat was a very forceful character, Mrs Neurath, co-owner with her husband, the late Walter, of Thames & Hudson. She turned up dressed totally in black leather and proceeded to hold forth through most of the meal. Being a well mannered girl, Jilly wrote to Ilsa the next day a thank you letter for dinner which said, among other things, that she'd had a lovely time but she didn't much care for 'that Nazi lady'. Since she did not know Ilsa's home address, although we had been there, she posted the letter to Thames & Hudson. Here of course was another example of corporate post open-ing. It turned out later that when the post was opened in the days after the dinner party the remark that Jilly had made about 'Nazis' was read out in front of Mrs Neurath, she of the black leather, much to the embarrassment of everyone around the table. It may well be a lesson – never write private letters to people at their offices.* Not long after this Ilsa told me she asked Eva to dinner. Eva said to Ilsa 'Walter thought very highly of you. I could never understand why.'

There were signs in the mid 1970s that the public was becoming more interested in military history. I think this may be because television had taken it up in a big way; John Terraine's series on the Great War was being constantly repeated and a lot of new documentaries and the marking of anniversaries were being shown. Newspapers also began

---

* Incidentally, it was as the same dinner party that Godfrey Smith of the *Sunday Times* met Jilly for the first time and that evening commissioned the first piece that she ever wrote for that paper.

to give more space to reviewing books of a military nature and good public relations in this field made all the difference. We had to maintain a high profile, which disguised the thin ice on which we were skating. The PR side of the operation was handled almost entirely by myself and one of my dictums is, and always has been, that if you pour enough drink down somebody's throat before he or she has time to think what's happening, they may become more malleable. Getting newspaper coverage is a skill. Few publishers would deny this. It is difficult to obtain, but is most important when launching a book. You must be sure to cultivate the Press. You must know the specialist correspondents, the relevant magazines and journals and as many hacks as possible.

We had to know a great deal about the defence industry too. Quite a lot of our titles had to be cleared by the MOD whom I never found very easy and who very often made tinkering noises just to pretend that they knew what was going on and so that they were noticed.* On several occasions we had to submit books to the D-Notice Committee, and on others to consult lawyers before we published anything that was slightly risky. We did have one narrow squeak, and that was with a book called *Our Enemies the French* by Anthony Mockler. This describes the fighting in North Africa between the French and the British at the beginning of World War Two. Not many people remember that the French took us on and were soundly beaten. One of the senior British commanders in the area was General Jack (known as 'Black Jack') Evvets. In the course of Mockler's account of some of the fighting in North Africa certain derogatory remarks were made about the General.** Had we not been assured by the author that the General was dead we would never have printed it. I'm not going to risk reprinting it here, although General Evvets is at least officially dead, but I do say, on his behalf, that he was a gentleman. After we had admitted liability his lawyers asked that we should deposit £300 with the Basingstoke Branch of the British Legion and remaining copies of the book must be pulped and destroyed. Second-hand dealers will tell you that it still changes hands at an exorbitant price. The irony of this story though is that when he finally did die, aged 93, all the allegations were found to be true!

* An example of nit picking: the MOD insisted on a passage coming out of a text which referred to the 11th Hussars 'acquiring' a carpet from a German officers' mess. The argument was that this was plundering and should not be referred to. They were of course talking about something that had happened in 1945. Amazing.
** One of them concerned a Druse princess.

**24.** 'General China' on trial in the courthouse at Nyeri under the watchful eye of Luo policemen. He used to be the local milkman. His real name was Warihu Itote.

**25.** Formation flying taken from the Lincoln.

**26.** Henry Nelson (left) – 'Ham Tea'

**27.** Tim Carew, wearing his 'very good MC' – 'The Experimental Stick' at Ringway, Manchester.

**28.** André Deutsch.

**29.** General Horrocks and the author at the Famous Regiments' launch party in the Royal Hospital Chelsea.

**30.** Jamie Hamilton and General Horrocks.

**31.** General Chambe and John Goldsmith.

**32.** Goldsmith shows the window through which he escaped from the Gestapo.

**33.** John Watson, *the* bomber pilot.

**34.** Portrait of John Guest by Jeremy Holt.

**35.** John Guest talks to Jilly Cooper.

**36.** Some players.
Laura Hesketh 'the urban
marmoset' *(top left)*,
Alistair Service *(top centre)*,
Cric Perkins *(top right)*,
Michael Glover *(middle left)*,
Lizzie Drinnan *(middle right)*,
John Service *(bottom left)*,
Jack Smithers *(bottom right)*.

**37.** The Kent Brothers.

**38a&b.** Unusual photograph of Mussolini and Hitler. The man in the middle autographed this print to the author at the Frankfurt Book Fair. He was Hitler's butler, Herr Linge.

**39.** The author talks to Eric Hiscock (left).

**40.** His Excellency *(left)*, the German Ambassador, the author, Herbert Sulzbach and Mrs Sulzbach at the German Embassy launch of *With The German Guns*.

**41.** A terrible trio – Tom Hartman *(left)*, Jilly Cooper and Tim Jacques.

**42.** On the Road to Malmédy.

**43.** Landing the Big Fish. Anything Tom Maschler can do the author can do better – almost! An 86lb Nile Perch taken from Lake Turkana during a visit post national service to Kenya.

On another occasion we came across, in a book we were going to publish, a derogatory passage about General Sir James Marshall Cornwall. It was fairly crucial to the content of the book. I deemed, however, that we must be cautious, so I wrote to the General saying: 'If I print this passage will you sue us for libel?' He replied by return of post, 'Yes, I shall,' so we dropped the passage from the book. Ten years later Sir James contacted us and asked if we'd like to publish his autobiography, *Wars and Rumours of Wars*, because he'd been so impressed by our honesty over the libel matter. It just shows you that good deeds sometimes pay off. Lest I'm accused of name-dropping from time to time, how's this? I lent my only copy of *Our Enemies the French* to the Duke of Wellington the other day and at the time of writing he has lost it, but at least I am in continuing correspondence with him!

Gradually our list began to expand. So too did our staff, and indeed my waist! We acquired a number of packers with university degrees; they were tailor-made for the job. In fact we used to get letters from graduates and indeed undergraduates asking for holiday work, some actually wanting to get into publishing direct. At one stage we had seven people with degrees working in the warehouse and they were certainly better educated than those on the editorial floors. We could manage one 'A' Level between us. One of the packers, an American called Cric Perkins, even drafted a novel with the title *Packing Room*. Cric, who is Felix's (my son) godfather, is the only person I know who has refereed a rugger match without ever having seen a game played! Later he made seven not out in a cricket match when playing against the Old Merchant Tailors, the name of which side he was never able to fathom. He also caught a blinding catch in the covers and he actually appeared in the newspapers. When he hit his first delivery he dropped his bat and ran for cover. I once had him umpiring too, but that is another story. We did achieve one marriage when a Canadian packer ended up with our Australian nanny. The nanny in question turned up at our hotel in Australia when we were doing the grand tour. Jilly had always found her difficult, but I was really rather fond of her and she brought with her some squawking children. We invited her up to our room and gave her a drink. The children behaved in the most impossible manner, trashing the place and ended up putting all the bathroom equipment into the loo. Jilly said after the nanny had left, 'Thank God she was as incapable of controlling her own children as she was ours.' We are still in touch with those two who are now living in Australia with all their children. That is the only marriage we actually achieved, but I have a suspicion that there were from time to time couplings that were taking place behind my back in the office after hours.

Anyway, with a packing staff to look after and the front office resembling a bomb site, we set to work to improve our working conditions. We converted the front part of the building into a military bookshop which was a rash thing to do, partly because we didn't know much about bookselling. It never really got off the ground but it looked good and was somewhere for people to browse when they came to call on us. We had a limited range of stock, mainly our own books, but just occasionally we'd go the whole hog on a book published by someone else and I remember we sold at least 300 copies of General Hackett's book *I was a Stranger* which is in my all-time top ten, and we also did a very successful mailing on the memoirs of R V Jones, one of the first revelations of the secret operations going on behind the green baize door in the war. Professor Jones himself was a remarkable character and often honoured us with visits to the office. People were beginning to discover where we were and quite often would drop in for a chat which usually meant a visit to the branch office. We were acquiring a high profile in the market place through word of mouth and, although an awful lot of rubbish came in, I was pleasantly surprised how quickly word got round that we were in business.

Later in this section I have created a sort of chapter within a chapter, which is really thumbnail sketches of some of the more distinguished writers, soldiers, sailors and airmen who passed through our doors. I have chosen those who were more than just visitors. In many cases they were authors already, some were incipient writers, while others just popped in for a drink. But our old friends made it seem a more cheerful place and a certain amount of interior decoration by a gang of three more graduates gave the place a new look. The warehouse was dusted down and an attempt was made to get the lift working (it failed). We picked up four or five small publishers who were prepared to let us handle their distribution. This was, I'm afraid, a mistake on my part because running the warehouse was an extremely expensive business, not least because you had to pay the postage or carriage on most of the goods and this meant more cash upfront. We weren't pulling enough in from the bookshop and by the time we'd reached the middle of the decade it was obvious that we were going to have to look for substantial capital investment or go under like one of Edwyn Gray's submarines, new paint and old.

Fortunately Alistair Service, a member of the Service family and a director of the firm, who'd been acting as a sort of guide dog in search of a merger or at least another umbrella, had some good connections with an organisation called The Municipal Journal Group of Companies. In fact he was married to the daughter of the firm's management. The Municipal Journal was a company which handled a whole series of journals and magazines, mainly covering business, local politics, second-hand cars and it also had a strong interest in exhibitions. Alistair very cleverly managed to introduce us to the Journal and we were given a charming Dutchman called Max Rodenberg and one of their freelance accountants, David D'eath, who were posted in to keep an eye on us. At the same time Alistair's father-in-law, Harold Hemming, a Canadian who had served with the British Forces in the First World War* and a very remarkable man, agreed to put a large sum of money, about £100,000, into the business as long as we could come up with some projects which would take us into the big time! We did in fact find two or three books for which we organised very large print runs both here and abroad, particularly in the USA.

The trouble was that putting these books together was rather more expensive than we had anticipated because inflation was galloping and our original estimates were, it was plain, very near the bone. We were going to use nearly all the money made available to us on a couple of projects which seemed to move backwards every day of the week. But the books did appear. One was *Swastika at War* – a book of colour photographs of the German war machine which was very unusual because colour work of World War Two was still in its infancy. Another project which did quite well was a book on the Normandy landings. But at the end of the operation and in the latter years of the decade, the books existed but the money didn't. We'd used it all up. From now on survival was the key word and what follows shows that we were working very hard to broaden the list and our figures were not looking too bad. It was going to be very difficult though. This did not, however, stop us from continuing to publish and, with the knowledge that the Municipal Journal was still looking at us in a fairly friendly way, we felt able to carry on for longer than we actually should have done.

The people who kept us going for a time were the aforementioned Max Rodenberg and the late David D'eath, the accountant. Storm clouds were gathering though and it did not take long to register the truth. We published against all the odds and we struggled like

* He was the author of a book about artillery which rejoiced in the title of *Flash Spotting*. This is a way of detecting how far away the enemy artillery were firing from.

anything to get the financial side right, but the country was going through a very tough recession and this made our task even more difficult. Although we did continue to publish, we were ever-conscious that we were being watched very carefully. In one way this was a good thing, but it didn't do much to inspire confidence.

I must say something more about the staff at this stage, because every time I think of them the images of their faces and their sense of humour come grinning back.

Alison Harvey, who had come to me from Macmillans, was without doubt the best secretary I have ever had. I was very frightened of her, but she was long-suffering and of great goodness as well as a brilliant rights dealer and a comfort to me, and it was she who later made my life at Warne's (one of our umbrellas to be) in Bedford Square easier and held my hand for a while. Toby Buchan was still around in the background but shortly about to leave us and join Cassells and later Davis-Poynter before eventually running his own firm, Buchan & Enright. A variety of girls came and went including a very pretty one called Annabel Windsor-Clive, my beautiful niece Amelia, and there was also Victoria Stileman who was with us in the early days and of course the famous Beryl Hill, probably the most constant employee we ever had. She was the toast of the regiment or at least the sliced bread! She had worked at Hamish Hamilton for Tom and then left and followed him to another job. Quite what happened immediately after that I don't remember but she got married and had children. Between these births she came to work for Tom and me on and off and was probably employed for some twenty years. Without doubt Tom could never have survived in the great world without her and I think I would say the same from the publishing point of view. She was absolutely infallible. She had an impeccable memory. Although she couldn't do shorthand you could dictate longhand to her and she very often knew what letter to write without asking me. Everybody loved her, everybody still does. She looked rather like Cilla Black and she was full of beans and full of fun. She came into her own at the Frankfurt Book Fair where she enjoyed the evening entertainment as much as anybody, but we'll come to that later. Beryl is now a very senior executive at El Vino's. I wonder where she acquired that taste for wine?

There were a number of memorable people in the warehouse, including the Kent brothers who were a double act. They had some association with one of those societies that dress up in German uniform. The Kents had a habit of putting their uniforms on and marching up and down outside the office and there was a photograph of them taken at the office party. I don't think they were very clever, but their father was a wonderful Gurkha Brigadier for whom I used to play cricket. The last I heard of them was that they were running a bookshop in Marlborough which was next door to a pub. I know where they got that idea from. As I said, the packing department went through constant staff changes.

Other staff brought to the office an atmosphere of jollity and irreverence which we needed at this time and several of them went on to distinguish themselves in the publishing field, not least Steven Williams who now has his own firm called Midas and who is probably one of the best freelance public relations operators in publishing to this day*.

I can't close this section of the book without mentioning one protégé of mine called Simon McMurtrie. He came to me through work experience along with a lot of other boys from Radley who had responded to my invitation when I went there to talk about book production. A number of the more intelligent lads saw that there was more to books and publishing than it would appear from a day-to-day reading. My usual trick on these occasions was to produce a new book and take it apart with a pen knife so they could see how many pieces and sections there were to deal with before you could put a book together. One of the first people to be impressed by this was Simon, a small and innocent-looking Radleian with an intellect which absolutely staggered me. He was blessed with enormous musical talent, was an organ scholar and he was everything that I might have wanted as an assistant. He couldn't keep his nose out of anything in the office. He was entirely free with his advice and more often than not he was right. He irritated a great many people because he picked things up so quickly that he ended up knowing more about the subject than they did. I found him astonishingly useful because he would do all the dirty jobs without grumbling and he had a ready wit and an intelligent way of applying it.

When standing in for Beryl (when she was on her family holiday) he was renamed Miss Firtree by Tom, which resulted in his being bought a pot plant for Christmas by one or other of our older Army authors under the impression that he was a female member of the staff! I am happy to say that he now earns a sum of money which in my days would have been equivalent to the turnover of a small publishing firm in a year. He is still in publishing. He is extremely talented, has got the

* Not forgetting Beth Macdougall.

rest of his life in front of him and has managed to get married and have children as well. I think he is one of the most brilliant young men I have ever come across and I take a great deal of credit for launching him and for his success. I have no hesitation in saying this. I am also very fond of him and I expect one day that he will appear in some honours list somewhere. He is certainly on mine.

There were other Radleians who did their stuff including one called Chris Perring who is now a publisher up in Edinburgh; another one became an actor and several others distinguished themselves in other activities. There was always a constant flow of these bright young things through the warehouse which I found leavened the bread and provided a great deal of entertainment. I must mention here that I had quite a strong disagreement with Denis Silk, the Warden of Radley. During my lecture on book production to leavers and sixth formers, I announced that all boys ought to learn how to type. The Warden, much to my surprise, took umbrage at this and said that the boys had enough on their hands without learning something else and that I wasn't to be ridiculous. This was of course before the days of PCs and I have never quite understood his attitude.

There were other minor characters who cropped up from time to time, not least a certain Laura Hesketh. She was small and birdlike and caused one author to remark that she looked like the sort of boy that he would take round behind the bike sheds. She was a socialite and with a name like Hesketh you never knew what to expect. Having said that, even I was staggered when I discovered that she'd run up a bill of over £300 in private calls on the office telephone. It may surprise nobody to learn that she eventually married the publisher Anthony Blond. It was a strange relationship, the mechanics of which can only be imagined.

One of my great friends and confidants during those days was the late Desmond Elliot who was always on hand to advise me. As I write, it is only ten days since he died and I have lost one of my best publishing friends ever. For some time he was Jilly's agent and, although they fell out towards the end, just before he died, it was plain that they were attempting to piece together a shattered friendship. Desmond, who was the star of the Young Publishers' Review, was one of the funniest men I have ever met. He was a brilliant publisher and his knowledge of the publishing undergrowth was second to none. I miss him terribly; he influenced the way I went about things and, although he was very small, his was probably the shoulder I cried on most during the worst days.

Not all days were bad. Of course we had our ups and downs, but it has to be said that some of our authors behaved in such an extraordinary manner that you couldn't take them seriously. The sort of books that I was publishing would never have been published by anyone else. Most of my authors weren't writers in the true sense of the word. Many of them simply had a very good story to tell and it was Tom's job to try to knock it into shape so that it appeared mildly literate. We had a way of categorising certain kinds of books that would come into the office unsolicited. They were known as the 'BOW School', i.e. the accused couldn't write bum on a wall. Likewise there was the 'Got Up Had Breakfast' variety. These were long, laborious diaries kept by thoroughly inconsequential people which always began with a lengthy description of their childhood, being born in Hornchurch and then brought up in Quetta and giving interesting accounts of pig-sticking and tent-pegging and how their daughter Molly fell in love with a punkah-wallah. They were kitchen-sink jobs really and only occasionally were there flashes of humour or material of any sort of interest to us or indeed anybody else. We got many submissions which started off: 'I am not intending to try and make any money out of this book but I am doing it for my grandchildren.' They weren't really. They were doing it for themselves. Most people like that believe that their own life is of enormous interest to everyone else. I'm afraid that is very seldom the case.

Another remark that tended to accompany these offerings was the justification of publication which would be helped by 'all my friends will buy it' – hence the title of this book. In my estimation most of us have very few friends, say six as a maximum. We have hundreds of acquaintances, but not everybody has even that number. Before I put pen to paper I thought long and hard about joining the ranks of those I grumble about, but I now understand how much more it meant to those incipient authors. Appearing in hardcover never fails to cause a buzz. There is, alas, a book in most of us, but not necessarily a very good one!

What follows is an attempt to explain what we were trying to do in the '80s and '90s. The time warp may be a little bit obvious because I find it difficult to remember past events with clarity in chronological order. One thing had a habit of blending into another so I must again crave my readers' indulgence and apologise if they spot that some of the dates don't make sense.

I fear the truth is that sometimes the results and sales figures were so awful for months on end that one tended to shove them under the blotter, so to speak, although there are lots of funny stories still to come and books to be published despite the feeling of gathering gloom. Nevertheless I felt the crunch was coming. The writing was on the wall. It was the wrong kind of graffiti. We could not go on trading like this much longer. That would make matters worse if anything. We'd come to the end of a decade and we were going broke. Money seemed to have slipped through our outstretched hands, or indeed down our throats. After ten years I was going to have to call it a day. It was all my fault. I had to think fast. The matter was not helped much by the fact that Alistair Service had had a run in with his wife (a director of the Municipal Journal). They separated and the breakdown caused an awkward situation for the Service family who of course had the freehold of the building which kept them sound, but Seeley Service & Cooper was not sound. You could say in artillery terms 'our flash had been spotted*'. But by the end of the '70s it looked as if things were coming to a nasty conclusion. It looked as if we were on the verge of trading whilst insolvent. We couldn't last long under those circumstances and it was decided that the only thing open to us was to call in the receiver. The nastiest person to emerge during these unhappy days was a young banking executive who was simply bloody-minded. He worked for our clearing bank and did everything he could to make life difficult. It was plain to me that he regarded himself as being groomed for stardom in the bank. I was eventually driven to be very, very rude to him indeed and I often wonder what happened to him. If I didn't strangle him someone else will have done**.

In a situation where the receiver has been called in, quite simply everything stops. You become superfluous in your own organisation. In our case very little time was wasted. After a final board meeting at the offices of the Municipal Journal, I and two of my colleagues returned to the branch office in the back of a taxi. By the time we'd finished at 3 o'clock and returned to the real office, the first moves had already been made and a receiver appointed. This did make sense in the end because every minute of further trading would have compounded the insolvency. It was my horrible task to break the news to the staff who I must say took it very well and headed straight for the branch office. Fortunately we were able to retain the services of one of the old ladies and we had a skeleton staff whom the receiver had

* See page 103.
** Throughout my publishing career I have never received any help, advice or interest from any of the clearing banks. They didn't understand publishing and most of the managers have never read a book in their lives.

promised to pay. However, that was the last of his concessions. In fact the man in question was distinctly sympathetic towards us. He had been aircrew during the war and was fascinated by a number of the books we'd published on such subjects. He did his best to make things easy for us and we were allowed to trade in a limited way. His assistant, a lugubrious Sherburnian with a great capacity for pints of bitter, meanwhile did all the dirty work. He was not popular with the staff who remained and I have no doubt he went on to a dramatic future tearing firms to pieces, but he was the man against whom our anger was vented and the people in the warehouse and other staff gave him a bloody awful time.

To say that the situation was undignified would be putting it mildly. I was embarrassed for my staff and angry with myself. The question was what to do, so I was thrown in at the deep end with the receiver and various representatives from the Municipal Journal, who obviously were likely to be the biggest losers in view of that large sum of money they had lent us for those two dramatic projects which I have previously described. The receiver had decided that the only thing to do was find a large publishing firm to which we could hitch our wagon, and if he could complete some sort of sale, he would at the same time pocket a percentage of the amount recovered. This is perfectly legitimate, but things like that don't happen overnight. There ensued a long period of what seemed endless days and weeks during which various publishing firms were approached to see if they would like to involve themselves with us and to a man they said, 'No thanks very much,' and wandered off. You can hardly blame them. Gradually accounts were being settled and a degree of revenue enabled us to pay quite a lot of people who might have suffered otherwise but there is no doubt that, apart from myself and Tom, a number of suppliers had been caught and this was almost the most difficult to cope with because they had trusted us. I did everything I could to mollify them, but I was not flavour of the month, as you can imagine. By this time I was virtually penniless.

Gradually we worked our way through the marriage market, but there seemed to be no grooms in the offing. Day-by-day business slowed down and we said sad farewells to various people. At last, though, there appeared a glimmer of light on the horizon. The receiver had an approach from Frederick Warne, the publishers of Beatrix Potter, who had shown some interest in our list because there were parallels with their own. For instance they had the famous Observer books and they had a line in books on transport, some of it military. I don't mean that our books were suitable for the rabbit market, but there was room for expansion on Warne's part and indeed, as the Potter copyright was heading for the public domain, they were seriously wondering what to do and how to safeguard their lines before everyone else started printing Beatrix Potter books or selling twee porridge bowls, dish cloths and cuddly rabbits in waistcoats.

Finally a deal was done and a certain degree of relief all round was tempered by the fact that the whole initial adventure had come to an ignominious end. What Warne's had at least done was to agree to take on all those publishing projects for which I was liable and also my work in progress, which meant that for the next eighteen months or two years, we probably had a throughput of books which still bore the Leo Cooper imprint and colophon. It was finally agreed to close down 196 Shaftesbury Avenue and move my stock, records, myself and my secretary Alison over to Frederick Warne's building in Bedford Square. The receivership was exclusive to Seeley Service and Cooper, which was then struck off, but the imprints of Seeley Service and Leo Cooper remained unsullied and, as it proved, very much part of the foundations for the future. I wasn't going to take this situation lying down. I'd already been trampled on enough but I am not grumbling about what happened. In the long term things worked out better than I'd dared to hope, but ahead there lay more choppy waters, no calm sea in sight and the forecast was lowering skies.

You soon learn who your friends are in a business like this. I must say that most of the people I dealt with were more than kind and sympathetic, but one did get a few angry people banging on the door and one just had to accept that this is part of the way that things happen. One ironic episode took place after the receiver, Mr Draper, had signed and sealed the deal with Frederick Warne. He sold his flying helmet which he'd worn during the war to one of the boys who ran the bookshop, who, with his Nazi uniform, wore it at our farewell wake at the old office. Fortunately I was able to retain the tenancy of the flat at 190 Shaftesbury Avenue, owned by the Greek Cypriot Karamanis, so I had somewhere out of which I could operate, while the office was being moved physically to Bedford Square which was only a few hundred yards away.

After the receivers and the kings had departed and the removal men had vanished to the pub, I sat one day contemplating the empty shell of 196 Shaftesbury Avenue to which I still had the keys. The ghosts were all around me. Where the dartboard had been there was a circle of dust. There was the wash basin in which James Essington-Bolton washed his feet and thereby earned the name James Smashington-

Basin, having broken it in the process. I recalled also my early arrival in the office one morning to find little Joe, the packer, fast asleep under one of the desks. He'd obviously been there all night because one could smell him. He was removed from his prone position and placed on the labour market. One day I got an infuriated telephone call from the doorman of the nearby hotel. 'What do you mean by giving this man Smith a reference as a porter?' he said:

> You gave me a written reference and it is of no value whatsoever. I employed this man on your word because I know you to be an honest man and all that has happened is that he is either sick or when he does come in he goes to sleep.

I said 'I hope you've read the reference that I gave you carefully. I will quote it to you. "When Joe Smith *does* work he is a thoroughly competent operator but that is all that I can say."' One does have to be careful about giving references and I must say I'd had a few pints with Joe in the past, but I was annoyed that he took advantage of that.

On the other side of the office there was one desk which looked as if it had been heavily smashed. This was where our Nigerian accountant (sent by the job centre) used to sit. His name was Adamolo. He was aptly named. Few people could have got it wrong more often than him and he was known forever after as Adam Allupwrong! Our cleaner, Mrs Whittaker, took pity on him at the Christmas party because it was obvious that he was feeling out of place and he didn't drink either (which was rare in 196 Shaftesbury Avenue). Mrs Whittaker took him aside and in a voice like a corncrake said, 'I know you don't like to have a drink Mr Adamolo, but don't let the others put you off. I think you are an 'uman bein' and deserve to be treated like one.' On that she flounced out and never came back, nor did Mr Adamolo. Perhaps they are in the Nigerian government by now.

Before we left 196 we gave a riotous party and asked as many of the people who'd worked for us that we could contact. The nicest aspect of that was that nearly all of them had now got jobs in publishing firms; not all of them were just packers or gofers; most had degrees anyway. Some of them now have very distinguished jobs. It would be unfair to mention that they cut their teeth with us but I remember them all with affection because we never had any trouble. This was partly alleviated by the easy access to The Oporto down the ginnel.

I moved on down to the basement and there was the old photocopying machine no longer able to wheeze out badly presented press handouts. It (the machine) had a gallant career culminating in being completely shamed by two young packers who had attempted to photograph their male members under the flap of the printer. I only discovered this when one of the girls, alternatively bright red in the face and giggling, handed me a crumpled piece of paper which she said she'd found in the basement waste paper basket. Sure enough there was a shape that I recognised, but only just. The feat of gymnastics required to be able to get the said member in the right position to register gave the impression that we were harbouring seriously deformed creatures in the basement, or at least an acrobat. I couldn't stop laughing. The perpetrator of that episode is still running around the publishing world. I last met him on Stroud station. He was really an enchanting boy, but I had to get rid of him. He wasn't called 'Tripod' for nothing.

Returning to the main room again I was looking at a pile of damaged books and watching the passers-by staring in at the now empty shop window when my eye caught something sticking out from one of the central heating radiators. On closer inspection it appeared to be a manuscript. With much difficulty and the use of various lengths of wood from Mr Adamolo's desk, I managed to prise out this object from behind the pipes and plonked it on a filing cabinet. It was indeed a manuscript. I found a rickety chair and sat myself down amid a sea of crumpled paper, old books and empty files. I started to read. About two hours later I had finished it and I knew that I had a potential bestseller on my hands. The light was fading and the electricity was shut off as I read the last page. It was quite extraordinary. I was staggered by this story of a 13-year-old girl left behind in German-occupied France by her parents at the beginning of the Second World War with the encouraging words: 'We'll see you in time for Christmas.'

Antonia Hunt – for she was the author – had written an account of her life which was to be given an ecstatic welcome by the press and not only that but it was plain at once that here was a mini triumph if we got our act right. I was so enthused by it that I picked up the telephone which, thank God, was still connected and rang the number on the manuscript. I was careful not to be too enthusiastic, but the first thing I had to do was to establish that the writer of this book was still alive. She was indeed and I had a little bit of difficulty in stopping her talking. At the same time I had some sympathy with her because the book had been, according to her records, in my office for six months and in the current atmosphere of gloom and doom I suspect it had just been shoved aside.

This incident cheered me up a bit. The book, eventually entitled

*Little Resistance*, subsequently became a tremendous success and went into foreign editions, paperback and sold a good many thousands in the United Kingdom. Antonia Hunt is still very much alive and I am in touch with her from time to time because I have always remained convinced that the story is so good that it will eventually appear as a film of some sort. There is an extraordinary postscript to this story. Part of the fascination comes from the fact that when the Germans discovered that there was a young English girl living among them, they promptly arrested her and she was put into a prisoner of war camp with adult civilians. Remember she was only 13. Eventually she was released, but it wasn't long before she got caught up by the Gestapo because, rather foolishly, she had decided to become a courier for the Resistance. By this time she had moved to Paris and was technically on bail, so to speak. From time to time she was interrogated and one Gestapo officer plainly fell in love with her. Modesty prevents Antonia from describing what happened, but it was a love affair, a bit one-sided, but not entirely. The point of this story is that when I eventually did publish the book I received in the post some six months later a letter from the Gestapo officer in question. He wrote that he had heard that there was a book on the subject and he enclosed in sterling the price of the book and money for postage. Sensing a public relations coup I immediately sent him a copy of the book and returned his money. It has to be said that he didn't emerge from the story very well, but Antonia was such an attractive girl that I understood his feelings. However, Antonia had let rip about him in the book and what he'd tried to do and indeed did do to her. It is a fairly graphic account. The Gestapo man was obviously absolutely horrified by the image painted of him in the book and he returned the offending article with no more than a note and the money. I tried to get in touch with him but I didn't make it. I am still trying but I don't expect I ever will. That story has haunted me ever since I first found it stuck behind the radiator. I also regarded it as a sort of symbol of starting all over again. The first submission to reach me after the break-up of Seeley Service & Cooper was a winner and so it proved for the next few years, but of course there was always trouble around the corner.

Warning shots. When the dust had settled and all the bits and pieces had been removed from 196 Shaftesbury Avenue, including a great many files, I was left to take my camp followers, or in this case camp follower, Alison Harvey, with me to Bedford Square where Frederick Warne were situated. It was a lovely house and at one stage it was rumoured to have belonged to Anthony Hope who wrote *The Prisoner of Zenda*. It was so successful that he had a squash court built (but that never came into our orbit) or it might have been next door. Anyway, Alison and I were given the basement office which was huge and had presumably once been the kitchen. It was not an attractive location but opened onto a little courtyard where there was a lone fig tree. Not, alas, big enough to cover our inadequacies.

I moved there one morning (I can't remember exactly what date it was) and Alison and I supervised the unloading of my pathetic remains from 196. It was rather like an Egyptian mummy excavation or one of Sir Mortimer Wheeler's expeditions. All our past was laid out on the floor in front of us where it had been dumped by the removal men. Actually it was quite helpful, because much of the material we hadn't seen for ages or had forgotten about, and it saved us the problem of searching the files because they'd searched themselves.

Anyway, there we were in Bedford Square and I was in the paws of Peter Rabbit & Co., appropriately enough underground. After arriving on the first morning, I sat down and made a few telephone calls to make sure that people knew where I was. Then I thought it judicious to announce my arrival personally and ascended from the basement to the first floor where the Managing Director and virtual owner of Frederick Warne, Mr Stephens, was in situ. He was somewhat surprised to see me and made it very plain to me that he'd forgotten that I was coming. He was a very roly-poly sort of man with a bought suit. I didn't know what to do so I joined him and his colleague, David Bisacre, the sales director, David Traube, and the production director, Susan Coley, who were sitting round a small side office table solemnly going through the post. Every letter that came into that office, regardless of whom it was addressed to, was read by this cabal who gathered together every morning. This was a method of management that I understood because it meant that you knew what everybody else was up to, but the more cunning among us, I discovered later on, would tend not to communicate by handwritten letters or indeed by telephone if anybody was in the room. There was an air of unease in the building.

I have to say that I think the two years I spent in that basement were two of the most miserable years of my life. Much as I loved Beatrix Potter and all her works I found it very difficult to equate her with the people who were running the business. Alison kept me sane. An example of Mr Stephens in action: when he had ascertained who I was and once the post had been opened he said, 'I want to talk to you, but before I do come downstairs to the basement.' I said to him, 'I've already been there.' He said, 'No you haven't' and I followed him downstairs. He produced a huge bunch of keys from his pocket and unlocked a large steel door in a part of the basement that I had not been aware of. On top of several filing cabinets was a large brown paper bag, the sort that American men in films come back from supermarkets with full of goodies carried under one arm. He put his hand into the paper bag and drew out a pair of muddy wooden clogs. 'What do you think of these, then?' he said, 'What do you think of these? What about it then? What do you think of them?' I said, 'Oh well, that's fascinating. They look like a pair of clogs to me.' He went bright red. 'They're hers,' he said, 'they're her boots. They're her clogs.' He was practically orgasmic. 'I bought them at Sotheby's last week.' Indeed he had and they were. So her presence at least from below the ankle meant that she still had a foot in the door. Then really turned on the heat.

Taking the keys out again he unlocked a series of cabinets and with one wave of a hand I was transported back to my childhood. Here were all the *original* watercolours of the Beatrix Potter books. When I say 'all', a certain quantity were actually either at the Victoria and Albert Museum or in the library at the National Book League, but it could be said that the majority of Beatrix Potter's artwork was at that time contained in this cellar room in Bedford Square. Such is the magic of those drawings that I was nothing less than dumbstruck.* It was almost as if I'd discovered the holy grail. This might seem an over-reaction, but in subsequent months, when I was able to compare the quality of the art work with the inadequacy of the people who were in charge of the outfit, I felt a great sadness. Frederick Warne didn't really know what they were up to. Also copyright was running out. There were no concrete plans for the future. They were, for instance, still reprinting time and again all the Potter books, but they were not re-originating the artwork. As a result subsequent editions of all the books were becoming less and less attractive to the discerning eye. The colours had lost their sparkle and the reason was that not only had Mr Stephens and his gang decided not to re-originate from time to time but the reason given (and it struck me as so bizarre that I almost hope it wasn't true) was that they claimed they were so frightened of letting the artwork out of the building to go to a printer because it would be pirated and so they were prepared to put up with less attractive images. I am glad to say that Nemesis finally did descend on them in the form of Penguin Books.

The first thing Penguin did, having bought the firm for what proved to be a very clever price, was to re-originate all the artwork. This was entirely due to Peter Mayer and was one of the most intelligent pieces

---

* As a treat I was given a free entry pass to the 'Potter Grotto' at Selfridges that Christmas. I am still haunted by nodding badgers and shifty foxes.

of publishing acquisition I have ever seen. It is also a fact that Warne had been, at the same time, employing artists to imitate Potter images for their drying up cloths, pottery, etc. because they wouldn't let the originals out of the building. They were really breaching their own copyright. I have learnt recently that they hated me at Warne and had even contemplated taking legal action over the method of my departure. Quite honestly I can't remember what I did do or say and it can't have been very important because someone managed to put them off and when the time came for me to go I was able to leave Frederick Warne and break into daylight without any more trouble. But I have not finished with them yet.

It is not quite clear even now why Mr Stephens bought the remains of me from the receiver. I don't think he knew either. Certainly they had various books on their list which came under the transport heading and they did publish the Observer books, which had one or two military titles therein. But it was plainly obvious that the Observer books were going out of fashion and that they had thought there was some connection between them and military history, but they didn't quite know what it was. It was very plain to me, fairly soon, that I had come to the wrong place. An all too prevalent situation you might say. I got on with them quite well but they weren't publishers as I understood it.

They had a fine warehouse and offices in Dorking and a lovely custom-built complex, because, despite the lack of quality printing, Beatrix Potter was still good news. They also ran an outfit within the firm called Potter Sundries – porridge bowls with rabbits on the bottom of them, stuffed animals, and so forth.

Initially I was involved in all the publishing meetings and the day-to-day running of the business. Talks to the reps, visits to bookshops, and indeed some publishing, were easy to handle because there was a momentum in the publishing programme I had brought with me which actually meant that some of the books that we did bore the joint imprint of Leo Cooper and Frederick Warne; I never actually stopped publishing during those dreadful years. My faith in my own imprint remained solid and I am happy to say I was eventually able to sail into calmer waters without too much trouble. This was helped by the arrival of a good friend of mine called Martin Marix-Evans who I'd worked with at Longmans and who came in as Editorial Director which was fairly obviously a job that I myself had been groomed for but had failed to make the grade. So they were lumbered with me and Martin and one of us had to go.

Martin was a far shrewder politician than I and he persuaded them (Warne) to ask him to write a business plan for the ensuing years which, among other things, would forecast exactly what Peter Mayer (who had been prowling round the imprint for some time) did when he eventually re-originated all the Potter artwork without Captain Hook in sight. Peter completely re-jigged the foreign rights and virtually changed the marketing image of Potter. All this had previously been suggested by Martin Marix-Evans who very quietly, and without realising it, completely wrote himself out of a job. So they had me whom they didn't want and they had Martin as well who very quickly realised that he had arranged for himself not to be wanted either. Frankly it was miserable chaos. Martin had done exactly the same to himself at Longmans. Now successfully freelance he can only blame himself if he drops out of that! Martin writes:

> I can't remember if the letter opening thing was still in force when I arrived but I do remember arranging for my staff to send me only their answers to letters, after they had gone out. I knew what was going on, but they had to decide what to say. Anyway, the business plan included selective use of the alternative Potter illustrations, ones not previously published, in the course of rescanning all pictures. That would have created new copyright as for previously unpublished scripts, muddied the waters and given us grounds for lawsuits. Anyhow, the merchant bankers told Warnes it was all too expensive as Potter was not worth above £500,000 and the whole plan was turned down. They were pissed off I would not sell back the shares they had made me buy to go on the board, and of course that paid off wonderfully when Penguin bought them up! The copyright issue went away when the European Union raised the period to 70 years from 50. Did you know I was summoned by the Editor of *The Observer* and threatened with a suit over usurping their name for the Warne series? I had to point out that name had been used since the '30s and in any case they'd look very silly so they dropped it.

To give you some idea of how hopeless the management at Warne was, a crisis arose very quickly when Mr Stephens fell ill while we were all at the Frankfurt Book Fair. Not only did Mr Stephens fall ill but he compounded the problem by dying. This put the fear of God into the remaining staff because it was plainly obvious that this was a one-man band. Both David Bisacre and Susan Coley were absolutely gobsmacked and Mr Bisacre, who was left behind in London while we were living it up in Frankfurt, was not in a position to help. I suggested that somebody ought to write an obituary for *The Times*. I rang up *The Times* and, although they'd heard of Beatrix Potter, they'd never heard of Mr Stephens and were singularly unhelpful. I reported this to my superiors who turned on me and said, 'Well why don't you do it yourself and make sure it gets in?' So I rang up *The Times* again and laid my cards on the table and between us we cobbled together a biography of a man who, though no doubt well intentioned, had not made the slightest impact on the publishing world as we knew it.

It was not very long after Mr Stephens' death the crunch came. Peter Mayer saw the target and went straight for the bull's eye. The first of these was the purchase of Frederick Warne for £6m. The Beatrix Potter copyrights then had no more than ten years to run, which may go some way to explain the startling fact that few publishers participated in the Frederick Warne auction. Eric de Bellaigue, the book trade guru, writes:

> The subsequent extension of copyright from fifty years to seventy years proved a considerable unanticipated bonus. Of the two under-bidders, believed to have been the printing group McCorquodale and the commodities group Booker McConnell, the latter was reported to have offered £4m. Penguin's bid – equivalent to twenty times Warne's latest pre-tax profits of £297,000 – looked to many wildly improvident. In the event, Penguin recovered its purchase price within two to three years. Costs were slashed with the virtual closure of the company, which had had a staff of seventy; assets, aside from Beatrix Potter interests, were sold off; Sally Floyer, recruited from Kestrel, orchestrated the aggressive exploitation of merchandising rights – and then there was the build-up of unit sales from the pre-acquisition level of two million to over seven million by 1986. Penguin's purchase of Warne provided the world of publishing with a business-school model of international marketing at its most effective. In April 1987, the books were republished in a new edition, incorporating new plates, to great acclaim.

I can never pass that building in Bedford Square without shuddering at the thought of the sheer horrors that went on during my two years. The staff were splendid and very good at their jobs, but were the victims of a reign of terror which perhaps some of them would prefer to forget. It was a subtle form of terror based entirely on survival of the most cunning. Mr Tod ruled!

Mr Stephens was related, I think, in some way to the Potter family. I discovered one thing about him when we were opening the post one morning. He opened one letter which was a press handout for something called The Book Bonanza so he handed this to me and said, 'What's this *Bozana*? Where is it – in Africa?' It immediately occurred to me, and indeed I was right, that the man was dyslexic. It turned out that he couldn't read. It seemed somewhat incongruous that the man running Frederick Warne and Beatrix Potter could not read. This was very much kept quiet. He was adept at dictating letters and using the telephone, but one never saw anything written by him. Martin discovered this at about the same time as I did. I, however, realising that once again the carpet was shifting under my feet, decided that something must be done. After two and a half years during which I'd had some ups and downs, I rang up Tom Rosenthal, Chairman of Heinemann and Secker, who had made a bid for my firm two days after Frederick Warne had bought it, and said to him, 'Do you remember two and a half years ago we spoke about the possibility of me joining you at Secker's and Heinemann?' and he said, 'Yes I do.' I said, 'Well as you know I had to answer you in the negative because two days before the deal had been struck with Frederick Warne by the receivers. I'm free again.' Tom paused for a moment and said, 'Come round and see me.' I went round to Poland Street where Tom was in charge of Secker (he was also Chairman of Heinemann at the time). I won't go into all the details but he was a man as good as his word and we put together a link which enabled me to gather my soul back and to recover my dignity and still keep the publishing going.

I can't resist recounting the story told to me by one of the lady members of staff. She was a buxom lady with a sense of humour. She and a senior colleague accompanied each other to some book fair in the West Country. She was in her hotel room one evening when the telephone rang and a familiar voice said, 'I bet you don't know what I'm doing now.' She recognised the dulcet tones. The voice went on, 'I'm sitting on my bed with no clothes on looking at myself in the mirror. Would you like to come and join me?' The lady quite rightly said 'No'. I wonder who it was?

In joining up with Secker and latterly Heinemann for a few years, I had some of the happiest times I have ever had in publishing. This was because we were at the centre of the Heinemann group with just enough autonomy allowed for people to run their own empires. As I said, Tom was in charge of both Heinemann and Secker, and then there was Barley Alison who had her own little imprint, The Alison

Press, and I was attached to the group on the same basis. They became my new umbrella. There was also the support of the Heinemann group generally, the sales force and everything else I needed and almost before I'd got through the door of Poland Street, I realised that this was going to be fun, although as usual in this story there were devils lurking around the corner, but more of that later. Little did I know at the time what momentous events were about to take place in the publishing world. To call them dramatic would be the understatement of the century.

# CHAPTER VIII

# *Secker and War Book*

*Mon centre cède, ma droite recule, situation excellente.*
*J'attaque.*
My centre is giving way, my right is in retreat;
situation excellent. I shall attack.

Maréchal Foch

The move to Secker in early 1982 went much more quickly than I had expected. I was allocated visiting rights, whilst maintaining my private office in Shaftesbury Avenue. This meant that I could attend most of the editorial meetings at Secker (more often than not chaired by Tom Rosenthal to begin with). Secker were in Poland Street, a mere nine-minute walk from my Shaftesbury Avenue office. I was allocated time and indeed the services of a number of PR girls, one of whom was the great Beth Macdougall, and as a result of all this was fairly involved in the day-to-day publishing throughout the group.

I was more than fortunate that the Falklands campaign exploded at the time that it did. It arrived just as I was linking up with Secker and I remember to this day an early editorial meeting at which I presented the eight new beautiful publishing ideas that had so far emerged after such a brief campaign. They stood us, and me in particular, in very good stead and showed that the imprint was again very lively and our ear was close to the ground. The Falklands War was quite simply a gift to us*. Apart from being very interested in the campaign itself, I was aware that this was going to be a very significant conflict in historical terms. I at least knew where the Falklands were which is more than can be said for Prime Minister Thatcher who thought they were in

* Curiously enough Secker had just commissioned a book on the sinking of the *Belgrano* at about the time I arrived on the scene.

Scotland and Jilly who didn't know where they were. The whole occasion seemed to be rushed when it happened.

We were actually *en famille* sailing from Portsmouth to Cherbourg for a fortnight's holiday on the Normandy coast. I must say that seeing HMS *Bristol* setting out for the South Atlantic with her sailors lining the deck produced in me an astonishingly atavistic feeling: pride and fear. It is not a scene that I thought I would ever have to witness again although I had actually seen, in the United States, the USS *Missouri* sailing under the Golden Gate Bridge at full throttle for the bi-centennial, but that was some years earlier. Anyway, we settled down near Cherbourg (in the house of one of our authors) where we were regarded with some curiosity by the French population. Truculent Frenchmen kept on coming up to us in cafés and restaurants asking what the hell did we think we were doing invading the Falklands and so on. It wasn't until we got back from Cherbourg and read the English newspapers that we realised that we'd lived through a piece of British history that will never cease to be carefully scrutinised. From my own point of view, I realised that there was likely to be a continuing interest in the conflict and that, although our forces were magnificent, we were under-equipped, but we were certainly not inexperienced. The campaign itself proved that the British Armed Forces were second to none in all departments except the RAF. I also realised that if I played my cards right and worked all my contacts there would be some rich pickings in the memoir and campaign history fields, and so it proved.

I found people returning from the South Atlantic only too anxious to talk and discuss the campaign and I'd like to think that I got there before most people. Within weeks of the triumphant task force returning, I'd signed up no fewer than eight authors, much to Secker's and Heinemann's delight. These, in no particular order, were *No Picnic* by Brigadier (now Major General) Julian Thompson – the Commander of Three Brigade; Ewen Southby-Tailyour – *Reasons in Writing*; Guy Bransby – *Her Majesty's Interrogator*; Nick Barker – *Beyond Endurance*; David Brown – *The Royal Navy in the Falklands War* and a book by Edward Fursden called *Falkland's Aftermath* consisting of material sent to *The Telegraph* but not printed. Also there was *Amphibious Assault* by Michael Clapp aided and abetted by Ewen Southby-Tailyour and, not to be outdone, a brilliant piece of action writing by Sharky Ward called *Sea Harrier over The Falklands*.

If you look at the bibliography in any of the other books published during or after that period, you will be surprised how many of the titles listed are credited to Leo Cooper. Not only was that the case but they all turned out to be money spinners, not least Julian Thompson's book, *No Picnic*, which actually got itself onto the general bestseller list, albeit briefly. *The Royal Navy in the Falklands War* by David Brown was also quite a coup, although there were certain things that we were not allowed to say. It is interesting to note that all these works had to be submitted to the Ministry of Defence for vetting and, apart from the odd niggle, I think we were very lucky to get away with publishing what we did.

No single book mentioned above was outstandingly better than the others, but I think that Ewen Southby-Tailyour's contributions take the silverware. He himself had been stationed with the Royal Marines garrison in the Falklands some years before and had published a totally unreadable book about the navigation problems around the islands called *Falkland Island Shores*. When it was realised that we were going to have to send a task force to the islands and to the other little islands like South Georgia, it was essential that somebody like Ewen Southby-Tailyour was at once co-opted because he knew the coastlines like the back of his hands. It was entirely due to him, I think, that the task force had so little trouble landing unopposed, although reading his book *Reasons in Writing*, you will see that there is a very interesting account of the unfortunate dispute between the Welsh Guards and the Royal Navy which resulted in the terrible casualties at Bluff Cove. Had people listened to Ewen Southby-Tailyour's advice this would never have happened. Anyway, not only did he write a brilliant book but he went on to help Commodore Clapp who wrote a more detailed book about the amphibious assault and these two books make a very interesting pair.

It has to be remembered at this stage that there was a degree of running conflict between Admiral Woodward, who was in charge of the task force, and a number of other senior ranking officers from all three services. A lot of this stemmed from the fact that Woodward, quite sensibly I think, insisted on withdrawing his battle fleet at the end of every day to lessen the chance of being attacked by the Argentinean air force. It was very obvious that when the Argies did get through they could create a lot of damage. The arguments about the deployment of the fleet still go on. I don't think anybody was really right or wrong, but it is a discussion that will continue for years to come and it certainly added to the bad blood between Woodward and some other senior commanders.

There is one interesting account, not published by me, which has only just seen the light of day. In *Five Brigade in the Falklands**, the problems with Brigadier Wilson's Five Brigade are highlighted. Very

---

* The book is in fact published by Pen & Sword but it bears my name!

few people would deny that Brigadier Wilson had rather a rough time of it but he also made some dreadful mistakes. He was, as you will recall, the only senior officer to receive no recognition for his part in the campaign. He was also responsible for what seems to have been a strange sideshow involving a Chinook helicopter. The tensions between Brigadier Wilson and his colleagues are probably best left out of a book like this. It is not for me to judge the rights and wrongs, but I have one advantage over most people and that is that I have read Brigadier Wilson's *own* manuscript. No publisher would publish it. This is just as well because it could have done him an enormous amount of harm.

The book I referred to earlier, *Sea Harrier over The Falklands*, is a classic of its kind. There is a description of flying sorties in a Harrier jet, not least off the flight deck of an aircraft carrier and it is a fine piece of writing. It shows just what a brilliant weapon the Harrier turned out to be. One of the things that fascinated me about its performance was a manoeuvre entitled 'vectoring'. This was all to do with the fact that a Harrier moved very fast, ostensibly running away from an Argie aircraft, then stopping suddenly, whereupon the Argie flew straight past, not realising the Harrier was going to stop, and got shot up the arse! As far as I can remember, Sharky Ward shot down two Mirages this way. Later he gives a dramatic account of what it was like to shoot down a Hercules aircraft coming into Port Stanley with supplies and with a crew of nine on board. This lumbering giant had absolutely no hope but Sharky describes aiming his cannons in on the aircraft and blasting the crew and aircraft to pieces. This was, and is, the horrid side of warfare. He told me that he saw a pathetic face peering out of one of the windows as he descended for the final attack and blew the plane to pieces. At the same time it is a vivid underlining of how you must be well trained and well motivated.

All the books referred to above were very successful and we certainly enhanced our reputation by being up to the minute and by capturing the right authors. It also helped us to make rather a welcome amount of turnover for, by the time the books were published, I was well dug in at Secker & Warburg and the Heinemann group where the next part of the drama, much to my surprise, was to be played out. This was political warfare.

I referred earlier to the signing up with Tom Rosenthal which offered us a specialist lifeline. The Falklands crisis did our reputation no harm at all and the Leo Cooper imprint was flavour of the month, but not for long. Something was stirring in the undergrowth. Hasty meetings were being called, whispered telephone calls were being made, people shut their office doors and Barley Alison was getting over-excited. I tried very hard to find out what was going on with little success, but whatever it was it was being masterminded from the Heinemann group headquarters in Upper Grosvenor Street.

Tom Rosenthal had now relinquished control of Secker and moved over to Heinemann full-time. Poor Peter Grose, an amiable Australian and ex-Curtis Brown, was left holding a very noisy Secker baby. Soon the name of Charles Pick, known to some as Pickiavelli, would be ringing the bells. That character had been operating behind the scenes on his own agenda for ages. Although he was Wilbur Smith's publisher, he was also his agent and was reportedly taking more than was the normal slice. It was also rumoured that he even made his wife travel second class when they went on business trips while he, of course, sat up front. When the going was good Pick always claimed that it was he who introduced me into the group and took all the credit, when in fact it was Tom Rosenthal and I who cooked up the deal. When things went less well, as they would in the future, you could guarantee that Mr Pick was nowhere to be seen.

The whole saga had really started with the formation of Paul Hamlyn Ltd which became successful despite several hiccups. When Paul's first imprint had been sold a new version, Octopus, appeared on the scene. As far as living up to its name is concerned no one did better than Octopus, which had now bought Heinemann, until they themselves were bought by Reed.

I am not going to go into detail about what happened and who took whom over and when. That would constitute a major book in itself. Fortunately a volume does exist which covers the ground from all the points of view. It is called *The British Book Publishing Business Since the 1960s* and is a reprint of the selected essays of Eric de Bellaigue which appeared from time to time in the trade press. Eric had made a speciality of financial journalism with reference to publishing and his book, even if you haven't been in the business, is simply riveting.

Reading the book at a sitting, years after the event, a whole lot of things fell into place that I had only guessed at, or indeed not noticed at all. Eric de Bellaigue chronicles a time of rampant takeovers. People were jumping out of windows, there was a recession going on and new printing techniques, and indeed selling techniques, were very much flavour of the month.

As I said I am not going to go into details. Suffice it to say there was a changing population, particularly of advisers and financial gurus, so one never knew who was in charge of what and who'd bought what or when however hard one tried.

You can see therefore that a small imprint such as mine really wasn't going to count at all, although all the right noises were made in my direction and I was initially included in plots and plans for the imprints that were shortly to be relocated.

This didn't stop me continuing to publish and I was in a better situation than some I think because I was self employed and was not subject to the whims and fancies of the financial boys except when they decided, almost immediately, that my imprint was no longer needed. I existed in this sort of limbo for seven years.

There were one or two people who gave me a fair wind it has to be said, but at the same time were empowered to decide that I didn't really need to exist any longer. One of these, peculiarly, was somebody whom I might call a friend named Ian Irvine with whom I had served in the Honourable Artillery Company. He was an extremely powerful accountant, having worked for Lord Matthews in Fleet Street and before that being responsible for breaking the Reuters Trust. He was a friend of Paul Hamlyn's. He viewed the world of book publishing with a certain amount of impatience and he appeared on the scene when Paul announced that Octopus was going to buy Heinemann.

Of him Eric de Bellaigue says:

Ian Irvine, as chief executive of Reed's book interests but until recently in the camp of the vendors, had the challenging task of justifying to the purchasers the substantial investment they had chosen to make. His personal quandary was somewhat analogous to that of Rabelais' Gargantua, who alternated between rejoicing at the birth of his son Pantagruel (sale price of Octopus) and lamenting the death in childbirth of his wife Badebec (declining fortunes of the business). The reality of his position was such that he could not spend much time openly rejoicing.

Ian Irvine's responses to pressure from the Reed board automatically turned the spotlight on his style of management. A Fleet Street newspaper background naturally breeds a certain toughness where the stick is used to great effect. It does not, however, automatically produce the right results when exported to the more tender environment of book publishing. Even less so when the wielder of the stick appears to view the industry with a certain degree of impatience. Indeed the suspicion that Ian Irvine did not find book publishing totally absorbing gradually gained ground.

From then on Octopus appeared to be putting its tentacles round the whole Heinemann empire. This was, frankly, the beginning of the end. The Ides of March was upon us. Heads began to roll and I kept mine very much below the parapet, because this looked as if yet again one of the organisations that I had relied on for an umbrella was proving not to be watertight. In fact, leaking copious buckets would be a better description for the scenario in which I found myself.

Finally, after all the rumours, the truth emerged. We were all summoned to Upper Grosvenor Street where a somewhat less than enthralled audience of employees were informed officially that the Heinemann group had been sold to the Octopus group and more changes were about to be made, culminating, not least, in the eventual sale of Octopus to Reed (the point at which Ian Irvine arrived)! The only thing to do was to go on publishing and see what happened, and this I did. For a year or so all went quite well, but it was plainly obvious that the operation at Kingswood, where the warehouse was located, and Upper Grosvenor Street itself were to be disposed of and instead the whole operation, except warehousing, were located in that architectural peculiarity in the Fulham Road called Michelin House in April 1985. This was the building that also housed the restaurant Bibendum.

There was nothing much wrong with Michelin House and in mitigation I actually saw great plans of various offices showing where everybody was going to be located and at one stage even an office allocated to me. Initially the expense eaters thoroughly approved of an office which had an oyster bar on the ground floor. However, things were changing fast and then there came the news that Heinemann had sold their share in Pan Books of which they were joint owners with Macmillan. This was apparently a serious political mistake because there had been a deal with Macmillan that should any sale be made they should be informed at the same time. The sale of Pan by Heinemann was, in fact, triggered by the sale of Heinemann itself to the Octopus group, thus throwing confusion on to the Pan co-ownership by Heinemann and Macmillan.

At one famous sales conference to which we were all summoned, held in some ghastly hotel near Maidenhead, all the editorial staff were called in and in an embarrassing meeting asked to stand up and say what they thought they could contribute to the group and what their plans for the future were. At one stage during the morning session Ian Irvine stood up and said, 'Authors don't matter', or words to that effect. There was a stunned silence, almost as telling as the silence that greeted the news that there would be nothing to drink at lunchtime. At the lunch break several of us discovered a bar in another part of the hotel to which we repaired. As soon as he could get to it, a colleague, who shall remain nameless, slipped out and got on the telephone to the trade press. Sure enough, it was all over the press the following week. Though I don't claim credit for it, it was probably my friend who tipped them off. I felt that it summed up all that was too prevalent about the business, i.e. nobody seemed to care any more about authors or imprints. It showed too, a total contempt for the long suffering staff; something that was to become standard practice.

There were good moments, of course, and one really engaging character I discovered on one of the many floors of Michelin House was one Piers Russell-Cobb. Ostensibly he was in charge of publicity. He was very good at it, particularly with regard to himself, but the one saving grace he had in my eyes was that he always kept a bottle of whisky in the cupboard by his desk. He also constantly got himself into trouble with the management, not least by giving expensive dinner parties in Bibendum which was in part of the Michelin building. On one such evening he entertained an author and several guests after a launch party at which the bill came to about £600. What he failed to notice was that sitting on the other side of the foliage was Paul Hamlyn and some other big dignitaries from the group who happened to hear everything through the potted plants. Piers didn't last long after that but they treated him appallingly when it came to the crunch. His child became very ill and was dying, or so it seemed, when they hauled him in (knowing perfectly this was the case) and sacked him on the spot. A number of people vanished in this way during those years. Management of human resources was not a record that the group could point to with any pride. In fact the behaviour of the organisation that looked after staff was thoroughly second-rate.

The number of names who could flit through these pages is enough to give anybody the willies. Small men one had never noticed would appear in offices wearing bad gabardine suits and pencil moustaches. On other floors there was a box and cox movement of sharing offices and it was all open plan and noisy. It reminded me of 'H' block in Northern Ireland.

All in all it seemed that every time I got linked up with another publishing house with a view to sharing services, finances etc., that particular firm ended up on the cutting room floor and the founders six feet underground; perhaps I was the kiss of death. For instance, although Longmans are still going today, they are nothing like the force that they once were. André Deutsch exists only in name and he himself is dead.

Hamish Hamilton is now only a name, he is dead too. The same goes for Mr Stephens of Warne and Barley Alison. The main protagonists at Secker were being filtered out and there was no longer a Heinemann image. Their names really only exist now as trade marks like mine, but at least I am not dead. The current Octopus group continues in its own acquisitive way and I am sure it is very successful, but I have lost track of the people who are now holding down the editorial jobs.

But to return to 1988, an unusual man called Charkin, who had the reputation of being something of a *bon viveur*, appeared on the scene. This well travelled publisher was inserted, that year, at the top. He was ostensibly brought in to start Mandarin, a new paperback imprint. The last I heard of him, he ended up at Macmillan where he is today.

I am saying all this because circumstances suggested to the people at Octopus, not least to Charkin, that they might as well get rid of me because I was a passenger who had not paid for his ticket – a not unusual suggestion. Charkin, I am now told, had to exercise his charm and put on a sad face at the thought of leaving me in the lurch again. Crocodile tears. He certainly decided that I was a misfit, but a series of meetings, in of all places the Cumberland Hotel, set up a structure that enabled me to continue publishing through the Secker imprint whilst once again looking for another firm to buy me, which they did and I was saved eventually. Fortunately Kate Gavron (formerly Kate Gardiner) was posted in to act as liaison and it was she and I who managed to save the ship from running on to the rocks and I am eternally grateful to her for all the help that she gave me. She married Bob Gavron, who had recently endured a heart bypass. I remember being stuck on a train with her on the way to some regimental headquarters. The train had broken down but I am glad to say there was a bar on board and after one or two gin and tonics Kate confessed how happy she was and that she would soon be married. Many wonderful hours were spent in her company, researching regiments, sharing bottles and generally setting the publishing world right. I owe more to her than almost anyone else.

In passing I must mention a very peculiar story in relation to the Cumberland Hotel, which has always been a dreadful name in the Cooper family. In the 1920s my father wrote a novel called *Nipper's Bar* published by Collins. A comparatively jocular remark made in a bar (in the aforementioned hotel) to a barman turned into the catalyst for a major libel case. The character in my father's book said to the barman, 'Give me a glass of really good sherry, not an Amontillado.' The libel laws being as they were in those days, there was an almighty row and my father was sued for £1,000 by the manufacturers of

Amontillado, which in those days was a brand name not just a district. This was a lot of money at the time, and the book was withdrawn from circulation. He didn't write another book for ten years, partly because the war was upon us but also because his confidence had been utterly destroyed. So again remember never mention the Cumberland Hotel to me.

It might now be worth saying a word about the Michelin building which was at the centre of the argument. Eric de Bellaigue says:

> In the history of Octopus, the Michelin building occupies a position that is infinitely greater than one might expect of a piece of real estate, however distinguished. In addition to its role as a workplace for the 380 people who moved there in April 1988, the Michelin building was where the strategies for the business were evolved, fought over, and implemented. For the critics of Reed's management of the Octopus publishing assets, it occupies top slot in their demonologies.
>
> At a practical level, however, it has had its admirers as well as critics. The administrative and operational advantages of having a business that shares a degree of common ground, whether it be in products or markets, is widely accepted but undoubtedly many of the seven imprints that moved into Michelin House found the change deeply shocking for a number of reasons. Going into an open plan office building with executive type gradings covering such matters as size of desk and heights of partitions excites either mirth or outrage. Conforming to rules of behaviour is irksome. No pets on the premises (ha, ha) being one that presented particular difficulties for a few dog owning trade editors*. Most of all there was the shock of being one of several hundred in a regimented office.

The trouble with all the red tape was that we minions, minnows or whatever you might have called us, were trying to get on with our work and never knew where the next board of directors was coming from or the next instructions, or approval. I think it says a lot for the staff of all the companies involved in this that they simply took their

---

* I cannot let the comment pass without recording an act of great gallantry by one Simon McMurtrie (mentioned earlier) who was found one day clearing dog turds deposited on the staircase of 54 Poland Street with the use of a credit card. The dog belonged to the future Mrs Michael Sissons.

courage in one hand if not two and got on with the job despite the growlings and grumblings as the sounds of warfare reverberated round the publishing world. It was interesting to note that over this period of time so many people who had appeared to be secure in their jobs, and indeed very good at them, became casualties*.

* Roll of Honour – victims of the amalgamations: Nigel Viney, Brian Perman, Nigel Hollis, Roland Grant, David Farrer, John Blackwell, Kate Gardiner, Lionel Foot, Bill Holden, Tom Rosenthal, Tim Manderson, Peter Grose, Beth Macdougall, Barley Alison, Serena Palmer. Some of these moved on, some retired, and the Grim Reaper claimed his fair share.

# CHAPTER IX

# *A Few Loose Ends*

*War is much too serious a thing to be left to military men.*

Talleyrand

I've called this chapter *Loose Ends* because there are certain sorts of cameo pieces that I wanted to include but couldn't quite guess where they should be put in the text. Rather than miss them out I decided to include them in the penultimate chapter which takes into account various other experiences, including those of entertaining and travel and hints at the fact that we might have found our saviour thanks to one Toby Buchan.

Whilst all the brawling and infighting was going on in Upper Grosvenor Street and ultimately in Michelin House, everybody got on with their jobs as best they could. I had one particular setback when Heinemann lost the whole of my mailing list which was one of the vital advantages that I had over a lot of my fellow publishers. Over thirty years I had built up and cared for a very sophisticated mail order list and we were selling, as we have seen before, large numbers of books direct to the customer. The loss of the mailing list was a disaster when trying to interest other publishers in the business. So we just got on with things. Books were continuing to flow into an increasingly uncertain market, full of confusion. Although we had sales conferences, one of them in Majorca, another at Blenheim Palace, another on Lake Windermere and one in Deal, the general momentum in the Heinemann/Octopus group seemed to have vanished. Frankly people were nervous about their jobs. There was no sort of leadership in evidence. Most of the people I knew and trusted were either retiring, being retired, or in some cases made redundant. Some even died.

Charles Pick, the much disliked chief director of the group, had his hands busy with intrigue.

It would be almost impossible to imagine, after what you have read, that I still had any energy or patience left. Once again Leo Cooper was on the market and this time there were fewer people than ever who were likely to snap up an unconsidered trifle such as my list with its track record of previous unsuitable attachments. To deliver the kiss of death obviously seems to have been my legacy. I was left once again on the lookout to see if, with one final shoulder to the wheel, I could last a little bit longer because I still had some very interesting projects to deal with. I should add though that at this stage the politics of the group became so confused that the only thing I could do is recommend again that you buy *British Book Publishing as a Business since the 1960s*. This, as I mentioned before, is published by the British Library and consists of a series of excellent essays by Eric de Bellaigue about the whole business of publishing politics. He gives a far clearer picture of the goings on than I could ever attempt.

A few words about literary agents and my relationship with them. Whilst never denying that they are sometimes necessary evils, I have to say that I had very little time for them, in both senses of that phrase. There is some point to having an agent if you start off successful, grow and develop and become an industry. For instance Jilly had no agent to start with for the first two or three years because trade followed the flag so to speak, but some people seem to think that it is absolutely essential to have an agent. Agents of course have got more wise to this recently and are tending now not to take on people at a whim or a fancy. More often than not they tend to pinch authors from other agents. Most of the bigger ones, such as Curtis Brown, A M Heath or Fraser & Dunlop, are fairly selective about who they choose to take on. I think it is a pity that agents aren't more adventurous. To this end if I wanted dealings with any of them I would tend to use the smaller individual operations. The one purpose I found agents had in my publishing days was that they were very useful for disposing of authors one didn't want to get involved with. Either that or they were useful in acting as a barrier between you and the cantankerous hack who doesn't think they are being given a fair deal. I suppose it is rather spiteful of me, but there have been occasions in the past where somebody has been such a nuisance that I have actually suggested to them that they go and help themselves to a literary agent. This would be knowing full well that the likelihood of Agent X taking them on was pretty remote. It at least gave them the opportunity though of referring to 'My Agent' rather like people refer to their solicitors.

Some authors, of course, are quite content to let their agents do all the hard grind, apart from writing the book. An example of a very successful relationship is given by Christopher Hibbert whose agent Bruce Hunter at David Higham Associates is tough but straight, efficient and creative. I have enormous respect for him. Quite a lot of the other one-man bands, much as one likes the idea of them, are no more than magnified post offices. There used to be a firm of family agents in London who were renowned for the eccentric way that they handled manuscripts. A manuscript would come in and they would claim to read it and send it off to anybody they could think of with a letter extolling its virtues. When it came back, as almost invariably it did, all that happened was the parcel was opened, the rejection slip or letter removed and a new label stuck on the front with a compliment slip and off it went to yet another publisher. I don't think they exist any more, but they were renowned for this manner of operation at the time. I always gave an author an opportunity of having an agent or taking one on, but I usually warned them that it was going to be even more difficult to get an agent to work hard than it was for a publisher to make an offer in the first place.

It is true to say, though, that a number of the smaller agents have actually got some purpose and I've had very good relationships with them on an individual basis. Today the market has changed and many of the jobs which were allegedly the province of the agent are now handled by publishers' rights departments which are growing in strength and this is, I think, the American influence being felt. The Americans, it seems to me, have a far greater respect for literary agents and they are a very much tougher bunch than you will ever find over here. One could learn a lot of lessons from them and one can pick up quite a lot of information by just talking to other authors who are thus agented in the USA.

I used to like one agent called Yuri Gabriel who was an Estonian. I don't know what happened to him, but I would have done business with him any day just to see a name like that on the letters. Also there is Laura Morris, who used to work with me at Secker and later on at Deutsch who has set up on her own and looks promising, as does John Beaton who recently started his agency working out of Scotland. Jane Gregory is another name to conjure with, a ball of fire.

My father, who was a writer, used to have a literary agent who shall remain nameless but he was very loyal to him. All the family hid when a letter from that agency arrived in the house because it was almost certainly going to be a rejection slip. This happened all too often towards the end of his career. When we were at home we were in the firing line. All in all I would say literary agents could and can be useful and indeed some of them are very jolly, but in principle if you are prepared to work your own patch you'd be far better off asking friends over a drink or doing the hard work yourself. It is perfectly true that first-time authors often regard their first contract as a minefield. It is also certainly true that quite a lot of the smaller publishers, and indeed some of the bigger ones, have very often offered contracts at an early stage (suspecting the author's innocence) that you could drive a bus through. It has happened in this household and I never cease to hear of examples and indeed have given friendly advice to people at the back door without necessarily making a song and dance about it. Agents are useful but only when all other efforts have been exhausted. There is one more alleyway which I do recommend and that is The Society of Authors who are always helpful, even if you are not a member.

Entertaining has always played a large part in my business life, as must be evident from these pages. We very seldom had a day in the week when we weren't having lunch with somebody or buying the drinks or chatting them up. This was as good a way as any of having one's ear to the ground, so to speak, which, considering our plight, was a must. On the edge of Soho we were blessed with many good restaurants, not to mention our friends the Karamanis and the excellent French restaurant Mon Plaisir and The Gay Hussar in Dean Street. There were plenty of sandwich bars, lots of pubs and it was very near the Garrick Club. We were very lucky to be in such a place and many of our sorrows were drowned in one or other of those establishments. Needless to say these encounters with authors and others were not without their humorous side. If we need some light relief, it might be of interest to hear a little about our entertaining policies or indeed the reputation we had for being very hospitable. Take parties for instance. 'Let's have a launch party,' says the author. My heart sinks. I am not against parties on the whole. Indeed I have spent a great deal of my life attending them or giving them, but one of the worst activities to be dragged into is that of giving an author a launch party when deep in your soul you know that it is a complete waste of time and money. One is having to contend with the absolute vanity problem. Nearly all authors think that by the time the book has reached fruition and is safely between bound covers, somehow the whole world is leaping up and down and getting excited about its forthcoming publication.

Of course we have given launch parties in our time and indeed attended a great many, but nothing quite beats the intransigence of authors who are determined, one way or another, to launch their books in what they regard as stylish fashion. My objection to these occasions was largely to do with cost. Just as most authors, or most writers, have absolutely no idea about the economics of publishing, so they have even less understanding of the nature of launch parties as long as you are giving them. To start with they are very expensive. Wherever you go, whatever venue you choose you are going to have to pay through the nose (you the publisher that is). It is quite pointless having a launch party unless you have been prepared to spend some money and indeed to be fair quite often authors do contribute or offer to. In the final analysis I know no better way of wasting £700 or £800 than giving a party for the author and his friends (all six of them) to celebrate a book which you know by the subscription (that's the number of copies ordered before publication) is not going to pay its way.

One advantage I had was that, owing to our military flavour, I was always absolutely certain of a decent venue. Based in London we had the Imperial War Museum, the National Army Museum, the Honourable Artillery Company, HMS *Belfast*, the Royal Hospital, the Cavalry Club and so on. This was never a problem and among the best people to deal with were always the IWM whose deputy director, Dr Christopher Dowling, is without doubt the best in London at giving parties for selected military people. The IWM were always incredibly kind to me and on many occasions allowed us to hold parties on their premises without making a charge. They benefited of course from the joint publicity, but it was such a good place to have a party that one realised it was worth a great deal more just to be seen to be pushing the boat out.

Apart from special parties which were given at the insistence of regiments and indeed very often paid for by those regiments, there were occasionally sad little episodes where one stood by the door with a bottle and a tray of drinks and very few people turned up. It didn't happen to us all that often and when it did it was usually when we'd warned an author that we couldn't guarantee much of a turnout. The way we played it was this. We opted at an early stage for giving what I might call corporate parties. We might seize on the publication of a particular book and say to the author that we were intending to launch it with some sort of celebration but we would like to include all the other authors on the list so that they could swell the numbers and in many cases act as professional guests as far as drinking was concerned.

To this end I suppose we must have given in our thirty-five to forty years of publishing something like twenty parties, many of them being more than memorable. We occasionally strayed out of London as well.

One of the parties I remember particularly was given at the Headquarters of the Liverpool Scottish in Liverpool to celebrate the publication of *Chavasse Double VC* who was one of only three men to win the Victoria Cross twice. There was a splendid turnout including the Bishop of Liverpool, Dr David Sheppard*, and, best of all, Chavasse's medals were escorted by rail all the way from Oxford (where they were billeted with his old college) to the HQ to be on display. To be in the presence of one VC is something one never forgets but in this case there were two, so to speak, if you count the bar to Chavasse's double. I was fortunate enough in several cases to come across a number of VC holders in my career. There was of course Brigadier Sir John Smyth and then there was Stan Hollis of the Green Howards whom I met in Leeds and alongside two naval VCs, Able Seaman Magennis and PO T W Gould. I myself was actually physically knocked down by a holder of the Victoria Cross. It was in my army days when I was an officer cadet. I was in the NAAFI Club in Aldershot and I had gone to relieve myself in the obvious place. As I turned to come out the door sprang open and knocked me absolutely flat on my back with my head in the urinal. A great dark figure loomed over me and the first thing I noticed was the ribbon of the Victoria Cross on his battle dress jacket. It was Private Speakman who was in as much of a hurry to get to the urinal as I had been. He picked me up and dusted me down and apologised profusely because of course it wasn't intentional and then we went and had a drink together. That at least was a fairly unusual experience.

We published another double VC biography. The subject Arthur Martin-Leake was the second doctor to win a VC twice, the first in the South African war and the second on the Western Front. He is buried in a grave in an unassuming little churchyard at Ware in Hertfordshire. We did in fact hold a launch party in Martin-Leake's old house which is only a few hundred yards from where he is buried facing the cemetery wall at the top of the churchyard. The only other holder of a double VC was Charles Upham, a New Zealander who won both his medals in the Second World War. He was an unassuming sheep farmer and a quiet, taciturn man, but alas, although we were just about to approach him, I never got to know him as he died about ten years ago.

Other great junkets that we've had to celebrate either regimental

* Ex-England cricketer.

138

histories or several books at a time were held at the Cavalry Club, an ideal location, the Honourable Artillery Company at Armoury House, the Royal Hospital in Chelsea where the Famous Regiment Series was launched, the Army & Navy Club (known as the Rag) and on several other occasions out of London one of them being in East Anglia for the Royal Anglian Regiment. This was the first of the amalgamated histories to be published. Several parties given at regimental head-quarters have faded from my memory. We were very lucky also, in most cases, to have been given facilities by the regiments themselves, not least the Foot Guards whose museum is an absolute must for parties and whose Officers' messes are well appointed. Certainly with the Grenadiers, the Scots Guards and the Coldstream we made the very best of these splendid surroundings.

It is difficult to say whether any of these junkets were worth it in the long run. I used the word 'vanity' earlier and with individual authors this was very much the case. Whilst happily watching another £700 or £800 go down the gullets of the press, I always felt in the back of my mind that the money would have been better spent on something else, but very often I couldn't think what that might be. Anyway, we did have a reputation for very jolly times. We had a full Gurkha band once for us at the Imperial War Museum. We had a brilliant little party at the National Book League to celebrate the publication of *Songs and Music of the Redcoats* where I, the publisher, performed part of the book by singing some early marching songs. We had a party aboard a submarine in the London docks and another at the Bovington Tank Museum. Also, when I was dealing with regimental histories I was frequently asked to dinner nights around the country as a thank you in many cases and as a familiarisation exercise just to make sure I was still going strong. These regimental dinners were tremendous fun and they took me back to my army days, particularly when one was given a bed for the night and woke up the following morning in the sparse cubicle that very often young subalterns were given to sleep in a strange officer's mess. Nothing had changed. Same smells, same noises, same bed and same tea.

Looking back on all this now I think I probably enjoyed the celebrations as much as anybody. The art of giving a good party is quite simply that you have got to be an electric host. You must meet people at the door, gate or tent. You must immediately guide them to a decent drink and introduce them at once to other people. You must do this time and again and then you must mix people up in the first hour. You must make absolutely certain that the people in the room know who you are, particularly if you are giving the party. I have been to so many occasions where other books have been launched and one walks into a room which is empty of familiar faces and there is nobody to greet you. I made an absolute science of hosting these occasions and I cannot emphasise enough the importance of being immediately available to everybody who comes through the door. That means not having a drink yourself until everybody's got not one but two or three inside them. You then take a bottle in each hand and you circulate the room making sure people's glasses are full. Always invariably they say 'No, no, no' and put a hand over their glass so you pour it through their fingers. After about half an hour you will find that no hand is put over the glass and the bearer of that vessel is seen approaching either the drinks table or you with the bottle in your hand. Even worse is when the author approaches with one in his. You know the flood gates are open. Things obviously tend to get rather more exciting later on, but there again you must be responsible for making sure that there is no trouble and also that your staff who usually hang back do the same sort of thing, i.e. go and mix people up. Everybody is shy on occasions like this. Those who aren't are probably bogus.

That is really all I have got to say about parties but I doubt very much whether I shall be seeing many more. I remember them with tenderness and they all merge into one great celebration.

Looking back at what I have written, I am horrified to note that virtually every episode in this book ends with some description of the consumption of alcohol in large quantities. If it is not parties it is drinks with authors; if it's not drinks with authors it's drinks with printers, binders, journalists, you name them. I am not ashamed of this. I wonder if I am alone in suggesting that it is an integral part of our make-up. I suppose I should be horrified because, when describing so many of my friends, I refer to their intake without necessarily referring to my own, but it certainly loosens the machinery and where we would have been without the odd bottle I simply don't know. Probably down in the basement among the empties with David Bruce, John Watson's partner.

Having started off with a sinking heart at the beginning of this section I now notice that my horror of parties seems to have changed to one of tacit approval when I look back on the number I have given. I missed an awful lot of them out because probably they are just as well not remembered, but I only hope that in confessing what I have, people reading this will understand what I am trying to get at. I am not, nor ever could be, a drawing-room publisher. I'd like to think I was hands on and if it is hands on the bottle that's just too bad.

## IF YOU . . .
(to be read in a voice redolent of pink gin and curry)

If you can write of hard-earned fame and glory;
Yet not complain when royalties don't come;
If you can make of REME a good story,
And when the Guards sell better, not be glum:
If you can wait, and not be tired of waiting,
For proofs that, when arrived, are badly set;
If you resist the drab delineating
Of every single general that you've met:

If you can hate the jacket and the binding,
And in that hatred still conceal distaste;
If you can find a scoop and, in its finding,
Be grateful that it does not go to waste;
If you can fill the unforgiven binder
With gin, and hear him in his fullest spate
This is your last, the ultimate, reminder,
And, which is more, we hope you'll make this date.

Thursday 17th April, 1980 at Services Bookshop,
196 Shaftesbury Avenue, London, W.C.2.

Drawing by Tim Jaques, doggerel by Major 'Buffy' ppoulkes-Hawses, late Indian Cavalry.

During the course of the years that I was running my own list I found very good reasons to visit the United States on a number of occasions and on one other occasion managed to wangle a trip to Australia with Jilly who was doing a round-the-cities tour to promote her book *Class*. This trip was paid for by Methuen who acted as our hosts down under and very kindly let me go along for the ride. Also, to be fair to Frederick Warne, because this offer came during their ownership, they offered to pay some of my expenses so that I could represent them in the book trade out there. We had a wonderful time, probably the best three weeks we've ever spent together in our lives, but it was not without its incidents.

But it was the USA that I found most interesting. My sort of publishing was not exactly fashionable over there, but we must remember that there are only three wars in previous history that we have not fought together, those being the Mexican war, the war in the Philippines and of course Vietnam. And you must not forget the one where we fought against them. I have a distant relation who got into a lot of trouble during the War of Independence. He was called the Reverend Miles Cooper and was the founder of Columbia University, New York. He was among other things a rather bad poet and here is one of his poems – 'An epitaph to oneself', e.g. himself.

> Here lies a Priest of English blood,
> Who, living, lik'd whate'er was good –
> Good company, good wine, good name;
> Yet never hunted after fame.
> But, as the first he still prefer'd,
> So here he chose to be interr'd;
> And unobserv'd from crowds withdrew,
> To rest among a chosen few;
> In humble hope, that Sovereign Love
> Will raise him to the best above.

I know he left America in a bit of a hurry on a British man of war but I am not entirely certain why. Perhaps it was his poetry.

I met some splendid characters in New York and Boston, among them Alan Williams of Viking Press and Jack Galaska, then of Scribners. Then there was an agent, Nat Sobel, a good friend. I did quite a lot of business with Sol Stein, but he was a slippery fellow. I remember one thing about Sol that makes me laugh. He gave a party at the Connaught where he always stayed when he came to London. He usually gave some sort of thrash and on this particular visit Jilly and I and Tom were all invited. Sol had pushed the boat out in a big way and allowed a large number of members of the publishing profession to be seen milling around the room. Unfortunately the penalty for this attendance was that you had to watch a mawkish film about Sol's office and how it worked. He was very flattered because the BBC had offered to send a camera crew to film the party and this they duly did. What they hadn't told him though was that they were doing a film about alcoholics and they could wrap it up in far less time by going to a publisher's party than going anywhere else. Sol was absolutely furious and sued them and won. Sol Stein and I published Charles Whiting together, but he no longer has a publishing firm and he became an author himself. He asked me one evening to his home, about an hour's drive or train journey from the centre of New York. It was somewhere up the Hudson River, I think. Several other British publishers were invited, including the late Desmond Briggs, who stupidly wrong footed many of the automobile wives who were meeting their husbands off the commuter train. He leapt off the train in an extravagant looking white suit and a large panama hat shouting 'Hello, dears,' and kissing me and Sol on the lips. Most embarrassing. Sol told me that you could always tell when they'd had English visitors in the garden because when they departed all the chairs were in a position facing the sun!

There is little comparison between my pathetic little outfit and the vast emporiums of the American publishing groups but they all gave me access, were courteous and in many cases did their very best to see if they could fit me up with some sort of deal. In the end I imported far more material from the States than I exported, but this was nice because it added another dimension to the list and I was very happy that so much cooperation was available. My thanks go out to Howard Karminski and his wife Susan, whom I have known for years, and then in Boston to my great friend Jay Williams, as she was (now Jay Howland), who used to work for Longmans and eventually Little Brown. I always left the States via Boston because it was such a civilised place. I used to stay in the Ritz Carlton Hotel for one reason alone. This was that it was the only hotel left as far as I know where if you leave your shoes outside the door they are not purloined. They came back, I'm happy to say, with a beautiful shine on them. It is so different, Boston, from New York and actually I did far more business with Little Brown and Houghton Mifflin than I did in New York. But I used to visit on a regular basis every couple of years and was always made welcome and I made a lot of friends who came over here and I was able to reciprocate very often asking them to dinner at home because people on long business trips tend to get lonely.

I found one thing about the Americans deeply irritating and that was their ingrained reluctance to reply to letters or indeed to write them at all. It is different today when you have email and all the electronics and everything else like that, but I did find it held matters up quite a lot so I used to resort to sending faxes rather than letters. I also made them carry the odd joke so that people who might not necessarily be familiar with me had some idea that there was a cheerful but needy soul at the dispatching end. If you pulled their legs it tended to work, but you had to pull very hard. Also they are very sensitive. I remember staying one weekend with Alan Williams down at Harvard in his lovely old, white, clapboard house. One of the many daughters of the house rushed into the kitchen where we were all sitting shouting 'Mommy, mommy, Donna [that was the dog] has gone to the bathroom in the living room.' Need I say more? Jilly included this in one of her articles about visiting New York and found that Alan was deeply upset by this reference. He was a man who I knew had a sense of humour, but it just shows how delicate you have to be. Another American agent who became a great friend was Nat Sobel – I had wonderful seminars with him when he used to pass through London. I wonder where he is now?

I mentioned earlier that Jilly and I made a trip to Australia under the aegis of Methuen, with a contribution from Frederick Warne. Neither of us had been to Australia before or had the slightest idea of what we were in for, although we knew a lot of people who lived there. They were mainly nannies or rather ex-nannies, but one or two people from the book trade as well. We were not really prepared for what happened, but the welcome held out by the Australians to us was just extraordinary. We managed to do every major city in Australia in the course of three weeks and that includes a visit to Darwin. We started with Brisbane and coincidences began there. We'd no sooner walked into our hotel room after flying for twenty-four hours or so when the telephone rang. I said something to Jilly like, 'My God they do start early don't they?' and I went to pick up the telephone. It wasn't a call for Jilly at all it was for me! My ex-warehouse man from Shaftesbury Avenue who had emigrated not once but twice was on the end of the telephone. He'd read in the papers that we were due to arrive and could he come round and have a drink and bring his father? Not only did he come with his father, he came with his wife and his brother and we then had a somewhat noisy reunion without them realising that neither Jilly nor I had been to bed at all for more than a day. It was in a way the right foot to get off on but actually the wrong foot. We never looked back. After that event we flew off to Sydney, Adelaide, Melbourne, Darwin and Perth, although not necessarily in that order. It included a visit to the Australian Booksellers' Conference which was not unlike that of the UK except that everybody wore shorts. However, the same grievances were aired – terms and deliveries.

In every city we went to old friends came out of the woodwork, some that I'd been at school with and many that I'd met at the Frankfurt Book Fair or through my twenty odd years, as it was then, in the publishing trade. Nothing could have been better organised than our trip. It included hardly any days off which was probably quite a good idea because if we had paused to think we would have dropped dead from exhaustion.

I heard a very funny story about a group of English publishers over in Melbourne for the Australian Booksellers' Conference which was on at the time that we were there. Simon Huntley from Thames & Hudson and a number of other English publishers hired a car for the day and decided to drive into the outback to have lunch. They solemnly put on their best suits and went in all innocence only to find that virtually every restaurant and pub was closed. The usual form is that when you go out to lunch outside the city you buy your own liquor because the licensing laws are such that there is no official drinking on Sundays. They drove for over 100 miles passing numerous cafés and bars on the way – all shut. In desperation they rolled up outside a suspicious looking shebeen (bar) and one of the English publishers got out and walked round a building because he could hear the noise of raucous laughter. The front of the building was empty. He knocked on the door and walked in. There was a deathly hush as large numbers of men with corks dangling from their hats turned to stare at him. 'I say,' he is alleged to have said. 'Can we get a decent lunch here?' There was a horrible silence and the voice from the back of the room said, 'Fucking Pommie C***'. The English publisher withdrew and remained unfed for the rest of the day.

I remember another episode when we were taken out of Melbourne on a Sunday to have lunch with the celebrated painter Clifton Pugh. Here I was introduced to a live wombat which sat comfortably on my knee and went to sleep. Later in the day I wasn't looking very carefully and the wombat's mother came wandering into the house. It was about the size of a small hippopotamus and I've never had such a fright in my life. There is a picture hanging in our hallway to this day of this small wombat asleep on my knee.

Jilly was writing a piece for the *Sunday Times* about our visit so she was playing two parts at every juncture. She did, however, have one unfortunate accident but this was more an intellectual one than anything physical. She was on some programme in the state of Victoria when she unfortunately let loose the 'f' word which apparently was the first time it had ever been heard on Australian television. The context was that she was quoting one of the children who said, 'Mummy says "pardon is a much worse word than fuck"'. This caused a sensation. The girl whose show it was was dismissed on the spot and it made headlines not in Australia so much as in the UK, where it was blazoned all over the tabloid press.

While Jilly was going around shocking people and being interviewed about the fact that there wasn't a class system in England or Australia, or there was, depending on how they felt that day, I took it upon myself to visit all the existing cricket grounds, although as it was May, the season had just finished. So I can say that I have been to the Gabba and to the MCG Oval and to Sydney and seen the Hill and the lovely ground at Adelaide, most beautiful of all I think.

There is no room to go on extolling the virtues of Australia. The nice thing has been that we made so many friends that it enabled us to send our children there in their gap years, as I believe they are called, to follow up our visit and they were welcomed with open arms wherever they went as are all Australians who came over here. There is a constant stream of them flowing through our house in Gloucestershire to this day. At this very moment I am also expecting a telephone call from an old school friend of mine who has just flown in from Australia and wants to pick up the pieces where we left off last time we met.

It is ironic that my two best school friends at Radley and the opening pair for the great Radley cricket XI of 1952 both emigrated to Australia. One was called John Waddilove and the other Christopher Walton, who captained Oxford and played cricket for Middlesex*. He told me a marvellous story about how it was that Bob Hawke, who eventually became Prime Minister of Australia, nearly managed to obtain a cricket blue. Actually Bob was a sort of honorary twelfth man in the Varsity Match. He had been, during the course of the cricket season in England, the owner of a Volkswagen van which was one of the few ways anyone could guarantee that the Oxford XI would ever turn up anywhere on time. The loan of his van and his constant attendance on Christopher Walton who was captaining Oxford was worth at least a half blue.

We met Bob Hawke in Australia. Jilly had an interview booked with him and we duly turned up (it was a Sunday) at his house outside

---

* I batted no. 6 in that team and only got nine innings in a season. One E R Dexter was the main reason!

Melbourne to find that he hadn't yet returned home from the races the previous day. This was before he was Prime Minister. He was currently running for the leadership of the Labour Party. We had just about given up any hope of him turning up when there was a noisy arrival outside the house and in burst Bob Hawke smelling overly of aftershave and looking like he'd spent the night in a wind tunnel. Mrs Hawke was not entirely pleased, but he nevertheless kept his date with Jilly and gave her a fascinating interview which was too hot to handle and was never actually published in the *Sunday Times*. Pity. I liked him a lot but I could see that problems were going to arise. To this day Mrs Hawke's remark to Jilly on the telephone is still quoted in our household of: 'He's not bek yit. He's still at the rices.' This is a euphemism we use frequently when somebody's not turned up on time – not back from the rices.

We eventually flew out of Darwin heading for Hong Kong. For me this was a particularly emotional visit because my mother's family had suffered under the Japanese during the war and my uncle had been on one of those prisoner of war ships (the *Lisbon Maru*) that was torpedoed by the Americans. I never knew him but I was able to visit the old house and the houses of various relations. My family were responsible, among other things, for helping to build the Peak Tramway, so some of our contribution is still in evidence. Everything else was lost. My Uncle Edmond eventually turned up at Kobe in Japan and was the first prisoner of war to die in the camp of natural causes. This is nothing to boast about, but I found his name on the memorial and that was better than nothing.

I loved Hong Kong (my mother was born there) and I wish I'd been able to see more of it, but we were off again the following day and never have two battered passengers descended from an aircraft with quite such groggy legs as we did, leaving behind a host of marvellous memories. Michael Turner, who was then running Methuen, took their Australian representative (called Bob something or other and over for a visit to London) to lunch at the Garrick Club. To start with, the Australian bookseller wasn't wearing a tie and was banned from entering until the porter produced one, then on being asked what he thought of the Garrick there was a long pause and he said, 'It could be improved by providing a few fruit machines.' There is the cultural difference. Anyway it was the experience of a lifetime and I think about it a lot even to this day.

Few accounts of a publishing career would be complete without some mention of the Frankfurt Book Fair. The space I am devoting to it here might seem out of proportion, but for me it was one of the most valuable experiences. It wasn't until I was working under my own steam that I actually managed to get there and my first visit was paid in company with Tom Hartman who was, like myself, totally ignorant of Germans, Germany and the language, despite having a name like Hartman*. This was emphasised by the fact that on one occasion I turned to Tom as we were motoring through Germany and said what an enormous place this town called Ausfahrt was; it seemed to go on forever. So did Eingang! I was unaware that I was commenting on the motorway exits as we sped into darkest Germany. We drove through the night because we hadn't got any hotel bookings and stopped at a wayside restaurant for breakfast. Here Tom came into his own for, having studied the menu for about half an hour, he finally put in an order which sent the waitress back into the kitchen laughing. Instead of ordering two boiled eggs he'd ordered two testicles. This was a very unusual beginning but one that set the tone.

When we got to Frankfurt the first thing to do was to try and find some sort of accommodation. Eventually we ended up in a hotel called the SVG which turned out to be the principal trade union hotel beloved of the *routiers* or their equivalent in Germany. Although there was a frontage to the hotel which suggested a degree of raffish elegance, in the back was the workman's café and the enormous car park which was frequently full of trucks, in turn full of young calves that mooed their way to death all night. Anyway, we were the first British publishers to slum it and our example was followed by quite a large number of the smaller firms who were finding it increasingly expensive to make their presence known at Frankfurt. We were very much trailblazers and I suppose we went on, over a period of twenty to thirty years, going there every year in one guise or another or under one umbrella or another.

When we did finally enter the exhibition hall I was already dazzled by the size, the buzz, the noise and the sight. And that was thirty years ago. I have watched the Fair grow and grow and I used to regard my visit as my annual holiday. This was because all my friends from overseas would be there and for a small publisher like myself it was a marvellous clearing house and I never came away from Frankfurt without having some deal or other in my pocket which had made it worthwhile.

It was the wild social scene, however, that attracted me. I have

---

* When we got to the border for the first time a somewhat cynical border guard said, as he thumbed through Tom's passport, 'Welcome home, Mr Hartman'.

always been very fond of most of my fellow publishers and this was the opportunity to have more than just a drink with them. We gathered friends like people gather nuts in May and we achieved a reputation for hospitality which constantly required us to put our hands in our pockets. We had, after a bit, seen this was a problem and did all our shopping in France on the way to Germany. This meant that we always had a large supply of liquor without having to pay the exorbitant prices that the Fair's management required. A glass of Sekt and a couple of Frankfurters cost a fortune. We instead had a cold box full of French pâtés, salamis, plenty of whisky, gin and vodka, and we made certain that this attracted people to our stand like bees to a honey pot. We usually gave an informal lunch on a couple of the days and people would come from all over the place, sometimes as many as thirty or forty so our supplies did not last very long.

I mentioned that we did our shopping in France and I always doubled up on the journey through France giving a tour of the battlefields to anybody who was coming with me. I usually took a secretary and sometimes one of the other junior staff to do the dogsbody stuff, but they had to endure a lecture on the battle of the Somme. Beryl not least became an expert on that particular battlefield tour. We stopped for lunch one day at a place called La Butte de Warlencourt which was a significant feature on the Somme battlefield. As we spread out our picnic at a deferential distance from the memorials I said to Beryl, 'All you have to do is to scrabble around with your foot in the soil and you'll find something metal.' Beryl then disappeared into France for ten minutes and came back holding half a 303 Lee Enfield Rifle less woodwork. 'Is this the sort of thing you mean?' she asked. Later on we found a lot of unexploded shells to which we gave a wide berth.

Very often the smarter publishers would earn their publicity by bringing over a distinguished writer to make a public appearance at the Fair, just showing off! Groupies like me, however, never can resist having a peek at somebody famous. Accordingly I can claim to have shaken hands at Frankfurt with the Japanese soldier who remained behind the lines for years in some distant Pacific Island after World War Two without realising it was over, Henry Kissinger, who needs no introduction, and Mohammed Ali, then called Cassius Clay. Another interesting contact I made was with a man who had been Hitler's valet, Heinz Linge, whose picture is on my study wall together with Hitler and Mussolini. You will see it if you turn to plate 38.

Another great contact was Herbert Walther. He'd been an officer in the Waffen SS and had taken part on the German side in the

Normandy landings. For many years after the war he was one of the chief executives at the Bundesarchiv and therefore to us military publishers an extremely useful contact because he knew where all the photographs were and indeed he knew where a lot of the Nazis were too. The thing about the pictures was interesting because up until fairly recently one was allowed to reproduce illustrations from the Bundesarchiv without permission and without paying under something called The Confiscation of Enemy Properties Act. This has now been stopped, but it was an extremely useful source of material at the time.

Herbert told me many stories of his military exploits and at one stage I had to lend him my bed in what was a single room. I slept on the floor and he slept in the bed but I remember watching him undress and when he was down to a pair of red y-fronts, I noticed that there was hardly a piece of his body that didn't have a hole straight through it or was not heading in the wrong direction; a human colander. He told me that he'd received most of these wounds riding a motorcycle and sidecar down a road with his officer sitting beside him. They'd got half-way down the road past a long column of tanks when Herbert suddenly realised that they were American tanks. Not only that but through the roof or lid of most of them appeared a large black man. Herbert had never seen a black man before and he didn't have much of a chance either because some of the tank men, spotting the sidecar, opened fire. They killed the officer and wounded Herbert badly. He, however, being a man of great intuition, crashed the bike, got out and dived over a bridge into a river. The trouble was it wasn't a river, it was a railway line and he awoke from unconsciousness some hours later to find a large black man hovering over him filling the wound in his head with ballast from the railway as a way of stopping the bleeding. He recovered in the USA as a prisoner. Herbert was truly a good friend and he was the author of a number of documentary books about the Waffen SS. Know thy enemy I suppose is the lesson, but I have always been eternally grateful to him for his help and understanding, not least his wit and hospitality, because he always came with a flask of schnapps, some beautiful women and tales of funny experiences. I don't know where he is now but certainly he can't have lasted all that long judging by the condition I found him in.

I suppose really the most valuable contact at Frankfurt was, or is, talking to the people from Australia and New Zealand and to a lesser extent Canada and the USA. There was a time when New Zealand was one of the biggest buyers of British books *per capita*, but this is no longer the case. Likewise Australia is now producing far more of its own books rather than importing everything from us. One gradually began to see the emphasis on trade shifting geographical markets. But apart from the one visit to Australia and the several visits to the USA the contacts with the rest of the Commonwealth were, particularly to me, worth their weight in gold.

After the day's events, which consisted usually of entertaining people or being entertained, we'd all go out for an evening on the town. I particularly enjoyed going to the beer hall round by the station where in the early days you got a lot of the refugees who'd remained in Germany after the war and were drowning their sorrows in buckets of beer. You also got quite a lot of German ex-servicemen with one arm, one leg and one eye and they were usually very vociferous; towards the end of the morning, and I mean morning (often 5 or 6am), they would call for marching songs and, with tears rolling down their cheeks, would suddenly become German again in all the wrong ways.

We had our fun though and this particular beer house is still going strong although I can never remember its name. I also remember a restaurant called Dippergucha, which was worth going to if only for the sound of its name.

The smart set hung out at the Frankfurter Hof or the Hessischer Hof or various other hotels such as the Marriott. If you knew your publishing field well, you'd make absolutely certain that you latched on to a rich publisher who would then buy you all drinks. Not least you could call on them at their hotel and hint that you might like to come up and sample their room service. People were very generous, particularly to the smaller publisher, and I remember with affection all the wonderful friendships which were made and cemented when attending the Fair.

My final memory doesn't show me in a very good light. I was having a shower in the hotel which we had now christened 'The Château Abattoir'. I went into the shower cubicle, shut the door and the handle fell off. I was locked in and all I had in my hands was a face flannel. Fortunately there was a window and, by soaping my body, I managed to slide through it and ended up on a pebbledash roof which was beginning to warm up from the heat of the early morning sun and which was under-laid with tar. I was still locked out of the building, totally naked, trying not to stick to the floor, within one hand a face flannel and in the other a door handle (the inside one). As there was a degree of to-ing and fro-ing on the floor below I eventually managed to contact a German lorry driver by doing a piece of mime with the door handle and flannel which reduced him to fits of laughter. I think he thought I was a lunatic. All of this was done to a cacophony of mooing from the calves that had spent all night in their lorries, and eventually a gaggle of fat lorry drivers looking up at me on the roof and pointing and laughing. Finally I convinced the management that I was in serious trouble and they came up and rescued me. They never forgot this and I remember for years afterwards I would walk in through the door on the first day of the Fair and the hotel staff would say almost to a man, 'Oh, not you again'. It seems trivial but it made us all laugh. Sadly the SVG is no longer. I rang up to book a final visit to the Fair and a voice said, 'Alas we will not be in business when you next are coming to Frankfurt. The hotel is being crashed.' By this I think they meant it was being pulled down and certainly when we drove past on our last visit it no longer existed, although I am sure a large number of small publishers will remember it with affection. It was about one third of the price of all the other Frankfurt hotels.

# CHAPTER X

## *Thumbnail Sketches*

*Lord Mountbatten also joined in the informalities,
shaking hands with every diner. No doubt he will
always remember ex-muleteer 'Tich' Fisher (late
38th of Foot) who, after dining most excellently
and swaying ever so slightly, with his eyes
streaming with emotion, shook the Admiral
warmly by the hand and said 'Good Old Monty'!*

Here are thumbnail sketches of some of the people who have walked (or staggered) through our doors, our many doors, over the years and an account of our relationship with them, not least where finance was concerned. They are not listed in any order of merit. They represent a sort of glorified index to some of the more exuberant or eccentric characters who appear earlier in the narrative. Just because somebody published by us during the time described is not included doesn't mean that they were any less well regarded than some who did make the list. Since most of my authors weren't actually professional writers, but rather more storytellers so to speak, I find it very difficult to make this selection as balanced as I would like. Those who wrote best were often the quietest and most unassuming people. They were usually modest. The noisy and less talented were much more fun and in many cases we did the writing for them. Some are only remembered for one thing, others for sustained eccentricity. However, when I used to sleep in my roll-down bed in the Shaftesbury Avenue flat, I would gaze up at all the books on the wall filed (allegedly) in alphabetical order. This represented all the books, one copy of each, that I'd ever published over the years. Gazing at the mute and serried rank of titles as they marched past my fevered brain, I suddenly realised that almost invariably there was more than one good story in every book. In the body of the work it is obvious, but invariably there was another story to be told about the author. There was seldom a contributor to the many books we published who didn't have something odd or peculiar about him (or her) or didn't behave in an odd way, or was just generally never to be forgotten, regardless of their book. This doesn't mean to say that I thought any less of the quiet or modest ones, but somebody like Birdie Smith, who was in fact a competent writer anyway, sticks in my mind as an example of what I mean. Not for his written work do I remember him but for being the man whose arm was amputated with a pen knife by the medical officer who was a fellow passenger in a crashed helicopter in Borneo.

Episodes like this alone can't be ignored so I have perhaps served up rather an idiosyncratic selection of characters. The whole tenor of this book has been, I hope, a chronicle of the somewhat eccentric relationships between the provider, i.e. the author, and the publisher. I do have to admit though that, in the research, most of which has been carried out in my head, I did occasionally come across books and authors which I had no recollection whatsoever of publishing. Frantic searches in backlists and catalogues quite often revealed that I had indeed published the books in question, but either circumstances attending to the quality of the writing or matters beyond my control meant that the book had died an obscure death, as has the odd author. There have always been venerable skeletons of contention between publishers and writers. Publishers seldom provide a comprehensive and accurate amount of information that an author would like to see and the authors resent this, quite simply as at least they should be allowed to know their earnings and the print number. In this department every publisher I know has to be an accomplished liar. Also these days, when sale or return is not only endemic but almost compulsory, it very often leads to confusion about how many books are actually sold as opposed to the number sent out to the shops and then returned.

All the bestseller lists can be taken with a pinch of salt and, rather like casualty lists in the First World War, with each nation offering its figures in a different way, the royalty statement or sale figures from one book publisher or another is bound to be confusing since not all the information is provided in the same way. Publishers are notoriously reticent about how many copies of a book they print. They often hide behind the fact that they are uncertain ('I'll look into it') which is another lie to start with. Not only that but they have to be careful to disguise the fact that some sub-rights deals were made at less than an advantageous price for the author, such as selling the book above 45% discount. This means that the whole royalty situation is in turmoil and the author is only paid a percentage of the net receipts, normally 10%.

Thus I hesitate to give any indication of the sort of sales that most of these books achieved, but in the specialist market it would be true to say that our average first print was 1,500 copies and if we were feeling cheerful 2,000, but also we had been in a situation in the past where we'd actually printed 10,000 and 25,000 copies of certain books*. Today, with the vast number of books hitting the shops every day, you are very lucky to sell into four figures an unknown author in a difficult market. For instance a book such as *A History of Landmines* is not going to become a bestseller. However, it's arguable that it was worth getting it out while the threat of these ghastly weapons still existed. My books really have a much longer life than is immediately apparent. This is borne out by the fact that a large number of them are now being reprinted by Pen & Sword and Spellmount with great success and they are enjoying an exposure to a market that they never had a chance of in earlier days. This was partly due to the difficulty of sales and distribution encountered by small publishers. Recently I put into a book auction a selection of duplicated titles and other file copies of books that I have published which I no longer needed. To my amazement they all sold as individual lots at sometimes twice the price of the original and in some cases three times. That points to the fact that the demand was always there, but one of my failings during the course of the years described was that my sales set-up was never good enough at the time. I hate to confess this but I don't think we were very good at selling.

## Lord Anglesey
Even if his name began with a 'Z', Lord Anglesey would appear at the top of this list as one of the most co-operative and delightful authors to deal with. Furthermore, he also became the most profitable in publishing terms over the years and has left behind more than a memorial to himself but to ourselves as well.

What began as a tentative venture, anticipating a four-volume work eventually ended up, thirty years after its conception, eight volumes long and the receiver of ecstatic reviews for all volumes, not to mention the award of the Templer Medal. This was of course the *History of the British Cavalry*. Since Lord Anglesey is referred to a great many times in this text I will not go into details of his life, although perhaps it is worth mentioning that he is the direct ancestor of the famous Lord Uxbridge who lost his leg at Waterloo. The completion of these eight volumes

---

* Our pricing policy was almost invariably 10x the unit cost and then see how it looked.

was, more than anything else, a triumph of great courage because during the middle of the publishing venture he suffered a severe motor accident and nearly lost his life. This added several years to the length of the programme and only a man of great strength and modesty could have handled the whole situation as well as he did.

Henry Anglesey was a delight to deal with on all fronts and he goes in at number one in the batting for us for all sorts of reasons, not just because he begins with 'A'. He was the pillar around which our edifice was built and he stayed until the last, giving us encouragement with great humour, tact and plenty of advice.

### John Attwood (Bombardier)

Although he doesn't feature in the text, everybody who has ever used Shaftesbury Avenue and the office there will have come across Bombardier Attwood at one time or another. A complete eccentric who might have been invented by Evelyn Waugh, he had a series of jobs, mainly prep school-mastering, and indeed had been expelled with some force from a number of them for a variety of reasons, but never for the most usual one. He was a fellow member of the HAC. He was loud, abrasive, funny and rather alarming. He used to live in the flat in Shaftesbury Avenue during the weekends when I wasn't there, but these visits had the habit of flowing over to the extent that some-times he was the only person in the office manning the telephone and this is where things would tend to go radically wrong. He also had the habit of washing his smalls in the bathroom and hanging them on the radiators to dry out, hence the office had a strangely acrid smell about it which people put down to a range of causes.

Attwood was also a cultured man, but there was something wrong with him, although I don't know quite what it was. He was well read and indeed his knowledge of London (to which he was a qualified guide) was much appreciated by Tom and they used to go church-crawling together. He was probably the most tactless person I have ever met in my life, but he had a heart of gold and he always took an interest, rather too much I fear, in the books that we published and on a number of occasions was found in deep discussion with an author on editorial matters, they not realising that he was not entirely *au fait* with the publishing process. In his declining years he became a sad figure, forlorn and lonely. He once had a packing job in a shop in Oxford Street and he said, 'I am now bottom man at Top Man'. He died not long ago and will be much missed by his fellow men from the HAC.

Mention cannot be made of Attwood without reference to one of his most famous escapades. He was at a TA weekend with C Battery HAC on Salisbury Plain. That night there was a leisure break and the Battery trooped into Salisbury in various vehicles. They were all dressed in HAC uniform. Very quickly someone, probably Attwood, spotted that there was a Conservative dance at the Town Hall. Several of the members of the company crashed the party before they were prevented from getting any further by the door keepers. Attwood witnessed this rejection and, together with my friend James Colquhoun, doubled round the back of the Town Hall and eventually saw a light in a first floor window which had a drainpipe leading up to it. Whilst James stood guard Attwood clambered up the pipe, managed to open the window and fell straight into the arms of a policewoman. He'd arrived in the ladies' lavatory. He was promptly arrested and heard the police lady talking on her radio saying that she'd got one suspect, because there had been a lot of burglaries from the cloakroom in the past, 'and what is more he had an accomplice called James,' she added. On being apprehended Attwood had just managed to shout, 'James, James, run, the police' before being arrested.

The ladies' lavatory was on the first floor landing and to get out and into the street with the policewoman, to whom he was manacled, required them to come down the steps and then across the dance floor. As they reached the edge of the dance floor Attwood said to the police lady, 'I don't think we can walk across; shall we dance?' The next thing we all saw was Attwood in the arms of a policewoman doing a gentle waltz across the ballroom and out through the front door. It was plain by now that this was an emergency and the couple were shortly followed to the police station by half C Battery HAC who tried to explain what had happened. In the end the police relented and saw the funny side, but I don't think any of us who were there had ever seen anything quite like Attwood and the policewoman as they pirouetted round the room.

Several other Attwood legends were forged during those years. On one occasion returning from Salisbury Plain with a 25 pdr gun on the back of his truck, he missed a turning and went straight through the vicarage wall and into the flower beds. Eventually the police sorted it all out. Some weeks later a similar incident took place and the policeman, who had a sense of humour, said, 'Bombardier Attwood please 'ave the next one off our patch'. This hadn't prevented Attwood getting down from the driver's cab after he'd gone through the wall and asking the vicar's daughter out to dinner. He was full of tricks like this.*

* One of the legendary episodes recorded in the annals of the HAC was that of Gunner Price who turned right at a level crossing with a 25pdr and limber.

On one other evening at the Bisley Hut, which was our TA headquarters in Surrey that weekend, we were all playing strip poker and the word had gone round 'Get Attwood'. Every time he lost an item of clothing it was removed from him and eventually thrown onto the roaring fire which was in the main room. Since everybody was gunning up on him, to borrow the phrase, he soon became clothesless. Everybody then went to bed. It was about 2 o'clock in the morning. The next morning on muster parade one was horrified to see Attwood in the front rank standing to attention wearing nothing but his boots. Brian Davies, our Battery Commander, who was inspecting us for the morning activities hardly batted an eyelid. As he passed Attwood he said, 'Boots need a clean, Attwood'. Of such things are legends made.

### Anthony Babington

Judge Babington was a truly remarkable man. Severely wounded in Holland in June 1944, fighting with the British forces, he had half his head blown away. This, the medics told him, would mean that he would never be able to talk again and certainly he had no hope of being called to the Bar or indeed of living an active life. I first read his book *No Memorial*, which had been published several years earlier and had won the Heinemann award for literature. When I had finished reading it I burst into tears. I had to republish it and I did. It told the story of how he fought back after the dismal prognosis and eventually learnt to speak again and to recover the use of his limbs and how he passed his Bar examinations and became a popular and well liked judge on the circuit*. Subsequently he wrote two more books for me, the most famous being *For The Sake of Example* which was about the execution of soldiers for cowardice during the First World War. There is a curious story attached to this book.

When I linked up finally with Barnsley, of which more later, I found they had in print a book on the same subject called *Shot at Dawn* by Julian Putkowski and Julian Sykes, but, unlike my book, which Judge Babington and I had decided would not name any names, their book contained a complete list of all those executed for cowardice.** In other words we had one title which gave no names and another title which gave all the names. There was nothing I could do about it. The books complemented each other but in a friendly fashion and the subject was

---

* He used to instruct his jurors when he was sitting at Knightsbridge Crown Court to go out and buy his books from Harrods in the lunch hour.
** A full list of names had been in an open file in the public record files at Kew all the time under our noses.

brought once again to the attention of the British public who are constantly lobbying their members of parliament to have the court martials declared null and void and a pardon made available to those shot for cowardice. It is a minefield, but I am grateful to Judge Babington for introducing me to not only that subject but to a number of others including his book *Shellshock*. Judge Babington, a fellow member of the Garrick, is a marvellous example to all of us. To say that he was courageous after what he went through is putting it mildly and his intensely moving book *No Memorial* is a classic of its kind. He was also the author of *The Devil to Pay*, another book on the Connaught Rangers mutiny. He died in 2003.

### Derek Bond

An unusual POW story is told by the actor Derek Bond who was captured in the desert and shipped up to Italy. He tells about his adventures in a POW camp in his book, *Steady Old Man, Don't You Know There is a War on?* The great irony of his story is that when he was eventually liberated and returned to England he took up his career as an actor again and the first role he was offered was set in a prisoner of war camp. Within six weeks of the ending of the war he found himself behind bars again and playing the role in the very famous film, *The Captive Heart*. Derek, whose picture is in this book, and his other POW friends, meet now and again for a reunion. They seem to have worn very well.

### Alex Bowlby

Alex Bowlby came to me as a result of a famous article described at the beginning of this book about my setting up a military imprint. He had written a book called *The Recollections of Rifleman Bowlby*\* about his service as a gentleman ranker first in the desert and later on in Italy where he saw some desperate fighting. He was certainly damaged spiritually by what he saw and I think still is to this day a victim of shellshock. Nevertheless, he had written a classic of its kind. It has seldom been out of print. To say that Alex was eccentric is putting it mildly, but he had a heart of gold and was a very generous man. He had curiously enough been at school at Radley which he had not enjoyed, but I felt there was a bond between us and I still regard the *Recollections* as one of the best books I have ever published. Although we have not a lot in common any longer, I see him from time to time

---

\* Curiously enough I had read this manuscript when I was at Longmans; they rejected it.

and I did publish two others books by him which were not quite so successful, and then a book about the battle of Cassino which was a valuable piece of history. We sold it in the States as well.

## Brigadier Calvert ('Mad Mike') DSO, MC

I first met Mike Calvert when I offered to reprint *Prisoners of Hope*, in which he tells the story of the first Chindit expedition behind the Japanese lines in Burma. As such it has become one of the classics of military history and Brigadier Calvert himself one of the enigmas.

'Mad Mike', as he was known to the public, was a man of many parts. Some of them were dark and uncontrollable. Others were sheer brilliance, with an ability to earn the respect of his men. He was a sensible, intelligent and responsible operator. He and I formed an instant friendship which developed over the years and ended up shortly before his death with our publishing *Mad Mike* which was really all that had been left unsaid after his own book but with a little bit more thrown in. Many people know the story of Mike's fall from grace and his homosexuality, so there is no point in repeating it here, except to say that in his final months he talked to me quite a lot about it and I let him ramble on. In the end I was left without very much more information than I'd started with. He did, however, tell me one unforgettable story.

We went out for a drink together. He was going through one of his abstemious phases and he explained how these phases came and went. One day he found himself in the Travellers' Club in the depths of depression. He'd started drinking again and he'd lost all his friends and nearly all his money. He decided to end it all. Later that evening he somehow or other hid himself in the Club without being discovered and managed to acquire a full bottle of whisky and a complete tube of aspirins or some such analgesic. At night after the lights had all gone out, he crept through a back door into the garden and over a period of about forty-five minutes to an hour he consumed the whole bottle of whisky and all the aspirins. He lay down under a laurel bush. If that didn't do the trick, he said to himself, nothing would. Next morning shafts of sunlight came beaming through the laurel leaves and woke him. He'd had a good night's sleep and he felt absolutely splendid. Beside him there lay an empty bottle of whisky and an empty aspirin tube. He got up, walked back into the Club, asked the porter to unlock the door for him and disappeared into London. That's the last time, he said, that he tried anything like that. But it tells you something more about the man than how depressed he must have been. He must have had the constitution of an ox.

He told me another story which happened some time after the Travellers' Club episode. He was doing menial work in Australia of all places, which shows how low he had sunk. He was apparently labouring on the docks. Someone got to hear of this and reported it to Bill Slim, Calvert's old Commanding Officer in Burma. Bill was, of course, by then Governor General of Australia. Learning what the situation was he immediately sent two equerries down to the docks to locate Mike and they smuggled him into Government House and there he stayed for a fortnight being dried out, washed and clothed and talked to, not lectured, by the great Bill Slim. Again someone had rescued him from the brink. At that time he also had another idea up his sleeve, which was to write an autobiography called *On the Grog*. This, however, never came to fruition, thank God, otherwise it would have really ruined his slender reputation post war. Apart from helping him with the *Mad Mike* book, I was also instrumental in arranging for his medals to be auctioned. He was desperately in need of money and it was arranged that somebody who shall remain nameless would bid for them. He was not at that time allowed to wear them, so it was academic in many ways. They went for a tidy sum and it was all over the newspapers. Alas, however tidy the sum, it didn't last long and Mike ended his days as a rambling mess in the Charterhouse Hospital where he was looked after by people used to dealing with such suffering. To me he was an inspiring man. He was very kind to me and to Jilly when we met and was full of anecdotes, although sometimes he tended to cry. Of all the people I have come across in my time I rate him as one of the most interesting and certainly one of the most charismatic. His homosexuality was a tragedy and, knowing the full story as I do, I can only bless the day that I met him and I only remember the good things about him. He was cruelly treated by the military. He was framed – there is no doubt.

### Tim Carew MC

Tim Carew, one of my first partners, was an accident waiting to happen. Almost invariably he got things wrong or got muddled or just quite simply did something ridiculous. A high spot of his career, apart from winning the MC at the battle of Imphal (where he was wounded in the buttocks), was an occasion in the Oporto pub when he had come up to collect his weekly stipend. He used to smoke cigarettes like all ex-rankers used to i.e. with two fingers with the light turned into the palm and he would suck greedily at the last remaining vestiges of tobacco before flicking the dog-end into the nearest receptacle. On this occasion he was smoking in quite such a manner and had just accepted a second large gin and tonic, one of which he was still holding in his hand. The tonic for the second he had lodged in his upper left-hand breast pocket where he normally would have kept a silk handkerchief. Arriving at the end of his butt he leant towards the open door of the pub to flick the dog-end out into the street. Unfortunately it missed. It went to the right of the doorway, right down the front of a very pretty girl in a low cut dress who was sitting next to the door. Not only did it go down her bosom but Tim, having immediately seen what had happened, rushed towards her to try and retrieve the burning object whereupon the tonic that he had planted in his pocket gushed out all over the girl and whilst putting out the cigarette (which it certainly did) ruined her dress and reduced her to tears and the rest of the pub to hysterical laughter. Fortunately the landlord's wife had seen what had happened and the victim was taken up to the flat to be redressed and came down to a round of applause but I have never forgotten that piece of management by Tim. An entertainer could never have invented such 'business'. I think it was the gushing tonic from the tunic pocket that did it.

On another occasion Tim was sent by *The Daily Express* to cover the return of the Canadian veterans (from the Dieppe campaign) of the Second World War. It was the first return officially organised from Canada and Tim was sent to cover it. At 6.30am, having enjoyed a boozy night on board the ferry, he staggered down the gangplank and hailed a taxi, saying 'Hotel Oceanique, please'. The driver of the taxi looked aghast at him and didn't say a word. Tim repeated himself 'Hotel Oceanique.' The driver shrugged. Tim was getting rather annoyed. 'I have said Hotel Oceanique, surely that is good enough for you,' he said. The driver, realising he had met an implacable enemy, gestured for Tim to get in and slammed the door. He then did a U-turn and stopped. Tim was able to read above the doorway of the building which was 100 yards away from where he'd hailed the taxi – Hotel Oceanique. No need to say anymore.

Apart from his various activities on the battlefield Tim was a member of the 'Experimental Stick' which was the original training wing of the Parachute Regiment based at Ringway near Manchester. He achieved his parachute wings with very few jumps and was lucky really to have survived for as long as he did because their early jumps were carried out by letting themselves down through a hole in the floor of a Whitley Bomber.

### Charles Carrington

I published Charles Carrington's book, *Soldier at Bomber Command*, because I found the subject of enormous interest myself. Charles was getting on in years when I came to him. His memory was fading but he had during the last period of the Second World War the opportunity, given to him by the MOD office, to be an inspector and interpreter of the effects of bombing on the German cities during and after the war. He was chiefly known for his own memoirs *Soldiers from the War Returning* which was one of the classic memoirs of World War One. His later book is about the investigation of bomb damage and is interesting because it actually proves that not half as much damage was done overall as the RAF claimed. This, however, makes no difference to the fact that RAF aircrew suffered over 57,000 (killed) casualties in the course of the war as did the American Air Force whose loss figure was almost exactly the same.

### John Colvin CMG

John Colvin came to us in a roundabout way which I can't remember, but he is not the sort of person you would forget easily. He had been the British Ambassador in North Vietnam and in Ulan Bator during the course of his diplomatic career, but what makes me put him on this thumbnail list is that he wrote a book about the battle of Kohima called *Not Ordinary Men*. This was a superb account of the battle. It became very much required reading for anybody with an interest in military history and it is now, I understand, in its third or fourth edition. It was a terrible battle and probably deserves its place as one of the greatest feats of arms of the British Army during the Second World War. Not all my geese turned into swans but this one did. John Colvin died recently.

### Dennis Dobson

A publisher by instinct, although not a particularly well organised one, Dennis Dobson founded a small firm publishing mainly children's books which operated from his flat somewhere in South London. He was notorious for failing to provide decent accounting dates, or indeed pay royalties if they were due. One day an author got so fed up with this that he marched down to Dennis' office and stormed into the room in which Dennis was on the telephone engaged in deep conversation. Having waited ten minutes the conversation still droned on and another phone rang on the desk so Dobson answered it whilst still keeping the other one on the boil. He dodged between the two calls and finally put one of the telephones down but on the wrong hook. This needed some unravelling but eventually he got one conversation going and just as that happened the other telephone rang again. The author could no longer take this. He picked up a manuscript which by good chance was sitting on the desk and began tearing it up in front of the publisher. This had the desired effect. Without finishing the telephone call Dobson said out of the side of his mouth, 'Now how much is it we owe you?' That is publishing for you!

## Christopher Duffy

Christopher is a well known and successful military history writer. At the time I worked with him on two books on *Borodino* and *Austerlitz* he was a visiting lecturer at Sandhurst. He invited me to attend one of their dinners and I duly rolled up at the Academy for drinks togged up in my dinner jacket. Since we managed to get changed fairly quickly, we had twenty-five minutes or so before we were due at the reception. Christopher then proceeded to show me how one of the cannons standing outside his quarter could be made to operate. Some 200 yards away in a field there was a donkey. We turned the cannon round and Christopher had a mixture of some sort of explosive which was loaded into the cannon followed by a tennis ball. This was then aimed at the donkey. The fuse was lit and we retired to a respectable distance. There was a loud bang and the tennis ball got a direct hit on the donkey which remained static. No need to say anything more about that episode. Curiously enough I had witnessed a similar scene once on one of my TA weekends where at a camp in Bedfordshire we found another similar type of field artillery piece outside the officers' mess. There was also a croquet lawn near by. Somebody had managed to obtain several thunder flashes and towards the end of the evening we decided to have a go at seeing if we could make the cannon work with one of the croquet balls. We succeeded rather more quickly than we had anticipated. The croquet ball went soaring over a playing field and straight through the bedroom window of a police sergeant who happened to be on night duty and was therefore still asleep. We had to do an awful lot of talking to get out of that one. Another good trick was to get hold of crow scarers and put them under a bucket where they exploded at regular intervals. No one ever finds the bucket in time.

## John Elwyn-Jones

John Elwyn-Jones totted up quite a record of escapes. His book was called *At the Fifth Attempt*. Indeed he did try to escape five times but this disguises the fact that in the middle of his incarceration somewhere in Germany he fell in love through the wire with a German girl and actually managed to break out of the prison camp to go and see her and get married. Such a dramatic relationship did not end in joy. He moved on. Few people, I suspect, had as many goes at

**44.** A motorcycle combination of the kind by which Herbert Walter was shot up.

**45.** Herbert Walter.

**46.** Herbert Walter
in his SS uniform.

**47.** Two old comrades – Leo Cooper and Robin Ray (40 years on).

**48.** The author with Beria's mistress The Red Spy.

**50.** Herbert Walter, the author, Mrs Walter and Laura Cooper (the author's daughter) at the Frankfurt Book Fair.

**49.** 196 Shaftesbury Avenue.

**51.** General Jack Evvets.

**52.** Bill Griffiths in action at Eton.

**53.** The hastily cobbled together party photograph for Cecil Lewis after the BBC had discovered that he was still alive. Michael Checkland is seated to his left.

**55.** Charles Whiting.

**54.** Doddy at last tastes freedom.

**56.** The indefatigable Beryl.

**57.** Tony Davis (third left, back row) and his escape party.

**58.** Publishers Cricket XI –v – The Times. Back row – Richard Tompkins; TM Jacques; John Charlton; Nigel Hollis; Bill Neill-Hall; Christopher Falkus; Richard Johnson; David Lines; Keith Lilly. Seated – Bruce Coward; John Letts, Erick Hiscock; Leo Cooper; Jeremy Hadfield.

**59.** The moment of rescue – *The Sederhana Johannis* meets a freighter and her fate.

**60.** The sinking of *The Sederhana Johannis*.

**61a.** The Derek Bond POW Set, *(left to right)* Captain Joshua Rowley, Captain Jasper Grinley, Captain Peter Langdon-Davies, Captain Rupert Woolcombe, Captain Derek Bond.

**61b.** The Derek Bond POW Set a little later!

**62.** The author making 126 for the Honourable Artillery Company against the Royal Artillery at Armoury House.

**63.** At the Supply Point, Neyri.

**64.** Bombardier Attwood on duty.

**65.** Ian Irvine.

**66.** The author *(left)*, John Waddilove *(centre)* and Christopher Walton *(right)* – the Radley Cricketers in Sydney, Australia.

breaching the defences of a prisoner of war camp as he did. He wrote his memoirs which were originally published in Welsh and I published the English edition with a Welsh foreword.

## Michael Glover MC

Of the many distinguished writers who appeared on the list during these years Michael Glover probably took the lead. Alas no longer with us, he produced a string of marvellously written books, many of them about Wellington and the Peninsular War and he wrote like an angel. Probably the crowning of his career was the official regimental history of the Royal Welch Fusiliers called *That Astonishing Infantry*. I remember him though for other reasons. He fought in Italy where he won the MC 'crossing the Rubicon' as he described it and was later captured by the Germans. He had a long-standing love affair with a girl whom he hoped to come marching home to and indeed he did and they were duly married*. He then worked at the British Council for a number of years but was meanwhile establishing a good reputation as a military historian.

There was one episode, however, that I always remember. We were sitting in the office one day when there was a noise on the staircase and in rushed Michael – flushed and obviously in great distress. He had been working in the London Library across St James's Square from the Libyan Embassy where, if you remember, there was a siege and a policewoman was shot by the inhabitants of the Embassy. The incident had been taken in by Michael who of course was used to the sound of shots fired in anger and this had brought home to him again the horrors. He was in a terribly distressed state. We managed to calm him down and I am reminded of that episode every time I pass through St James's Square by a little memorial to WPC Fletcher, who was killed by the sniper. The point about this anecdote is that it was the first time that I'd seen somebody genuinely frightened and almost as if he felt that the bullets were aimed at him. Having been shot at myself I quite understood Michael's reaction. Here is the announcement of the episode as it came through on the tapes.

*1984: Libyan Embassy shots kill policewoman*

A police officer has been killed and ten people injured after shots were fired from the Libyan People's Bureau in central London.

---

* There is an unpublished account of his courtship of Daphne. Someone ought to publish it – it is very moving.

WPC Yvonne Fletcher had been helping control a small demonstration outside the embassy when automatic gunfire came from outside.

She received a fatal stomach wound and some of the demonstrators were also severely injured.

WPC Fletcher, 25, died soon afterwards at Westminster Hospital.

Her fiancé, another police officer, who was also at the demonstration, was at her side.

After the shooting people were cleared from surrounding offices in St James' Square.

Some had witnessed events from their workplace.

Film maker Ray Barker said people were stunned by what had happened. 'Several of my colleagues burst into tears. It was unbelievable that sort of thing could happened at such an insignificant demonstration,' he said.

*Marksmen*

Journalist Brian Cartmell was in St James' Square just feet away from Yvonne Fletcher when she was hit.

'She crumpled to the floor clutching her lower stomach and groin and rolled on to her right-hand side with a look of total surprise on her pretty face,' Mr Cartmell said.

The Libyan building is now surrounded by armed police officers including specialist marksmen.

However, Home Secretary Leon Brittan has said the police are prepared to wait and deal with the situation in a peaceful way.

Police officers are in touch with those inside the Libyan People's Bureau via a special telephone link.

The Libyans, led by Colonel Gaddafi, are blaming Britain's police and security forces for 'attacking' their embassy.

Libyan soldiers have now surrounded Britain's embassy in Tripoli trapping 18 diplomats.

## Billy Griffiths

The bravest man I ever met was Billy Griffiths. Serving in the Royal Air Force as an 'erk' in the early days of the Anglo-Japanese war in Singapore, he was given the task, after having been captured by the Japanese, of helping to clear an airfield and humping spent and volatile ammunition into a dump which was going to be destroyed. Unfortunately, one of the loads he was carrying blew up, blowing him almost totally to smithereens. He lost both his eyes and both his hands. He was given up for dead by everybody but there was little chance that Billy was going to let them get away with it. He survived with the help of one of the most remarkable wartime surgeons, the Australian 'Weary Dunlop'. With skin grafts and ingenious operations, carried out with home-made instruments, he saved Billy's life and gradually repaired him. The Japanese couldn't understand this, life being not so precious to them, and they would come up to him and say 'Why you no die?' Well he didn't. He survived despite all the tribulations and on his return to the UK made a success of his family business, which was transport, up in the north of England. He became a major celebrity, fronting many of St Dunstan's promotional activities. There is a picture in the book of him addressing the boys of Eton. He was, and still is, an utterly delightful man with a wonderful wife whose devotion to Bill knows no bounds. An example will show you what I mean.

They were in a cathedral town not long ago where he had been giving a talk and he was suddenly taken short in the street. Fortunately his wife spotted a policeman on the other side of the road standing, would you believe it, next door to a public convenience. She very quickly explained to the policeman what the problem was and the PC nodded and escorted Billy down into the depths of the urinal. He didn't appear for about five minutes but she didn't think that was unusual. A further five minutes passed. No sign of Billy. Finally plucking up her courage she went down to the gents and there the horrible sight of Billy Griffiths cradling the policeman, who was unconscious in his arms. The policeman unfortunately had not realised that there was more to having a pee than just going down to the urinal and that he had been expected to do all the attendant services. It was at this stage it was that the policeman fainted. I think that is a lovely story and Billy never ceases to tell it and it still doesn't seem stale.

He really is a wonderful man. He has met everybody you can think of and more. He goes swimming, he gives lectures, he can sing and as an example of human courage in the face of adversity I do not know of anyone who has quite so bravely faced up to the deprivations that he suffered. His memoirs were published under the title *Blind to Misfortune*.

### Sir Stephen Hastings MC
I first met Sir Stephen Hastings when he was a member of parliament and a confidant of Mrs Thatcher. It was during the time of the Frolik affair, about which I wrote earlier, and it was plainly obvious that Sir Stephen was of the security services. Working as he was on behalf of Mrs Thatcher he asked me to come and see him on the strength of the fact that I had been introduced to Joe Frolik and could I give him any information at all which might be used by Mrs Thatcher in her campaign for the leadership of the Tory party? In other words they were looking for dirt on the Labour Party and the Unions. There wasn't a lot I could do but I remember being invited to his flat near the Albert Hall and I remember the beautiful paintings on the walls and this eventually led, some years later, to my being offered his auto-biography, *The Drums of Memory* and I am glad to say that the book was a success. He was a force for good and knew a lot about horse racing. He died as this book went to press.

### The Holts
Among the most unusual and delightful people to deal with on the publishing scene who go back to 1985 are the Holts and their battlefield tours. Tonie and Valmai had come to me when I was at the Heinemann part of my career. They had written one or two not particularly interesting books but had some ideas for battlefield tours which has always been of interest to me. They produced material for a couple of pamphlets which ran to about sixteen pages each, wire stitched. I liked the idea enormously because I had learnt much in the previous years and indeed had visited, very often with friends, battlefields in northern France. There was, it seemed to me, potentially a market, as the geography of France became more available to the day tripper and the continued interest in military history made itself apparent. I cannot say that they received a very good reception when I put forward the proposal and Tim Manderson at Heinemann, the

sales director and a man whom I respect enormously, said that he thought they were a complete waste of time and would never catch on. I am glad to say how wrong he was.

The Holts (Tonie & Valmai), who insisted on calling themselves by their rightful names, much to my regret, were known in the office as *The Hairdresser's Guide to the Battlefields* which was perhaps rather unfair. However, they began to expand their activities and put together more comprehensive and better researched battlefield tours. They now head the market. Their books on the Somme, Ypres, Normandy, Gallipoli and Arnhem are acknowledged as the absolute top of the battlefield tour market*. There was of course a stage when they conducted the tours themselves, but they sold the tour business and stuck to producing these quite simply remarkably good books. Writing now some years after they began, I can say that they are being marketed in the best possible way by the Holts in conjunction with Pen & Sword Books and I am happy to say that they contribute greatly to the enormously increased turnover that the tour market has achieved. They have also produced a number of other excellent First World War books, not least one about the efforts of Kipling to try and locate his Irish Guards son's grave which he eventually did. They also produced an excellent book on the war poets and continue to be lively and highly professional, not least in the excellent maps that they design to go with their texts. I am very proud that I was in on the ground floor of the operation and even prouder still that the dismal Jimmies were proved wrong.

### Lieutenant General Sir Brian Horrocks KCB, KBE, DSO, MC, LLD (Hon)

Of all the people that we dealt with during our business years no one could have been more helpful and charming than Brian Horrocks. As I mentioned earlier in the book I picked him up as a result of his battle series on HTV which immediately led me to believe that we could translate a form of them into books. It was the beginning of the Famous Regiment series. He eagerly accepted the idea and some twenty years later we could look back and see that there were over sixty regiments to which he had contributed a knowledgeable introduction. One only had to mention the name of a regiment and he would immediately come out with some story about it off the cuff. He was a delight to deal with and made us feel extremely important.

His nickname in the army was 'Old Plausible' and he did use his

* Guide to the Western Front – North is just printed

charm to great effect, but he knew his stuff and his staff. The interesting thing about him is that he never really did any regimental soldiering. He joined the Middlesex Regiment at the beginning of the First World War but was very quickly sent into action and was promptly captured by the Germans. At the end of that war he was made a prisoner of war in White Russia and when he got back to the UK, after having been in prison for some considerable time, five years in fact, he promptly moved on to the Staff College in Camberley. He became a champion expert of the modern pentathlon and was eventually posted to the 9th Battalion TA of his regiment (where he learnt all about the Territorial Army). Later he went on to command 13 Corps in the Desert War where he was wounded and eventually ended up spearheading the ride into Brussels with 30 Corps. In fact he only ever soldiered as an ordinary infantryman for six weeks. His father was a very distinguished army doctor who invented, among other things, a device known as the Horrocks box which was a machine for purifying water. Had this been available during the Boer War it could have saved thousands of lives because in that conflict disease accounted for two thirds of the casualties – most of them coming from contaminated water.

Anyway, Horrocks was an enchanting man to deal with and was a fund of marvellous military stories. He once told me that his most bitter regret was failing to make the rescue of the parachute divisions beleaguered in Arnhem and his failure to realise he was heading towards Arnhem on a one-vehicle front on a very narrow road where the verges were mined. He said it haunted him to that very day and I can understand that because he used to get very emotional talking about it. He was a splendid soldier and he always had the interests of his men at heart. At one stage he rather trod on people's toes by suggesting that some form of official brothel be set up in occupied Germany because the troops were getting too randy. This was frowned on by HQ back in London and he scored very bad marks for that.

He later became a director of Bovis, the builders, and is renowned for a public feud fought out between himself and General Templer. Horrocks, as a director of Bovis, wanted to build a single-storey National Army Museum in Chelsea and top it up with several floors of flats. Templer, on the other hand, did not like this idea of property development and wanted all the space to be devoted to the National Army Museum alone. In the end Templer got his way and Horrocks was not able to find more work for Bovis. They clashed frequently and at one stage the story leaked out that Horrocks had made some indiscreet remarks that Templer was the only man he knew who had been wounded in the war by a grand piano. This was true. What had happened was that a convoy of the staff of one of the units moving up the body of Italy came across a piano in an empty villa and lifted it. The next day they put it in a 3-ton truck and it was driving up the road followed by General Templer in his jeep when it hit a landmine which blew the cover off the lorry and the piano sailed gracefully through the air landing on General Templer in the following jeep, putting him off games for some months. It should be added though that Horrocks himself received a rather unusual injury when he was fighting in the desert with 13 Corps. A spent Ack Ack shell landed on his chest, went straight through his body and out through his anus. He used to say that it was the best enema a man could wish for. He was a hero to me and to many others and I am eternally grateful for the way that he looked after us.

### Sir George ('Loopy') Kennard
I include Loopy Kennard because you can't leave him out of anything. He was an eccentric cavalry officer and commanded his own regiment, The 4th Hussars, which he loved more dearly than all of his family put together. He wrote on spec an incredibly funny autobiography called *Loopy* which became quite a *cause célèbre* in army circles and totally surprised everybody by selling six or seven thousand copies. I think it should still be in print. Books like that, and another wonderful one by Lady Ranfurly called *To War with Whittaker,* still available in paperback, are the sort of memoirs which are pretty indiscreet but tasteful and often appeal to readers other than military authorities. Loopy was attached to the army and his regiment by so many umbilical cords that one knew it was just about the only thing he ever thought about. He eventually married, for a fourth time, somebody who was the Queen's best friend and towards the end of his life he was getting very deaf but my goodness what fun he was to publish and I am sure people reading this will remember him.

### Sir Derek Lang
One of the most unusual capture and escape stories was that of General Sir Derek Lang, as he later became, who was captured at St Valéry in 1940 and managed to go on the run. He had a distinguished military career (because of course he wasn't a General when he was captured) and he eventually became Chancellor of Stirling University. It was in the rough and tough days of demos and long hair, but he took up his appointment. His first major operation was to mastermind the

Queen's visit to the university. This went utterly haywire. The students rebelled and laid on violent demonstrations against the Queen and threw things and generally made the visit a disaster. A week or so after it had happened our office doorbell rang and there was a very distressed General Lang on the doorstep. He had just come hot foot from Buckingham Palace where he had received in person a major bollocking from Her Majesty and he was, to all intents and purposes, dismissed from his post. He was a nice man and he didn't deserve that but I have never seen a man look as shattered as he did having come directly from the Monarch's clutches.

## Cecil Lewis

Cecil Lewis became a hero overnight after the First World War when he wrote a classic of the Royal Flying Corps entitled *Sagittarius Rising*. I wanted to try and reprint this book and was in the process of getting agreement from my masters at Poland Street when Lionel Leventhal* (publisher and owner of Greenhill Books) nipped in before me and managed to get the reprint rights. I was left to pick up the crumbs and Cecil, who was getting on in years, allowed me to publish *Sagittarius Surviving*, but the really interesting thing about him was that he was a founder member of the BBC and they, the BBC, when I told them, had forgotten that he still existed. I saw him on several occasions when he was approaching the age of about 100 and I had alerted the BBC to the fact that I was going to publish this sequel to *Sagittarius Rising*. There was immediate panic at the BBC because they hadn't realised that one of their founders was still alive. A party in celebration was hastily cobbled together and the reception took place at the BBC head-quarters. Cecil was a remarkable old man and he didn't quite make his century but I am very proud to have been associated with him and indeed for having alerted the BBC to the fact that one of their oldest and boldest was still operating.

## Sir Charles Mott-Radcliffe

I include Sir Charles for one reason. We stepped out of line slightly and offered to publish his non-military memoirs, which we duly did. There was one episode in his memoirs which caught my eye. Apart from being a distinguished MP, he owned the living of a number of churches in East Anglia and was renowned for placing an advertisement in the local paper which revealed he was looking for a

---

* I salute my fellow publisher Lionel as he has done so much in publishing military history. It was he who made it respectable.

curate for one of his parishes but it was essential that he should be an off-spin bowler as well. This seems to have got the values right.

## Michael Nelson

Michael Nelson was an old rogue. He was the first man to write a novel about homosexuality after the Second World War called *A Room in Chelsea Square*. Later on he did two volumes of memoirs based on his somewhat dubious military career. The books were called *Captain Blossom* and *Captain Blossom Soldiers On*. They were all about his life as an officer in the Royal Army Service Corps during World War Two and his connections with the black market. He was a very funny man, very much a product of the pre-war years in Fitzrovia. At one stage he was in charge of the late- night God slot on independent television but was frequently inebriated when he came on at about 11.30 or whatever time it was. Very few people realised this. He was an energetic and exhausting author to handle, but he was civilised and his two books are classic anti-heroic volumes about soldiering and ring all the more true for that. He lived on a boat on the Thames.

## Geoffrey Powell MC

Geoffrey came to me via an old school friend who had married into the family. Geoffrey had fought at Arnhem and had served in the Green Howards for most of his military life. His memoir of taking part in the battle of Arnhem duly reached me and I read it at a sitting. It is one of the two books that made me cry when I first read it. It was called *Men at Arnhem* (my suggestion) and was a vivid account of the battle seen from a company commander's point of view. He managed to get some of his men back from the battle over the river but his company had taken the most appalling casualties. He originally insisted on publishing the book under a pseudonym largely because he was still employed by the Ministry of Defence in various activities, but to this day, as an account of a young officer's battle experience, I know no better in that field of military history. It has been recently updated and reissued. Happily now he has surrendered the author's anonymity. He is no longer Tom Angus but really is Geoffrey Powell. He went on to write others books for me, including the splendid account of *The Kandyan Wars* and he also became a bookseller of great distinction in Chipping Camden. It is very dangerous having an author who is also a bookseller! His son, too, commanded the Green Howards and Geoffrey was a shining star in the military firmament. He died, aged 90, as this book was going to press.

**Harry Seaman**

Harry, who is no longer with us, wrote a very valuable book called *The Battle at Shangshak*. This was a crucial action in World War Two where a parachute battalion held up the Japs to enable the British forces to relocate around the perimeter of Imphal and Kohima. It was an Indian parachute regiment and Harry was one of the white officers. It so happened that the Japs were held up on this hillside trying to burst out of Burma on the way to India. A fierce battle lasted a number of days until, having really been defeated but not totally conquered, the surviving troops were told to make their own way back to the British lines. They had fought a magnificent delaying action and they had probably enabled Slim to win the Kohima and Imphal battles by holding up the Japs for so long. What I didn't know at the time was that Harry himself had been involved in a horrible occurrence. Making his way back as instructed to the British lines he came across one of his colleagues, a British soldier very badly wounded, who implored him to put an end to his misery. Harry did this. It haunted him for the rest of his life, even to the extent that, when he went back to Burma, he located the very spot where the incident had taken place. He then, not surprisingly, had a nervous breakdown and for two years produced not a word, although he was under contract. I understood what the situation was, so I didn't press him. Being an honourable man, he delivered the manuscript with no mention of that incident, but his book threw light on probably one of the most important actions fought by the British Army in the Burma campaign and it is to this day hardly remembered as it should be, as should Harry who died not all that long ago.

**Brigadier E D ('Birdie') Smith CBE DSO**

I include Birdie Smith because, apart from being a prolific writer on Gurkha subjects and on military history generally, he did something which I think is so brave that I shudder to think of it. He was a passenger in a helicopter during the Borneo confrontation when it crashed and he was trapped in the wreckage by his arm. Having tried every means he could to free himself he decided the only course was to get the medical officer who was with him to take a penknife and amputate his arm without an anaesthetic and he lived to tell the tale. He was not called Birdie without reason. He was small and fluttered about but he had a steel will, vivid imagination and was all that you might expect of a Gurkha officer – quite superb.

## Ewen Southby-Tailyour OBE

I forget how Ewen came to me but I bless the day he did, with his first book, *Reasons in Writing* – an autobiography based on his life in the Marines and the Falkland Islands particularly. The son of the Commandant General Royal Marines and brought up by Blondie Hasler, the Cockleshell hero, he was bound to succeed and indeed he did. He had a superb career with the Marines and was noted for a degree of eccentricity and frequent high spirits. It was the Falklands War that really brought us together. I referred earlier in this memoir to a particularly dreadful book he wrote called *Falkland Island Shores*. I am in fact really pulling the reader's leg because, although it appeared that there was a small market for such a book, this particular one became flavour of the month at the beginning of the Falklands campaign because Ewen was one of the few people in the world who knew where the Falkland Islands were.

He had distinguished himself during his career in the Trucial Oman states and had received the Sultan of Oman's medal for bravery when he took part in several pretty hairy military operations during the Dohfar War in that part of the world. Dohfar so good! Having completed a tour of the Falkland Islands, he returned to normal duties and fortunately when the Falkland crisis arose somebody remembered that he'd written that book and also that he'd already had two years with the Marine detachment in the Falklands which was a permanent garrison. It was they who were captured by the Argies in the initial phases of the battle.

Ewen got an OBE for his efforts in the South Atlantic and there are many people who believe it should have been a much higher reward. He, for instance, preached long and loud about the Welsh Guards being detained on board the *Sir Galahad* instead of being put ashore as fast as possible. There was an argument between the Army and the Navy which was one of the most unpleasant situations that arose during that campaign. It was Ewen who selected the landing beaches and indeed who led them into battle in very hairy, or at least stormy circumstances. Later on he became, of course, invaluable and he certainly trod on a few toes at the same time, hence the somewhat meagre award he received.

Fortunately for me, he then went on to develop his literary career and this was very much to both our benefits. *Reasons in Writing* was a great success and was followed not long after by Commodore Clapp's book *Amphibious Assault* which was largely written by Ewen. He then embarked on a life of Blondie Hasler, his former guardian and former Cockleshell hero and this book again was widely reviewed and has just been reprinted. He has also just published a book about a little known but very gallant SOE operator called Hué and he is now currently at work on the biography of *HMS Fearless*, one of the ships that made her name down in the Falklands.

I'd go anywhere with Ewen at any time of the day or night and indeed have done on several occasions. I shall never forget him making a rousing speech at the Imperial War Museum on the launching of his book *Reasons in Writing*. For some reason I can't now remember, he ended up giving a speech standing on a table and when he jumped off he very nearly injured himself badly. Nothing, however, quite like one of the curators at the museum who, having left that party in a jolly state, followed the crowd to the pub behind the museum and was run over by a taxi, or it might have been a bus, but not fatally thank goodness. By then Ewen and I had managed to escape. However, the party went on for quite some time afterwards.

Ewen is, among other things (and obviously), a sailor of distinction and has his own boat, *Black Velvet* which he uses from time to time when he is not selling Hovercraft. He has been 'Yachtsman of the Year' in his career and heaven knows what he is going to do next. That he is unpredictable goes without saying, but whatever it is he is going to do it will be done with panache and no little laughter. Many is the bottle of port that has vanished down our throats in postprandial discussions; I have enjoyed his company hugely.

### Bill Sparks DSC (Last of the Cockleshell Heroes)

While we were working on Bill's book *The Last of the Cockleshell Heroes*, I got to know him very well indeed. He told me a lot of background material which was not included in the original text. The most interesting story was that on a number of occasions, when taking refuge in a farmhouse, or with peasants, 'Blondie' Hasler would always insist that Bill had his meals in a separate room from them – this was maintaining the rank and file order that you'd expect to find in an officers' mess! Bill had a termagant wife who was constantly bullying him and actually made him sell his medals which he felt very bitter about. Fortunately I believe they were bought for the Royal Marines Museum where they remain on display and then Bill went on, not under my tutelage, to write another book but that's another story.

### Dr Martin Stephen

A schoolmaster by trade but a poet and a literary man at heart, Martin was quite one of the most delightful authors to cross our paths. Currently he is the High Master of Manchester Grammar School and is about to become High Master of St Paul's. In other words he has opened the batting at both ends.

Apart from all this he finds time to write books. I came by his work quite fortuitously. He wrote *The Fighting Admirals* and *The Price of Pity*. He was into poetry and he was one of the most important people on our list. He is a very humble man and very witty. How he finds time to do all those things I simply do not know. It is a pity the world lost him to education and I am sure after the experience of being High Master of St Paul's (following in the footsteps of another author of ours, Dr Howarth*) that he will become, without a doubt, a powerful figure in the political future with regard to where education is going in this country.

## Herbert Sulzbach

Not many people fought on different sides in the last two wars but Herbert Sulzbach did. He was a German Jew, birdlike and intelligent and famous for his contribution to the de-Nazification process after the war. I got to know him very well when I published a book on his First World War experiences called *With the German Guns* which was a stunning success because books by Germans about either war are rarely translated into English. In this case, having been interned on the outbreak of the '39–'45 war on the Isle of Man, he was released when it was realised that he could be of more use to the war effort in the United Kingdom than he would as a prisoner. Herbert began to work passionately for the restoration of respect between enemies after the Second World War and he is chiefly responsible, or was, for running the Featherstone Camp in Northumberland where the senior Nazis who were captured were sent to be de-Nazified. They were not released until they'd given up their allegiance. So brilliant was Herbert at this *rapprochement* operation that he became an icon and, since he had got an Iron Cross twice in the First World War, he was duly recognised in the Second. It is ironic that when he was released from the Isle of Man and went home, he found that his house had been one of the first to be destroyed by the blitz in Hampstead. There is no justice. Herbert was a constant help to me and on a number of occasions assisted me when dealing with German military historians. He was also an enormous help in promoting his own book. I am at least able to claim that I have made a speech about warfare at the German Embassy.

* Dr Howarth wrote *Monty at Close Quarters* which became known in the book trade for its cod title *Monty at Hind Quarters*.

## Douglas Sutherland MC

There are a number of individuals who deserve a wider treatment than I am able to give them in these thumbnail sketches, and I feel that the late Douglas Sutherland deserves a longer innings, as indeed did the late Brigadier Calvert.

I have already mentioned Douglas Sutherland several times. He is not easy to forget. Alas neither he nor his wife Diana is now alive but I still feel I had better be careful what I say. Douglas worked in Fleet Street before the war as a cub reporter and then he went to war and got what is described as a 'good MC'. He was a great raconteur and became famous in more recent years for his series of books based on the English gentleman published by Debretts. Gentleman he wasn't really, but near enough to know how to get by. His best war story in *Sutherland's War*, of which I doubt the veracity, was when he was advancing with his troop towards some German tanks and the lid of one of them popped up and a man stepped out with his hands raised and Douglas recognised his old German tutor from pre-war days, so took his surrender. As I said, I doubt the truth of this, but it is a good story. There are legions of other tales about Douglas and his behaviour. He once bought a house called Pasture House so that he could say 'passed your house this morning' – a weak joke if ever I heard one. He wrote a very good life of Lord Lonsdale called *The Yellow Earl* and a history of The Border Regiment.

When he was working for one of the national papers he was commissioned by the editor to go and do a piece about Glamis, the family home of the Queen Mother. He travelled all the way up to Scotland on a sleeper and got a taxi to Glamis. When he arrived at the gatehouse the general factotum on duty said there was little point in showing him round because the house was completely closed down for the season. Douglas had persuasive ways with people which usually involved waving bottles about. In due course he returned from the village bearing two bottles of whisky and this not only opened the gates but gave him an accompanied journey up to the house itself and a back door was unlocked. Heeding the gate keeper's warning to behave himself he found himself alone in the castle without a single other person in sight or in sound. Unfortunately after he'd been in the house for about ten minutes he was taken very short indeed and had to rush and find a lavatory somewhere. After a frantic search he located one and managed to relieve the tension so to speak. Alas what he had not allowed for was the fact that to start with he was in the Queen Mother's own en-suite bathroom but much worse the water was turned off. As there was gross evidence of his occupation for all to see he realised that he would be in enormous trouble and so would the gate keeper if evidence of his visit were to remain. The next problem was to obtain enough water to flush the lavatory. This was almost impossible because virtually every WC that he went into had no water in. Eventually by the use of a milk bottle and pounding up and down several stairs he managed to get enough in the bowl to remove the evidence. He tidied up as best he could and crept out of the gate. He even slipped past the gate keeper. No piece ever appeared in the paper because, of course, there was nothing to report.

There was another occasion when his wife, Diana, who was quite free with her favours, had left a party that they had been attending at Claridge's with Douglas going in one direction and she going in another with another gentleman. Several hours later a man rang up and said to his friend whom he'd seen leaving with Diana, 'Have you seen Diana anywhere?' and the chap, lying through his teeth, said, 'No, no I haven't. What's the trouble?' 'It is Douglas's heart pills,' said the man. 'Diana has got them in her handbag.' The handbag needless to say was under the bed but Douglas did survive.

He was a very good host and entertained Jilly and me a number of times. One place I remember was called Rohallion, a rented mock gothic castle in Scotland. Among the guests was Victor Briggs, whom I mentioned earlier, and who was Douglas's agent for a time. He swore that the castle was haunted and that he heard strange noises in the night. What he heard was revealed later when Diana complained that Douglas used to beat her, which was unwise. I miss them both, because they were part of the eccentric Bloomsbury set and there was also plenty to drink and plenty of laughter when they were about. Douglas, among other things, wrote a fine regimental history of The Border Regiment, *Tried & Valiant* and another brief regimental history as well as his memoirs *Sutherland's War* for which the launch party was held at Stirling Castle. After the party was over Douglas got lost once again and found himself locked in. He managed to climb out of the castle to claim his car and was just getting into it when a police car drew up behind him. All the effort of getting over the wall of the castle seemed to have absorbed what alcohol he'd taken in and having being breathalysed by the suspicious policeman he was given the all clear. He got into his car and roared off, but unfortunately in reverse, rendering the police car incapable of movement. Seeing that his only chance was to step on it and guessing that they hadn't had time to take his number, he put his foot down on the accelerator and disappeared into the northern part of Scotland for several days. He was never apprehended.

On another occasion I remember him making a speech at the launch party for the book on *The Argylls*. People started laughing fairly early on in his speech and the hilarity began to grow and it wasn't until I asked my next door neighbour what the fuss was about that he pointed out that Douglas's fly buttons were undone from top to bottom and his trousers which apparently were not sustained by braces were about to fall round his ankles any minute. He was rescued with an office stapler.

One morning at about 7.30am the bell rang in the flat at Shaftesbury Avenue. It was a little bit early even for me but when I got to the answer phone a voice said, 'Is that you, Leo?' to which I of course replied 'Yes.'

I recognised instantly the voice of Douglas Sutherland and before I had a chance to say anything he said 'I want to see if you can lend me a pair of socks.' Knowing Douglas as I did there would certainly be an interesting tale behind this request so I pressed the button and let him in. He came upstairs and it transpired that he had spent the night sleeping under the arches near Charing Cross Station having not quite made it back home to wherever he was staying. During the night somebody had removed his shoes and socks but left the shoes behind and run off with the socks. Very odd. I was presumably one of the only publishers who kept a stock of socks in the office and was able to kit him out and off he went properly dressed. I then sent a memo to the royalty department of Heinemann who dealt with all these things asking that they debit his royalty statement for one pair of socks. Alas they did not see the joke.

### John Terraine

John Terraine was probably the most distinguished author I was ever lucky enough to publish. He is mentioned several times in this book but he is owed a little more than I have already given him. As you know John scripted the great war series for the BBC for whom he worked for many years and later on did the Mountbatten life on television. He was a prolific writer whose first book *Mons* very quickly established him as one of the leading writers on World War One. I have already said that he was difficult to deal with, but he started work on World War One at a time when not very many people were interested and he gradually built up a reputation which made him, alongside Correlli Barnett and John Keegan, one of the finest military history writers that this country has ever produced. Why he was never honoured I cannot say. His book on the Battle of the Atlantic, *Business in Great Waters*, is a classic, as was his history of Bomber Command, called *The Right of the Line*.

## Sir Robert Thompson KBE, CMG, DSO, MC

Earlier on I referred to people who qualify for the thumbnail sketch if only for one particular incident. Sir Robert had a distinguished career which began in the Malayan Civil Service in 1938; he then took part in the outbreak of war in the Pacific when he was stationed in Hong Kong from which he made a hurried and dramatic exit. Later on he became an expert in counter-insurgency and gained experience in anti-terrorist operations which was eventually to lead him, as a special adviser, to Vietnam and to be a confidant of Washington. En route he was privileged to meet many of the most influential and controversial figures of his time, from Wingate and Templer to Kennedy, Nixon and Kissinger. His comments on these and many others are candid and revealing. His book was called *Make for the Hills*. Among other books, he wrote a *History of the Royal Flying Corps* in the Famous Regiment series and is worthy of inclusion for that alone.

## John Watson DFC

John Watson features frequently in this book. After his dismissal from Mayflower and Consul and his attempt to forge a name as a TV presenter and novelist in Scotland, he decided that he'd start a publishing imprint instead. By some extraordinary piece of luck he had obtained an introduction to somebody called David Bruce MC who was Somerset Maugham's nephew. He'd been a very gallant Welsh Guards officer in the war but was not endowed with very much brain. Rather like Tim Carew, he had his stipend paid to him by his family's stockbroker. The same situation applied with David Bruce. His family arranged for him to have a lump sum and a small income as long as he could invest it in a viable business. And so David Bruce & Watson the publishing house was founded. It is difficult to remember quite how long the business lasted – not long I fear. It was his (John's) accountant who rang me up and asked if it was usual for the entertainment and expenses column in the accounts to be larger than the production costs. He published a few books, including *A Life of Sid Field*, the comedian and a book about Bomber Command by Alistair Revie.

Fairly early on John obtained the rights to a photographic book of sexual positions. It was perfectly tastefully done and utterly harmless. I will never forget, however, the repercussions when the book was delivered to our warehouse in Shaftesbury Avenue. The book was considered to be obscene and it was my job to get rid of it as fast as possible. John, however, was one step ahead of me and managed to do a deal with an Australian remainder merchant which meant that 5,000 copies (it might have been more) of this totally harmless, rather pathetic book showing a couple in various positions of sexual activity found its way to the state of Victoria. A worse venue could not have been found. There was more trouble to come. A complaint was received from Australia saying that in at least two of the illustrations, should the couple involved do whatever was being advised with any degree of violence, both positions would result in the breaking of the neck vertebrae. So the book travelled all the way to Australia to be pulped there and never saw the light of day.

The only really successful book they published was a collection of pieces by Cyril Connolly, and it was the last thing that appeared in print by him, called *The Evening Colonnade*. This publication was celebrated by a party at Brown's Hotel. Neither of the publishers, Bruce or Watson, was able to pay the bill which was something like £1,700 and a terrible row ensued until one of Watson's close friends dug into her savings and rescued him. I never pass Brown's Hotel without remembering that star-studded party and the air of doom that surrounded it. David Bruce, like Tim Carew, also broke his neck, in this case falling down the basement steps when dumping the Christmas empties. He was given a funeral with full military honours at the Guards Chapel and that was probably the nicest thing that ever happened to him.

### Colonel Jeffery Williams

Jeffery Williams was a Canadian soldier who at the end of his career worked as a Defence Attaché for the Canadian Government in London. Before that he'd commanded his regiment, The Princess Patricia's Canadian Light Infantry, and had also been present at Dieppe and taken part in the Korean War. After his retirement he took up writing, his first book being the History of the Princess Patricia's for the Famous Regiment Series. Subsequent to that he became a biographer and won the Canadian Governor General's Award for his excellent life of Byng of Vimy. He wrote a number of other successful military tittles, winning a great following in Canada itself. He also wrote a very good piece of military history called *The Long Left Flank* which was an account of the actions that took place on the left-hand side of Europe as the Allies strove towards Berlin leaving the low countries exposed to heavy and damp fighting over a prolonged period.

I can't resist including Jeffery because he is such good value anyway, but I know that during our publishing of the Byng of Vimy book my partner, Tom, came across a marvellous limerick which has to be taken with a pinch of salt and you can read between the lines if you want:

*One day in his bath Viscount Byng said*
*'What memories Vimy does bring*
*Of that pretty young trooper' No, No! Gladys Cooper*
*My goodness that was a near thing.*

## John Winton

John was a thoroughly professional naval historian and I published several books by him. He was not an easy man to deal with and he had been born with the name 'Pratt'. He changed this for his writing purposes to 'Winton' and I suppose I understand why because he rather lived up to his original name. Anyway he wrote some very good naval history books and was a great help when we set up the naval history part of our list.

# CHAPTER XI

## *Downhill all the Way*

*Nothing except a battle lost can be half so*
*melancholy as a battle won.*

(Despatch from the field of Waterloo,
Duke of Wellington, June 1815.)

Out of the blue one day the telephone rang very early in the morning in my flat in Shaftesbury Avenue. It was Toby Buchan, now aged 50, on the line. You will recall how he had had a sort of in and out career with me in the past. He told me he had some useful information to give me and could we meet for a drink*. Toby, it turned out, was now working as a freelance editor for an organisation called *The Barnsley Chronicle* group of newspapers based in Barnsley, South Yorkshire. Among other things they had developed a line in military history largely by publishing comprehensive histories of the PALS Battalions which were raised in the First World War in many of the northern towns and cities, particularly in mining areas such as Barnsley. The owners of the *Barnsley Chronicle*, the Hewitt family, had previously owned the coal mines and indeed it was Grandfather Hewitt who raised the Barnsley PALS battalion from his own coal miners. For this he received a Baronetcy.

They had found, almost by mistake, that there was a strong nostalgic military market for these Battalion histories and they were milking it, quite rightly, for all it was worth. The books contain, among other things, complete nominal rolls of all those who served in the various PALS battalions – these nominal rolls are invaluable for families researching their ancestors and it is comforting for them to know that there is a record (very often the only one) of their relevant ancestor for posterity. Also they (the Hewitts) had seen the signs that military

* He had previously worked for Reg Davis-Poynter and Cassell's before setting up his own firm Buchan & Enright. In the end he had to be bought out, as I mentioned earlier.

history was catching on in various places and were, Toby thought, in an acquisitive mood. Perhaps this could be the answer I thought wearily to myself once again.

I trusted Toby's information because he was always accurate. He kindly offered to introduce me to the *Barnsley Chronicle* which was all the more intriguing for me because, as a Yorkshireman myself, I believed, like most of us do, that I was different from the rest as far as general demeanour was concerned, but I have to admit that I was not prepared for the people of South Yorkshire. I come from the West Riding, as I still call it, where the people are very different. That's not the point though. The point was that any link-up might entail considering the prospect of doing some work up north which did not appeal. Nevertheless we set up a meeting in London where the people from Barnsley came down and we started discussing how we might bring life back to the Leo Cooper imprint while keeping the momentum going.

It was July 1990. By this time I was beginning to tire in the home straight. I was being distributed and represented by *Air Life* at the time. They too must have suffered from the curse of Cooper because they went bust only the other day. When they were working on my behalf I had no complaints at all and they were very nice people to deal with, but I am afraid Reed and Octopus, who were now doing my distribution, didn't rate them and eventually the whole distribution was taken over by Barnsley. The prospect of another long battle about prices, negation of contracts, rights and all sorts of other bits and pieces had worn me down. The number of stock checks, inventories, accountants' reports and everything that goes with merging businesses was rubbing the edges off me. I am not suggesting that this was superfluous or unnecessary. I felt that I was the person who was superfluous and unnecessary. Nevertheless a glimmer of hope had appeared on the horizon again and I can now give an account of the events that led to the formation of Pen & Sword Books and to my eventual throwing in the towel.

The final act of this story and the beginning of the next that you've been reading, assuming that you've got this far, took place at the London Book Fair at Olympia. It reads now rather like a game of consequences. Toby Buchan met John Mitchell and John Bayne, now deceased but who was one of the directors of the *Barnsley Chronicle*, and they fell to discussing the plight of Leo Cooper who was once again a refugee. Toby at this time had been working full time for Barnsley*, and on the loose from Reed/Octopus, as an editorial

---

* The colophon Pen & Sword was not in use yet. It was, of course, based on the graphic symbol (see page 56).

adviser. This meant that the poor man had to spend at least four days a week living in Barnsley which he did for about six months. During this time Toby was required to edit books for them and to advise them generally on publishing.

I don't know what went wrong, but Toby obviously didn't quite hit it off with some of the directors of the *Barnsley Chronicle*, of whom more later. Nevertheless, John Bayne must be given credit for the fact that he went back to Sir Nicholas Hewitt and, whilst not exactly praising our name, said that we were available and that we had a very good reputation. Various conversations took place after the one at the Book Fair and eventually we thrashed out the possibility of a deal. This among other things was going to involve us in the transfer of all the contracts that had travelled with me throughout these various ownerships and I learnt a new word, novating. This meant that within reason the *Barnsley Chronicle*, should they wish to acquire us, would have what rights any author was prepared to sign over to them. I am happy to say that without any pressure at all only one author refused to travel with the circus.

It seems only fair to say a few words about the *Barnsley Chronicle* here, who, as far as I am concerned, were my last port of call and I suppose you could say rescued me and the stranded imprint. They had scant general publishing knowledge, but they had another imprint, Wharncliffe, through which they published the PALS books. They also did local history and they had on their stocks *Shot at Dawn*, a similar volume to mine on the executions in the First World War called *For the Sake of Example*. These two titles eventually cohabited without there being any clash between them.

I have already said that South Yorkshire people are much different from those who live farther north in the county, but the Barnsley people are fair and outgoing and they made me feel very welcome, though for a few months we circled round each other taking stock of the situation. I think I was regarded with some curiosity by the management at Barnsley because, among other things, I went as far as taking members of the staff out to the pub for a drink at lunchtime. I am not saying this was frowned on but it certainly wasn't what I'd call *Chronicle* style.

Apart from Sir Nicholas Hewitt, who ran the joint, he was ably supported by his brother Timothy, who sadly died in January 2004, and the late John Bayne, who had been in on the earlier discussions and was an ex-Fleet Street man and with a degree of military knowledge which was helpful. He was also a peacemaker. The idea being developed was that I would make visits on a regular basis to

Barnsley, whilst Tom would continue to carry out his editorial duties in London with the occasional visit to Barnsley. John Mitchell would also be retained for the time being so he could handle the production, but we were very much aware that there was a division between north and south which did not exactly help communications. There was, fortunately, plenty of opportunity in the Barnsley office complex for the beginnings of the imprint and not long after we put our heads together a very shrewd piece of property dealing was done when Sir Nicholas purchased the old TA Barracks bang opposite the *Barnsley Chronicle* offices. This became a highly efficient warehouse and office block through which we did all our packing and dispatching, and as far as I was concerned and assuming that it is operating to this day, is as good a distribution system as I've ever had to deal with.

Initially the transfer took rather a long time and looking back on it now, over fourteen years ago, I'm amazed that we got our act together as fast as we did. The deal became firmed up on 20 September 1990. There were uneasy moments when culturally we seemed to be miles apart, but on the whole Nicholas had taken a tremendous risk in acquiring the imprint and he was very brave because it was quite a gamble. I think it is safe to say now that it was a gamble that paid off. I kept most of my entrepreneurial responsibilities which stopped short of the funding of projects and left the negotiating to HQ. This was probably a good thing because I needed reining in and, whilst the future looked uncertain, we were certainly well controlled by Sir Nicholas who, if nothing else, was miserly, but in the kindest sense of the word. He didn't believe in paying advances and has proved himself to be right. The fact is that such is the desire to appear in print that many authors and potential authors were only too happy to accept either low advances or none at all. What had particularly appealed to Sir Nicholas was the lucrative official regimental history market. What he appreciated about that was the fact that the money was there up front or guaranteed and this gave the whole operation a tremendous amount of momentum and kudos.

I cannot leave this brief description of the activities of Barnsley without referring to Barbara Bramall, the production manager, who has just retired. Learning from scratch, she turned herself into one of the best production executives that I have ever worked with and I know that Tom feels the same. She picked up the job remarkably quickly from a standing start and her print buying was impeccable as was her choice of supplier and indeed the quality of the work that was produced over all. She was an absolute wizard at timing and she was never flustered, although she used to pretend that she was. To do what she did in a matter of ten years was a truly remarkable feat, and had she been operational on the London market, I am quite certain that she would have been one of the most sought-after production directors in the metropolis. The fact that she quite rightly opted to stay and live in Barnsley was a tragedy for me because I liked working with her so much. I really do owe her a tremendous debt of gratitude for being so helpful to me when we first joined up with Barnsley. This reads rather like a thank you letter, but it is only meant to give credit where credit is more than due and as you will realise from the earlier pages of this book, giving credit is one thing, using it another.

It would be wrong to say that times were easy. This was 1990. I had virtually signed my life away and it was Sir Nicholas who suggested that we called the imprint Pen & Sword Books, but he also added that he would like to continue, for the time being, using my name on the title page and so to this day books land on my desk ostensibly published by myself of which I have never heard. So far I am happy to say that nothing has arrived that I am ashamed of.

Among other adventurous decisions taken by Sir Nicholas was the appointment of Henry Wilson (Brigadier) who had previously commanded the 1st Battalion Irish Guards and who had retired from the army and was obtained by advertising in the Officers' Pension Society Journal *Pennant*. Henry Wilson applied for what was partly my job which was the entrepreneurial side and he was very quickly dropped in at the deep end. Nobody could have known less about publishing than he, but he was literate, he was funny, he was modest and altogether a thoroughly nice man. The difficulty arose really though with his location so to speak. He had a house south of Barnsley in the Midlands somewhere and when he did go up to Barnsley it took rather a long time. Likewise being a London-based man when he was a soldier, he was south as much as he was north. He was a member of the Rag which helped so we could always meet there and he used to come to the office to start with, but gradually he gained confidence and whilst not in any way disadvantaging me he took over the role of book creating and at this he was very good indeed. He now lives in Hampshire. I should perhaps again mention here that there were certainly cultural differences between not only the north and south of Yorkshire but between Yorkshire and the south of England. I was still beavering away but beginning to see that the rope was tightening.

I don't think it is worth saying very much more at the moment because the imprint would appear to be flourishing and many pigeons have gone home to roost. I am particularly delighted that the backlist is being intelligently exploited, a thing that a lot of other publishers fail to do. Many of them are sitting on potential selling properties in their backlists without realising the rights are available. Pen & Sword by intelligent combing of the backlist produced and published a number of editions of books that I had previously done many years before. A willing market was found straight away and it was nice to see old friends coming back into print again. Much of the credit for this must go to Charles Hewitt, Sir Nicholas's son, who, with no knowledge of publishing whatsoever, virtually took over the management of Pen & Sword from his father and I certainly have no complaints about the material that he has been producing. This all sounds rather sycophantic but it is not meant to. I was tiring and I wasn't being much use to anybody and looking back on the past it is hardly surprising. I was emotionally and it turned out physically drained.

There is absolutely no doubt that this strong division between north and south does exist, not only in attitude but in general outlook. For instance the Hewitt family were mad on horse racing which is the sort of thing that left me absolutely cold. The local people who worked in the firm, be they compositors on the paper or designers or just general factotums, were nothing but marvellous, but in many ways deferential. They were very much like the days of Longmans when we had Mr Mark and Mr John and Mr you know what. We certainly had Sir Nicholas. I was fortunately never known by any other name than Leo which I think they found a bit too informal because it didn't fit in with the homage required. By now I'd blown my gasket. It is difficult to explain.

I am from a northern family, born and bred going way back to 1598 (as far as records show), and there is absolutely no doubt that we are different from those people south of Watford. All the more confusing though is the fact that I had lived and worked in London virtually all my life and somehow or other lost touch with the true north. It was a problem which I don't think I ever really cracked. Who was I? I loved my part of Yorkshire where I grew up, but there was no way that I could have ever done what I did in my life if I'd remained in the county. Publishing can only be done, in most cases, from London and so it was. However, Pen & Sword seem to have bridged the gap and have realised that a lot of the action does take place in the south and there has been a much better communication between both sides as a result of this awareness. I have got no more to say now except to tell you what finally pushed me over the brink.

I was entertaining an author (who must remain nameless) in the London office in an attempt to persuade him to allow me a little bit more editorial freedom with his new book. He was insisting on having coloured maps on various pages and a coloured frontispiece and you name it. I had to try and explain to him that you can't do that sort of thing and everything depends on where the illustrations fall and pagination and all the words that publishers use. He dug his heels in and became almost abusive if not sarcastic. I am afraid I'd had enough. I got up and quoted the immortal lines to be found in King's Regulations, 'I will soldier no more'. I walked out of the office. I went down the stairs*. I hailed a taxi to Paddington. I eventually got home and went to bed. The following day I realised I couldn't go on and as far as I know the author was still sitting waiting for me to come back to the office. I didn't and over the next few days, or was it weeks, or months I made it plain to Nicholas that I didn't fit in and I think he felt enormously relieved because I didn't. Not only that but I had been offered a research job for one A Cheetham (which also ended in tears). The question is where did I belong or where do I belong? The answer to that is I simply don't know. The shutters are drawn, the telephone is off the hook and that is the end for the moment.

Sadly, during the writing and production of this book (some fourteen months), no fewer than eleven of my authors have died.

### Envoi

I am allowing myself a few last words. Here we are at the end of the journey through part of my life. Some of it has been a delight to record. Much of it is rather shaming; a fair amount eccentric. I make no apology. As you might remember, if you recall the early pages of this work, I entered the publishing world with some trepidation. That I am still alive after forty-five years service in the cause is an object of some considerable surprise to many people, not least myself.

Looking back at the past, I think I may not have made one or two things clear enough. I am now going to try again but in brief.

People keep asking me why I got into the military business in the first place. I still don't really know. Deep down in my soul, however, there is a strong admiration for all those people whose exploits are here recorded, who described their participation in horrendous episodes of what is now called history. I would not be here but for the actions of people like many of those who appear in this book. Nor would you. They maintained their equilibrium selflessly, reluctantly in nearly all cases and modestly too, also with great courage and quite often terrible suffering. They fought through those dreadful times,

---

* The very same stairs down which I had once physically thrown an author.

both physically and psychologically. I am thinking of such people as Birdie Smith and the penknife, or Michael Glover, shattered by the Libyan Embassy fire fight, or Alex Bowlby shivering in a slit trench in Italy and the many ordinary people who have either been blown up, shot down in flames*, endured the attentions of the Gestapo, escaped from prison camp, taken part in what are today regarded as great battles or been torpedoed in icy cold waters. Many of those survivors walk among us today. All these men and women are heroes to me. I have no idea how I would have acted in similar circumstances.

I have always been interested in the software of military history, i.e. the people who make it and the people who carry out the plans of those who appoint themselves our leaders. By software I mean people, soldiers, sailors, airmen, civilians and even animals**. I have never been that interested in hardware. Hardware means, to me, the sort of weapons that were to be found under my bed in the nursery all those years ago as well, of course, as machine guns, submarines, bullets, lorries, tanks, anti-tank guns, revolvers, bombs, aircraft, battleships – I could go on forever. Nor have I been particularly interested in uniforms or regalia. On the other hand, for some extraordinary reason, I do have a fascination with military badges. This may be because one of the best-selling books I ever published was *Military Badge Collecting*, which is now in its sixth or seventh edition. I am moved again to refer to those famous words from the Apocrypha: 'Let us now praise famous men . . . and some there be that have no memorial'. I hope I have given, over the years, an opportunity to as many people and regiments as possible to erect their own memorial, to leave their mark on history, aided and abetted by me. Here are tales of derring-do, of courage and of fortitude and some of mere adventure. Here too are shattered landscapes, crumbling buildings, smashed aircraft, sinking ships (sounds rather like publishing!), lost causes and deep, deep sadness. But the pen is mightier than the sword.

That's really all I have to say. Mine has never been a morbid interest, as many people suspect. I am not dazzled by glory either but, among other things, pride in a regiment's long history shines out of the pages of the many Regimental Histories I published. What a man says in his diaries, letters, regimental history, or even conversation is sometimes far more telling and more immediate than the sound of machine gun

* 57,000 aircrew were killed in WWII. The Americans suffered about the same number of casualties in Europe. There were 57,000 casualties on the first day of the Battle of the Somme.
** Eight million horses died in the First World War.

fire in the distance, a screaming shell or a deafening explosion. Reading accounts of military conflicts one cannot fail to marvel at the courage of the average man sent to kill other average men at the behest of distinctly non-average people, the politicians. Perhaps I have arrived at an answer and that is that my publishing had behind it a driving force, an enormous reserve of anger in me ready to burst out yet remaining, reluctantly, contained. These men and women put their careers and lives at stake and fortunately lived to record the events. I myself had no chance to test my own courage. They were the people who had to go round shooting, dropping bombs and indeed killing people for various reasons. Many of these men and women still carry on living among us. We should treasure them and listen to what they have to say. All I wanted, and hoped to do, was to give these people a voice. I trust I've succeeded.

# The Famous Regiment Series

This series ran to fifty-eight volumes. My original intention had been to cover the history of every regiment of the British Army. Alas, galloping inflation saw to it that I did not succeed. The market for the books was obviously strong in the regimental domestic field, but gradually it became clear that we would have to print far more than we could sell to keep the series going and reluctantly I had to pass. The series is much loved and now changes hands in the second-hand market for very large sums of money. It would have been nice to have completed the job but now I know I never will.

*The King's Royal Rifle Corps*
*The Queen's Royal Regiment* (West Surrey)
*The Royal Fusiliers*
*The Royal Norfolk Regiment*
*The Royal Flying Corps*
*The Gordon Highlanders*
*The Black Watch*
*The Royal Berkshire Regiment*
*The Somerset Light Infantry*
*The Green Howards*
*The Royal Hampshire Regiment*
*The 17th /21st Lancers*
*The South Wales Borderers*
*The York and Lancaster Regiment*
*The Scots Guards*
*The Suffolk Regiment*
*The Wiltshire Regiment*
*The Highland Light Infantry*
*The 11th Hussars*
*The Argyll and Sutherland Highlanders*
*The Worcestershire Regiment*
*The Rhodesian African Rifles*

*The Duke of Cornwall's Light Infantry*
*The Royal Horse Guards* (The Blues)
*The Royal Northumberland Fusiliers*
*The Royal Tank Regiment*
*The King's Own Yorkshire Light Infantry*
*The Bedfordshire and Hertfordshire Regiment*
*The Dorset Regiment*
*The Royal Army Service Corps*
*The Oxfordshire and Buckinghamshire Light Infantry*
*The East Yorkshire Regiment*
*The North Staffordshire Regiment*
*The Red Devils*
*The Duke of Wellington's Regiment*
*The Lancashire Fusiliers*
*The Buffs* (The Royal East Kent Regiment)
*The Queen's Own Royal West Kent Regiment*
*The United States Marine Corps*
*The Royal Irish Fusiliers*
*The East Surrey Regiment*
*The Durham Light Infantry*
*The Corps of Royal Marines*
*Britain's Brigade of Gurkhas*
*Princess Patricia's Canadian Light Infantry*
*The Life Guards*
*The 7th Queen's Own Hussars*
*The King's Own Regiment*
*The Royal Scots Greys*
*The Devonshire Regiment*
*The Welsh Guards*
*The Northamptonshire Regiment*
*The WRAC*
*Queen Alexandra's Royal Nursing Corps*
*The Kenya Regiment*
*The Grenadier Guards*
*The Shropshire Light Infantry*
*The 10th Hussars*

# APPENDIX II

# *Official Regimental Histories*

This lists all the regiments and formations with whom we cooperated and acted as an adviser on their official regimental histories. This particular area was one where we became enormously successful having replaced, by good fortune, Gale & Polden who used to be well known for regimental history publishing.

*Among Friends* (Scots Guards)
*Annals of the King's Royal Rifle Corps*
*A Pride of Gurkhas* (2nd Gurkhas)
*The Blues & Royals*
*'C'Battery* (HAC)
*Cap Badge* (The Bedfordshire & Hertfordshire Regiments)
*Challengers to Chargers* (Lifeguards)
*The Charging Buffalo* (Kenya Regiment)
*Cold War Warriors* (Berkshire & Wiltshire Regiment)
*The Coldstream Guards*
*Crater to Creggan* (Royal Anglians)
*Craftsmen of the Army* (REME) (two volumes)
*East of Katmandu* (7th Gurkhas)
*The Emperor's Chambermaids* (12th/20th Light Dragoons)
*The Fighting Tenth* (Submarine Flotilla)
*First Aid Nursing Yeomanry* (FANY)
*Four Five* (45 Commando)
*The Glider Pilot Regiment*
*The Life of a Regiment: Gordon Highlanders* (three volumes)
*The Glorious Glosters*
*A History of Indian Artillery*
*The History of the RASC & RCT*
*Horse to Helicopter* (RASC)
*India's Paratroopers*
*Jai Sixth* (6th Gurkhas)
*Johnny Gurkha*

*The Light Dragoons*
*To the Last Round* (South Notts Hussars)
*Music in State Clothing*
*Once a Grenadier*
*Queen's Dragoon Guards*
*Remember with Advantages* (11th Hussars)
*The Royal Military Police*
*The Royal Scots in the Gulf*
*The Steadfast Gurkhas* (6th Gurkhas)
*The Scarlet Lancers* (16th / 5th Lancers)
*The 17th/21st Lancers*
*The Suffolk Regiment*
*Ten Commando*
*That Astonishing Infantry* (Royal Welch Fusiliers)
*The Vital Link* (Royal Signals)
*Tried and Valiant* (Border Regiment)
*Wait for the Wagon* (RASC)
*Britannia's Daughters* (the WRNS)
*Greensleeves WRVS* (Women's Royal Voluntary Service)

# Tom Hartman: In his own words

Since I joined Leo very shortly after he had started the firm, and indeed remained with him until he retired, he has asked me to explain how this came about.

My first job in publishing was in the production department at Hamish Hamilton as assistant to the then Production Director, Max Martyn. I have to admit that Max was not an ideal boss, though later we became very good friends. Book production in those days bore very little resemblance to the methods used today and all that I learnt then has long been totally out of date. Books were set in hot metal, using linotype or monotype machines. This was done by the printers who then printed the book after the proofs had been corrected and sent the sheets to the binder who produced the finished book. Nowadays it is all done photographically. Printers' reps, of whom more later, played a large part in our lives and distributed quantities of largesse at Christmas time, a pretty blatant form of bribery. Nowadays one is lucky to see so much as a calendar.

Later on I was moved to the Education Department as an assistant editor. The department was run by Dennis Napier, one of the kindest and nicest men it has ever been my good fortune to meet. It was at about this time that Leo joined the firm as Publicity Manager and we soon became good friends. A year or two later I was approached by a friend of mine called Andrew Kerr who worked as a sort of personal assistant to Randolph Churchill. He told me that Randolph was looking for someone with experience in publishing to help with the life of his father which he was compiling. In his usual awkward fashion Randolph refused to cooperate with the Production Department at Heinemann, who published his book, claiming that he was quite capable of producing copy already marked up for the printer. I went to see Leo, who knew a great many people in the publishing world, and asked him if he could think of anyone who would fit the bill. Leo said he would think about it and let me know. A day or two later he came to me and said, 'I don't think that there is any future for you here.

I think *you* should apply for the job.' So I went to see Randolph and was taken on. When I went to say goodbye to Jamie Hamilton he was appalled and said to me, 'I cannot understand how you can want to go and work for such an appalling shit,' to which I replied, 'Well, Mr Hamilton, I've had some experience in that respect.'

I remained with Randolph for about eighteen months until he died at the very young age of 57, although he had always seemed immensely old to me. We had one blazing row very soon after I arrived and I told him that if he was going to talk to me like that I was leaving; whereafter I never had another cross word with him.

After Randolph died there was a rather unseemly squabble between the various parties involved as to who should take over the writing of the book, and eventually the lot fell upon Martin Gilbert, who had neither the means nor the inclination to retain the services of the team which Randolph had assembled to help him with the work. So I was without a job, an awkward moment to find oneself in such a situation as I had just got engaged. However, I went to see my friend and former boss, Dennis Napier, who told me that there was a job going as an editor at a firm of educational publishers called Evans Brothers. I applied, was interviewed by a man with the rather unfortunate name of John Thomas, and was given the job. I think I was there for about eighteen months and I can't say that I found it a very stimulating place to work. Anyway, Leo and I had kept in touch since I left Hamish Hamilton, and by now he too had left and had set up on his own. He was about to join forces with a very long established but by now virtually moribund firm called Seeley Service and asked me if I would join him as editor. I left Evans Brothers with few regrets and we both moved into the Seeley Service offices at 196 Shaftesbury Avenue which were truly Dickensian in every way, including the staff.

Hardback publishing is an expensive business. To be successful one needs plenty of capital as you usually have to pay your bills long before anyone pays you for what you have produced. We had virtually no capital and were therefore always heavily dependent on the goodwill of our suppliers. Leo achieved this on the whole by setting up court in a pub behind the office called The Oporto. There, purely on the strength of Leo's personality, would foregather at lunchtime the reps of nearly all our suppliers who, after a few drinks, didn't feel in the mood to press us too hard for payment.

The sessions in what became known as the Branch Office are worth recalling. Almost daily there would come together a gaggle of people who had some connection with the business, however tenuous. Not all were looking for a cheque. Often on parade was Tim Carew, who was one of Leo's original backers. Where he found the money God only knows, for he never seemed to have much. He had had what is called 'a good war', from which he emerged with 'a good MC'. He had written a number of books and it was he who really taught me that to be illiterate doesn't stop you being an author. I think that he and I were vaguely related, as we both had many relations who came from Devon, where inbreeding is very common.

'They married and asked in marriage and danced at the County Ball,' as Belloc put it. Certainly Tim was related to my aunt, Theresa Farquhar, but I forget how. She had a large house near Chudleigh which later belonged to the former Countess Spencer, who, one is told, found Devon society beneath her. My most vivid memory of the place is being made to swim in a pool on the top of which a dead owl was floating!

As I said earlier, the reps, as they were known, played a large part in our lives. Not only did we rely on them to arrange the production of our books but it was vital to be on good terms with them, as, inevitably, they wanted to be paid for their work, or that of their firms, which was not always easy. Whether by accident or design, Leo managed to gather around us a very easy-going and, on the whole, bibulous bunch of reps who could be found in the Branch Office on most days at about 12.30. This amiable group played a significant role in the publishing world in the 70s and 80s and they deserve to be remembered individually. There was 'Andy' Andrews from the binders James Burn. At first he struck me as rather a grumpy old stick, but he had a heart of gold and, as far as I recall, never put the screws on us. Kenneth Innes also worked for a firm of binders, G & J Kitcat. He was so modest that it was years before we discovered that he was actually Sir Kenneth. The kindest and gentlest of men, one cannot imagine him putting the screws on anyone. Then there was the printing mob, of whom we used three or four, the choice generally depending on who was owed the least money. The most notable figure in that lot was Peter Parley, who worked for the Pitman Press. Peter gave the impression of always being a little the worse for drink, and certainly could be a crashing bore, but on the other hand it has to be said that he didn't have an ounce of malice in him. It was said of him that he never left a production manager's office without a typescript to be set. They would give him anything to get rid of him! Peter had a colleague called David Hodson who had been in the Life Guards during the war. I never found him very relaxing company.

Of the printing gang the liveliest were from Ebenezer Baylis. Their

London rep, Laurie Long, was an unlikely person to have found himself in such a job. He was the epitome of gentility and charm; quite unlike his two bosses Jack Baylis and Tom Foy, who would turn up with all guns blazing, buy several rounds and leave in the best of humour. Certainly Jack lived life to the full and Tom Foy kept pace with him.

From Hazel, Watson & Viney came Lawrence Viney, brother of Nigel who ran the production department at Heinemann. It was said of Lawrence that he had had an accident during the war when he jumped out of an aeroplane, his parachute failed to open and he landed on his head. Rumour had it that this had somewhat impaired his mental faculties but it did nothing to detract from his charm.

In those days the publisher bought the paper on which his books were to be printed from a paper merchant, who then delivered it to the printer and held it in the publisher's name until it was used. Nowadays, I believe, on the whole publishers simply rely on the printer to provide the paper from stock, which they buy from the paper merchant. We had to buy our own paper, which we did through an excellent chap called Gordon Lees, who worked for a firm called the Hale Paper Company. Gordon had a thick north Scottish country accent and I always called him Bill McLaren, which he didn't seem to mind. I think Gordon usually did manage to leave with a cheque.

These are the people who I remember most vividly from what may be called The Oporto Years, but there were many others who came and went and probably left having paid for a round of drinks, but without the cheque for which they had been hoping! I had no doubt that it was Leo's charm which kept the ship afloat, leaking though it was.

Through all this time we had a succession of devoted secretaries, some of whom became part of the family, as it were. Beryl Hill stands out among them. She came to work for me at Hamish Hamilton and I have to admit that I gave her the job because I thought she was so sweet and pretty. Whilst I was with Randolph she typed all my private letters; when I went to Evans Bros she came with me; when Leo and I joined up she came too. Off and on, taking into account time off to have a couple of sons, she was with us very nearly until Leo retired. She was then offered a job at a salary which we couldn't possibly afford and one cannot blame her for accepting it. I'm happy to say that to this day she remains one of my dearest friends.

Others came and went, most of whom I think I can say with honesty enjoyed their time with us. Alison Harvey was certainly the most intelligent and efficient. How she came to work for us is a mystery. She left to get married and is now the highly efficient chatelaine in Tiverton Castle in Devon.

Annabel Windsor-Clive came to us because I had just been staying with her parents in Cyprus where he'father commanded the Sovereign Base Area at Dhekelia. Her mother told me that Annabel was looking for a job so I said I was sure Leo would give her one. I don't think she was much good as a secretary, but she was a huge success in every other way. She was very pretty, had unlimited charm, and, through her father, knew, or knew about, most of the old soldiers who became our authors.

Once when there was a hiatus in sight, I put an advertisement in some paper asking for applicants. I said in it, 'A pleasing manner and appearance is of more importance than a scholastic record', or words to that effect. This attracted rather unfavourable criticism from some quarters but it did result in a charming girl called Sadie Wickham sending me a photograph of herself with a note saying, 'Will this do?' She got the job. She was a Star. Her father was an Air Marshal and her grandfather was J B Priestley, so her upbringing had accustomed her to both the Services and the literary world.

Since it was my responsibility to look after the editing and production of the books, nearly all of which were commissioned by Leo – I say nearly all because sometimes I would take on a book and very occasionally I would recommend to Leo one of the unsolicited manuscripts of which there was an increasing flow and which it was my job to vet – I came, in most cases, to have more contact with our authors than Leo. In our early days together most of our efforts were concentrated on the Famous Regiment Series which Leo had started while he was with Hamish Hamilton and which finally reached the impressive total of fifty-eight titles. These books came under the general editorship of Sir Brian Horrocks, which really just meant that he wrote the Foreword to each title. His knowledge of the British Army was encyclopaedic and I found him a joy to work with, but occasionally he could be surprisingly obtuse. He once began a Foreword with the words, 'Although this regiment comes quite high in the Army list, on any list endeavouring to show the relative social status of the regiments in the British Army it would be very near the bottom'! I said to him, 'You really can't say that, Sir Brian. Leo and I have got to try and sell the book to present and past members of the regiment and it doesn't help if you start off by telling them how common they are.' To which he replied, 'But they are, my dear boy, they are!' On the whole Sir Brian was disposed to think the best of his fellow men, but he did have a deep and abiding dislike of Field Marshal Templer and lost no opportunity to have a dig at him. Luckily he was always quite ready to tone things down a bit if I asked him to and later on, when we got to know each other well, he would send me a draft and give me carte blanche to amend his contribution in any way I saw fit.

Apart from the Famous Regiments there was a steady flow of 'general' books, but always with a military theme. Leo built up a solid core of faithful authors who could each be relied upon to produce a book every year or so. Notable among these were Michael Glover, Jack Smithers, Douglas Sutherland, Bill Moore and Charles Whiting. Indeed Charles Whiting seemed capable of producing a book a week if asked to! Jack Smithers has a penchant for using totally obscure words and when I said that none of our readers would have a clue what a certain word meant he simply said, 'Well, it'll do them good to look it up. Then they will have learnt something!'

Bill Moore, alas now dead, as indeed are Michael Glover and Douglas Sutherland, was a journalist by profession and suffered from some obscure complaint of which I have now forgotten the name but which left him with a permanently scarlet face. The first time I met him he took me to lunch at the Waldorf Hotel. He ordered a lobster and after lunch he called the waiter over and said to him, 'That lobster was delicious and, by God, it's got to be a good lobster to be able to look me in the face!'

Douglas Sutherland was an amiable rogue, but great fun nevertheless. He once persuaded Leo to publish a sort of autobiography he had written entitled *Sutherland's War*. In it he told how he came by his first job as a travelling salesman for Unilever, which he said came about as a result of a chance meeting on a train between Lord Leverhulme and his father. 'All the odder,' he wrote, 'as my father very seldom left his estates.' I thought that this was going a bit far, so I changed 'estates' to 'front garden', expecting a good laugh from Douglas when he read the proofs. Alas, Douglas was much too idle to read the proofs and I forgot all about it, so that is how it appeared. Luckily he was big enough to see the funny side of it when I confessed to him what I had done a year or so later.

In 1971 we published a book called *Little Hodge* which was made up of the letters and diaries of an officer who served in the Crimean War and was edited by the Marquess of Anglesey. Thus began our association with His Lordship which was to last for about the next thirty years, during which time we published the eight volumes of his monumental *History of the British Cavalry 1819–1919*. This culminated in his apotheosis as the winner of the Chesney Gold Medal, which is awarded, but only occasionally, for services to military history. The event was marked by a remarkable party at the Royal United Services

Institute attended by no fewer than eight field marshals and one royal duke. During those years Henry Anglesey and I became great friends and I think I can claim that it was a happy and fortunate liaison on both sides. It is certainly very unusual for an author to have the same editor over such a long period. Henry and I still see each other frequently and he once said to me that I was the equivalent of the dinosaur, as editors are now an extinct species. Most of the independent publishing firms have been gobbled up by the conglomerates which are not run by 'bookmen' but by accountants, who see no need for editors, a fact borne out by the frequency with which one sees attention drawn to the myriad howlers the reviewer has spotted.

The fault may lie with me, but I am often surprised by how seldom author and editor remain friends once a book has been published. During what one might call the gestation period, that is to say from the time a finished manuscript is delivered until the bound copy appears, author and editor are constantly in touch with one another and inevitably a certain bond is formed. Apart from the old stalwarts I have already mentioned, most of our authors could be classed as 'one book' men, so maybe it is not surprising that one never heard from them again. Notable exceptions to this were Henry Anglesey, who was certainly not a 'one book' man, and George Wright-Nooth who certainly was. George had the misfortune to join the Hong Kong police just before the war began and when the Japanese joined in he inevitably became a prisoner. He was fortunate in that he escaped the horrors of the Burma railway but was banged up in a camp at Stanley on Hong Kong Island. He wrote a book about his experiences which he called *Prisoner of the Turnip Heads*. Leo didn't like the title as he felt that it would prejudice any possibility of sales in Japan but George was adamant. 'That,' he said, 'was what we called them,' and he stuck to his guns. Luckily it didn't seem to make much difference to sales and I believe that the book is still in print in paperback. George and I became very firm friends and frequently lunched together until, sadly, he died last year.

Almost every book gave rise to some curious or hilarious incident, all of which it would be tedious to relate, but some deserve to be recorded. One I particularly remember concerned a book we did called *The Drums of Memory* by Stephen Hastings. Stephen had had an adventurous war, after which he became some sort of spy and later a member of parliament and a knight of the shires. He told me that he had found a man who was prepared to compile the index for his book. 'Does he know how to do an index?' I asked. 'Oh, he's very intelligent,' said Stephen. So when the proofs arrived I sent the man a set with a note telling him to get in touch with me if he had any problems. But I was rather taken aback when, a day or two later, he rang me and said, 'Now about this index, does it have to be in alphabetical order?!'

Following, and partly arising out of, Stephen Hastings' book we published the war memoirs of a couple of other ex-MPs, Carol Mather and Bob Boscawen, both of whom had had very adventurous wars. One sentence in Carol Mather's book, improbably entitled *When the Grass Stops Growing*, emphasised better than any other I have come across the vital importance of the humble comma. Carol was on the staff of General Montgomery and, at the beginning of what came to be known as the Battle of the Bulge, he was sent to tell the American General Hodges that Montgomery was taking over the direction of the battle. Carol wrote, 'When I arrived at General Hodges' Headquarters he was asleep in bed, with his ADC in another room.' Take out or move the comma and you get a very different picture.

A good back list is an invaluable asset to any publisher, for obviously reprints are more profitable than books which run to only one edition, but when you are starting from scratch as we were this is not easy to build up. One obvious basis on which to build is that of reference books and in 1971 we were lucky enough, or Leo was clever enough, to publish a book called *Military Badge Collecting* by John Gaylor. This doesn't sound very exciting to the uninitiated but it is amazing what a popular hobby it is. Now, over thirty years later, the book is still in print and in, I think, its fifth edition, for naturally it has to be updated from time to time as regiments are amalgamated and so on.

One invaluable work of reference which can never need updating is Arthur Banks' *Atlas of the First World War*. Arthur was a remarkable character whom I first met when I was working for Randolph Churchill. He had done a number of historical atlases with Martin Gilbert who again called upon his services when Randolph decided to produce a 'quickie' about the Six-Day War. He was an amazingly talented draughtsman whose skill I always felt was never fully appreciated. He had an unhappy life and the last time I saw him he was scrabbling about in a skip outside my house in Battersea.

Most of our books were concerned with the army or people who had served in it, but we did do a number of books with a Royal Navy theme. Luckily for me Leo didn't want to touch anything to do with the Royal Air Force; I say luckily as I know next to nothing about aeroplanes. Our 'stalwart' on the naval front was Edwyn Gray who wrote several books about submarines. Edwyn also wrote saucy stories for soft-porn magazines and one day he rang me to say that he had sold an extract from one of his books to a magazine of that nature. I went out to buy a copy and was admiring the gatefold in the centre as I walked back from the shop when who should I bump into but our old boss Jamie Hamilton. He gave me a very odd look! Submarine disasters seem to exercise a morbid interest in many people and Edwyn's book on the subject, once called *Few Survived*, but now updated and called *Disasters of the Deep*, is still in print.

In our particular field the occasional war was not to be deplored and the Falklands campaign of 1982 produced a whole shelf of titles. First to come out was Julian Thompson's *No Picnic*. Julian commanded 3 Para Brigade in the Falklands which made history with its famous 'yomp' across the main island when all the helicopters in which they should have travelled were sunk before they had been unloaded from the ship *Atlantic Conveyer*, which had brought them south. Julian, who was later promoted to Major General, looked, and indeed still looks, amazingly young. When he came to see me to go through the text, my godmother was staying with me and when I introduced her to General Thompson she looked at him and said, 'General! What of? The Boy's Brigade?'

After *No Picnic* came Ewen Southby-Tailyour's *Reasons in Writing*. Ewen was a delight to work with as he never failed to show his gratitude for one's work on his behalf, which is by no means always the case. Ewen was also partly responsible, with Michael Clapp, for another Falklands book which we published called *Amphibious Assault*. Michael was in charge of the Amphibious Forces 'down south' as the jargon of the time had it.

Nick Barker was Captain of the Antarctic survey ship *Endurance* at the time of the Falklands War and inevitably he and his ship got involved in the campaign. He wrote a book about the part played by him and his crew which he called *Beyond Endurance*. He came to see me with his wife who said to me, when he left the room for a few moments, 'I hope that it will not take you long to produce the book as Nick is dying.' Alas she was right; he died shortly afterwards, but we did manage to get the book out in time for him to see a copy.

Leo managed to fill the gap left by Gale & Polden of Aldershot, who for many years had had almost a monopoly on the publication of official regimental histories, and over the years we did quite a number of these, which were quite separate from the Famous Regiment series. Such books are a minefield for the poor author, as all the old and bold want to have their say and many are bound to feel that they have not been given their due. They are also, in theory, meant to be submitted to the Ministry of Defence in case they contain anything which might be regarded as a breach of security. It makes things easier if the author is the most senior officer who served in the regiment. Murray Naylor, who wrote *Among Friends*, a history of the Scots Guards, was a Major General and no one felt much like arguing with him, whereas poor Oliver Lindsay who wrote *Once a Grenadier*, was only a Colonel and had to cope with a multitude of officers senior to himself, all of whom felt entitled to have their say.

Another regimental history author, who bore with a degree of impatience not always associated with him a good deal of interference, was Henry Keown-Boyd, author of *Remember with Advantages*, a history of the 10th and 11th Hussars from the end of the war up until the time of their amalgamation. Henry is one author who has become a very firm friend – indeed I am writing this in his house in Herefordshire – but I did not mention him earlier because our friendship is based on several common factors which have nothing to do with the publishing world. We were at the same school, we did our National Service in the same regiment and we were both brought up in Herefordshire, but as he is a few – not many! – years older than me we had never met, so when the Regimental Secretary, then Peter Upton, rang me to say that a former officer had written a book about the campaigns in the Sudan in the latter part of the nineteenth century I at once agree to go and see him at his home in London. When we discovered that our backgrounds had so much in common we inevitably started talking about a great many things except, I'm afraid, the book. However, I reported back to Leo who was quite keen on the idea, but said that he wanted to see a synopsis. So I got in touch with Henry, explained the situation and told him what to do. The synopsis duly arrived and Leo said that it was the best he had ever read. The book was published in 1986 under the title of *A Good Dusting* and was very successful.

Not long after that Leo and I were having lunch with Henry and he and I started rabbiting on about the many friends and acquaintances that we had in common. I had never bothered to tell Leo that Henry and I had such similar backgrounds because it didn't seem very important and suddenly Leo banged on the table and exclaimed, 'My God, I've been set up!'

Some years later, I think in about 1992, Leo was approached by General John Friedberger who was the Colonel of the Royal Hussars, and asked if we could suggest an author for a combined post-war history of the 10th and 11th Hussars, recently amalgamated to form the Royal Hussars. Naturally I suggested Henry Keown-Boyd, who willingly took on the task, blissfully unaware, I am afraid, of the many minefields which lay ahead of him. The typescript, when finally complete, after a good deal of interference from the old and bold, was sent to the regiment for submission to the MOD. Unfortunately, whoever was meant to do this forgot all about it and it was not sent to the MOD until the book had already been set and the index compiled. The MOD took grave exception to some passages and John Friedberger and I were summoned to Whitehall to be grilled. Henry at the time was in Greece, which was perhaps fortunate. We were faced by three civil servants who started going through their objections. The most voluble of the three was a woman who said that it was written in the book that when the 11th Hussars reached Berlin in 1945 they removed a carpet from the Reichstag to furnish their mess. 'You can't say that, General,' she said. 'You are saying that you stole from the Germans, who are now our allies.' I remember John, who was sitting next to me, putting his head in his hands and saying sotto voce, 'I can't believe I'm hearing this.' But on it went, each objection more ludicrous than the one before. John finally agreed to make the alterations they wanted and we left. On our way out I asked the Brigadier, who was detailed to escort us to the door, what would happen if I just went home and rang Leo and said, 'It's OK, they don't want any corrections.' The Brigadier answered, 'Fuck all.' I said to the General, 'You heard what he said,' but the General insisted, so I had to make the necessary corrections. When, however, I did tell Leo what had occurred he was most intrigued and gave the story to the *Sunday Times*. They were delighted and actually sent a photographer all the way from Birmingham to Bromyard to take pictures of Henry who by then had return from Greece, and another to take pictures of me in Battersea, which took him about three hours! Only the story appeared; the pictures were never used!

At about this time a rather curious occurrence took place when André Deutsch, who had previously employed Leo, rang him up and asked if he could recommend anybody to write a life of Field Marshal Slim. I suggested, among others, Ronald Lewin and Leo relayed this to André. Leo, assuming that the publisher would be expected to come up with an advance which we could not possibly afford, then rang André to say that we had found him an author and would now bow out gracefully. But André, with a degree of magnanimity not always associated with him, said, 'No, you've done the work and somehow or other we must see to it that you publish the book.' Well, somehow or other we did and in due course it won the WH Smith Book of the Year Award. There was a big lunch at the WHS headquarters to which Leo and I were naturally invited, but felt very small compared to the great and the good who made up the rest of those present. We did, however, find Duff Hart-Davis there, who in those days worked on the *Sunday Telegraph* – maybe he still does. The three of us were standing together in a corner trying to identify the other guests when Leo said, 'Who is that incredibly scruffy man over there?' 'That,' said Duff, 'is my father.'

After the lunch various people got up and made speeches. Duff's father, Sir Rupert, made a speech about himself, the point of which was hard to grasp. Lord Trevelyan had obviously read the wrong book and made a speech about Orde Wingate. When editing the book I had gained the impression that Field Marshal Slim was inclined to see the best in every man, but could find nothing good to see in General Wingate, so this was rather unfortunate on the part of Lord Trevelyan. As we were all shuffling out of the dining room I found myself next to Lady Slim, the Field Marshal's widow, whom I had got to know quite well during the gestation period of the book. 'Oh dear,' I said, 'that was rather embarrassing.' 'Nonsense, dear boy,' she replied putting her arm round my shoulder, 'It's occasions like that which justify the continued existence of the House of Lords'!

A very dear friend of mine, alas now dead, was Barley Alison. How she came by such a first name – one can hardly call it a Christian name – I have no idea. She ran her own imprint called The Alison Press, under the umbrella of Secker & Warburg. One day she rang me up and asked me if I would do a bit of freelance editing for her. It appeared that her distinguished kinsman, now General Sir Michael Rose, had persuaded her to publish a book by General John Strawson. She told me that during the war she had served as a private in the FANYs and still trembled at the very word 'General', so would I please cope with him. When General Strawson and I met we got on fine; indeed I did a couple more books with him. One day he sent me a typescript with a note asking if Leo and I would be interested in publishing it. It was an autobiography by a former Commanding Officer of his regiment, the 4th Hussars. His name was Sir George Kennard, better known as Loopy. I was enchanted by the book and had no difficulty in persuading Leo to take it on. Indeed it proved to be one of the most successful books we ever published. Curiously an unsolicited review appeared in *The Spectator* submitted by a man who would remain nameless even if I could remember what it was. It was strange that Mark Amory, the literary editor of *The Spectator*, decided to print it for in the review the writer implied that the book was a disgrace and that it was the likes of Loopy Kennard who brought the British Army into ridicule and disrepute. This brought howls of disagreement from officers who had known Loopy in the Army and for weeks afterwards letters appeared saying what a fine solder he had been. It was the best publicity we ever had.

# *Air Drop*

I had never flown before and it was with some dismay that I received my instructions to report to Kenya's Eastleigh Airport at six o'clock one morning, to take part in an air drop – as a member of the despatch crew. This, it had been explained to me, was an essential part of any RASC officer's training, and I was lucky to be given the opportunity of taking part in a real drop and not just a practice. 'Wear warm clothes and gym shoes,' added my OC as an afterthought.

Nairobi was still sleeping as the Land Rover roared through the empty streets to the airport, which seemed to be in a similar state judging by the lack of activity. It was hardly light as the truck rolled to a stop outside the operations room. All was silence. Dimly I could make out the forms of aircraft crouched on the tarmac. A light shone in the control tower. I sat and waited, my eyes drawn to where the sun feebly hinted that the night was over as it struggled from behind the jagged hills. Without any warning the air was filled with an ear-splitting roar of engines which came from a number of Lincoln bombers on the far side of the airfield. I watched fascinated as, after they had warmed up, like lame birds they slowly moved onto the runway to take off just as the sun broke through the last of the dawn clouds, and the sky became a bright ceiling again. They were off on an early morning raid over the forest. The day had begun.

The campaign in Kenya at this stage had reached a point where big mopping-up operations were being carried on in the Aberdare forests. With such large-scale operations came the need for the troops to be supplied by air and to assist with this a special Air Despatch Unit had been sent down from the Canal Zone* to organise the supply drops. It was with this group that RASC officers, very sensibly, although I did not think so at the time, were being flown for experience.

Not long after the bombers had taken off a truck arrived and then a landrover and in no time supplies were being loaded into a Valetta

---

* A squadron of Lincolns and a squadron of Harvards and a few Vampire Jets.

which stood, doors open wide, a few hundred yards away from the control tower. I, with the despatch crew, watched and waited. I had butterflies in my stomach which were made worse when I found out that I would not be wearing a parachute ('You'll fly too low to be able to use it') and that there would be no doors on the aircraft, even in the air. However, when the time came I put on a brave face, which must have looked grim compared with the nonchalance of the rest of the crew. We boarded the aircraft at 7 o'clock and in no time we were roaring down the runway and finally, to my horror, leaping into the air. At once everything slowed down – the ground fell away beneath us and soon we were heading relentlessly for the Aberdare Mountains.

I watched tensely from a side window for a while and then moved back to begin work. I had been given instructions as to my task. First to load bundles onto a platform, then to watch for a red light, at which signal I had to raise my side of the platform and then, when the green light came on, tip and away the bundles would go out of the doorway and fall on the designated spot. Then, as we circled for the next run in, the board must be re-loaded and so on. All this I had to do wearing a belt to which was attached a running line, made up of what, at the time, seemed like thin string, this being my only link with the aircraft. The draught from the door was wicked and cold and I was thankful for the chance of activity to keep myself warm. Soon we sighted the first smoke signals over the forest and descended. The ground beneath looked like an endless series of hills and valleys covered with green cauliflowers. Higher up, at one stage actually higher than us, the moorland plateau leading to the black crags of the mountain tops stretched away, brown and lonely in the early sunlight. It was hard to believe that I was actually flying for the first time in my life as I gazed at the flitting scene below.

After a dummy run over the first DZ, we descended even lower and the jungle seemed to race past below as we approached the appointed clearing which I could see marked with the conventional signs. The red light came on – I lifted – then the green, I heaved – away slithered the bundles with everyone except myself, who cowered against the back wall, peering out of the doorway, hair blown by the slip-stream, to see if the parachutes had landed in the right place. After the first time I began to get used to it and even edged forward a little to watch the coloured parachutes float gently down and to see them all draped, like Monday's washing, on the trees as we flew over a second time. We completed eight drops on four different DZs and with each my confidence increased. I even began to look forward to the gradual descent, acceleration and then final swoop as we pulled out of a valley and watched the forest recede and the mountains revolve round us as we banked.

Heading for home was like a sightseeing trip. We watched the forest spread for miles below us – we saw a herd of elephants and there was Mount Kenya glistening in the early sunlight with her unexpected, snow-capped peak. Soon the forest changed to the Reserves, patterned and quilted by agriculture, snailed by roads and spattered with mushroom huts. Nairobi appeared, sudden and geometrical and then the airfield, brown and flat. Bump – bump and we were down. It was all over. I descended from the plane with regret. We had only been up for about eighty minutes. I was determined to fly again as soon as possible to convince myself that I liked it.

Opportunity appeared in the person of my fat platoon sergeant whom I saw, looking rather sheepish, standing by the control tower talking to some RAF personnel. He saw me too and he knew as well as I did that he wasn't meant to be there but back in the camp, safe in the routine of another day. 'What are you doing here?' I asked. 'I was just going up in one of the Lincolns with my friend,' he said. 'Why don't you come, Sir,' he added hastily, 'he'll fit you in. Won't you Ron?' There followed a whispered conversation. Sgt Jones anxiously gesticulated towards me. He could hardly afford not to wangle me a ride!

Eventually he succeeded. I wasn't one to look a gift horse in the mouth. This time I was actually issued with a parachute and attended a proper briefing. It was like the Dam Busters all over again as we trooped out to the waiting bombers which had been re-fuelled ready for the second sortie of the day. I was told to go into the nose turret with the bomb-aimer. It was very cramped and technical inside, a mass of wires, piping and instruments*. However my companion for the flight, a stringy, bespectacled looking youth in a flying suit, showed me where to sit and how to fix my helmet with the intercom. This time as we took of it was even more alarming. I was able to see not only all around me but there was glass underneath through which I watched the ground race by. I just had to grin and bear it, although my alarm was mingled with excited anticipation. We were the third to take off and followed closely behind the other two Lincolns. Behind us came five Harvards, clumsy looking aircraft but ideal for such types of operation. After circling around the airfield we eventually formed up and flew off in tight formation. This time towards Mount Kenya, on whose slopes, ridged and densely forested, our target area lay.

Once again we were soon there and after a few preparatory runs we

* See illustration number 23.

prepared to fly in and drop our bombs. There was no specific target but just a general area to be saturated. We watched the other two Lincolns go in first but I was unable to detect their bombs explode although I did see them spiral away from the bellies of the huge aircraft as they dived and banked. In a way it was rather disappointing not to see vast explosions, smoke and flames. All below seemed quiet and undisturbed. The bombs were just swallowed up by the dense forest.

After us the Harvards, like little wasps, flitted about below, diving and spinning – having, it appeared, a wonderful time. We circled above them until it was our time to descend again and rake the area with the machineguns mounted in the nose turret. The stringy youth gestured to me and showed me how to fire the guns. When he gave the signal I pressed the button and was shattered by the effect. The whole cockpit shuddered and roared and I flapped about on the end of the weapon like a jack-in-a-box. Thick cordite fumes swirled about us and then in no time it was all over. The forest had eaten up a few thousand rounds of ammunition, probably to little effect, and honour was satisfied. It was exciting though. I had fulfilled a boyhood dream – to fly in a real bomber, drop real bombs and fire the deadly guns at an uneasy enemy! The lack of opposition or apparent result was immaterial.

After a bit of sightseeing, during the course of which we must have covered a few hundred miles, we turned to catch up the other aircraft which had formed up and were heading for home. All the time on the intercom I could hear the ceaseless banter from plane to plane – very amusing some of it. Soon we caught sight of the others ahead of us and it was agreed that we would fly up above them to take some photographs of their formation flying. Steadily we caught them up and then rose higher and higher until we were directly above them, five Harvards closely and symmetrically flying, as if attached to one big Lincoln while the third flew behind us. I pointed my little black box camera through the Perspex and pressed the button, with, as it turned out later, surprising results*. It was indeed an impressive sight. 'Like a mother and her chicks,' said my companion in an unexpected surge of poetic feeling.

I was unprepared for the horror of landing as seen from the nose turret. The ground and the red tarmac roared straight up at us. It seemed inevitable that we should crash nose first or at least overshoot the runway – but all was safe. With a lurch we were down and it was

* See illustration number 25.

all over again. The only excitement left was when my platoon sergeant, who had been travelling farther back in the same aircraft, pulled his parachute rip-cord in the fuselage before he got out. Amid much merriment and no little derision the voluminous silk slithered all over the place. 'Well, at least it works,' he said philosophically. I returned thoughtfully to the camp in Nairobi trying to assimilate all that had happened in a few brief hours that morning. The whole thing had been a wonderful experience.

# Index